Adventure Into
BBC Basic

Adventure Into

BBC Basic

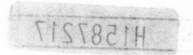
Miles Ellis
Computing Services
University of Sheffield

and

David Ellis

JOHN WILEY & SONS

Chichester . New York . Brisbane . Toronto . Singapore

Library of Congress Cataloging in Publication Data:

Ellis, Miles.
    Adventure into BBC Basic.

    Includes index.
    1. BBC Microcomputer – Programming. 2. Basic (Computer
program language) I. Ellis, David. II. Title.
III. Title: Adventure into BBC Basic.
QA76.8.B35E44   1984   001.64′2   83-16998
ISBN 0 471 90171 7

British Library Cataloguing in Publication Data:

Ellis, Miles
    Adventure into BBC Basic.
    1. BBC Microcomputer – Programming
    2. Basic (Computer program language)
    I. Title   II. Ellis, David
    001.64′24   QA76.8.B3

    ISBN 0 471 90171 7

Typeset by Pintail Studios, Ringwood, Hampshire.
Printed in Great Britain by the Pitman Press, Bath, Avon.

Preface

This is an unusual book for several reasons.

The most obvious way in which it is unusual can be best appreciated by looking at the contents list and comparing it with almost any other book on Basic programming. You will find that the order in which the various topics are discussed in this book is very different from most others. You will understand why this is so once we have discussed two more unusual features of the book.

The least obvious way in which it is unusual is that one of the authors (David Ellis) was only 12 years old when the book was written and was, therefore, much less experienced than the other author (his dad!). He knew enough about the BBC microcomputer, though, to suggest the fundamental approach which is used throughout this book and which makes it different from other books on programming.

This leads us to the third unusual feature, which is that the book has an accompanying cassette (and disc) containing a series of Basic programs which, together, create an enjoyable and challenging Adventure game to play on your BBC computer while you are learning to write your own programs. It isn't essential to buy the cassette or disc – the programs are listed in full in Appendix A – but it will save you a lot of typing if you do.

The fundamental philosophy of this book is that programming should be an enjoyable activity. It is almost always intellectually challenging, but that certainly doesn't mean that it has to be dry, theoretical and boring. We therefore start with an enjoyable game and show you how it produces different sound effects. From here it is only a small step to writing programs to play tunes.

But sound without pictures can be rather boring, so we then start to explore the world of graphics. The BBC computer has remarkable facilities for both sound and picture generation, and you will find that you can produce your own "personalised" version of the Adventure program and write a number of interesting demonstration programs without having even started on what most books consider to be the essential first steps. Once we do start to discuss the more conventional aspects of Basic, therefore, you will find that you can write really enjoyable and interesting programs – and not only to play games!

As we mentioned above, one of us was relatively inexperienced when this book was started. The idea for the approach used came from him, however, as did a number of the details of both the Adventure program and other example programs throughout the book.

He was also responsible for verifying that the book was easy to use and to understand while it was being written.

Having two members of one family involved in preparing and writing this book has, inevitably, had an effect on family life, and we would both like to apologise to Maggie (wife and mother), Sarah (daughter and sister) and Richard (son and brother) for the disruption caused to a normally chaotic household by our involvement with both computer and book!

Finally we should like to add a word of appreciation to Ian Shelley, our editor at John Wiley, for his support for the rather unusual approach used in this book, and for all his efforts in sorting out the various problems in producing a book, program cassette and disc. The text of the book was typed by Judith Denton directly onto a "floppy disc" using the Wordstar word-processing program on a SuperBrain microcomputer, and we are very grateful to her for all her hard work. The discs were then used by John Wiley to drive a photo-typesetting machine without the need for any further typing. The programs in the book were all written and tested on a BBC model B microcomputer and then listed directly from the computer to a Diablo printer – so you can be sure that they all work!

We hope that you enjoy learning to write programs for your BBC computer and that this book helps you to make the most of what is an extremely versatile and powerful machine.

MILES ELLIS
DAVID ELLIS
Sheffield

Contents

1

What's it all about?

1.1 THE BOOK

One of the most astonishing success stories of the last few years has been the personal computer. Until the mid-1970s, computers were large (or at any rate substantial) boxes of electronic and mechanical equipment that were used almost exclusively for commercial, industrial, academic or other "professional" purposes (see figures 1.1 and 1.2).

Figure 1.1   A large computer from the 1960s (courtesy of IBM United Kingdom Ltd.)

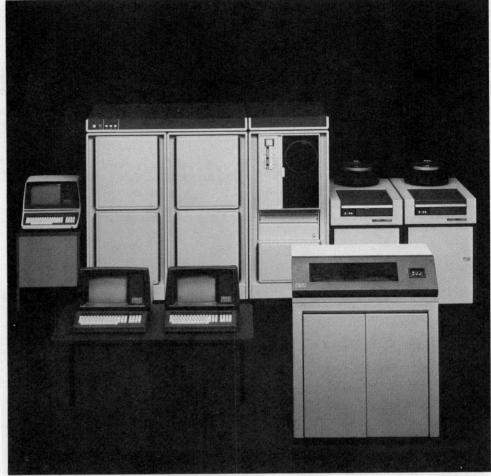

Figure 1.2   A medium-sized computer from the 1970s (courtesy of Prime Computer (UK) Ltd.)

In the mid-1970s, however, all that began to change. The development of integrated circuits which contained several transistors, resistors and capacitors on a single slice of silicon (a "chip") led inexorably to the production of a computer on a chip – or at least to the heart of a computer, the central processor, on a chip. This new type of integrated circuit was called a microprocessor.

Almost immediately the early microprocessors were incorporated into simple, self-contained, boxes containing all the other components necessary to create a desk-top sized microcomputer. One of the first of these was produced by the calculator manufacturer Commodore (figure 1.3), while the most famous of all was developed in a garage in California (figure 1.4).

At the same time as microprocessors were being used to create a new breed of computers, however, they were also being used to found a totally new form of entertainment – the video game. At first this was a simple "bat and ball" type of game (figure 1.5), but after only a brief pause came a range of highly sophisticated all-colour action games such as Defender, Pacman, and the grand-daddy of them all – Space Invaders (figure 1.6).

Figure 1.3   Commodore Pet

Figure 1.4   Apple II

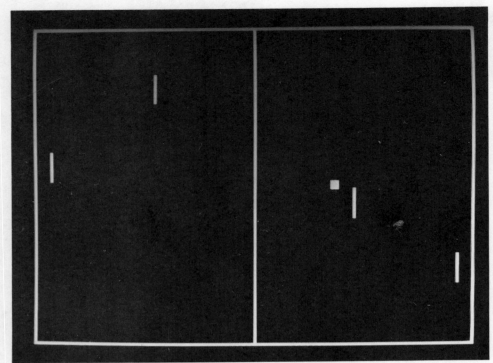

Figure 1.5   A simple "bat and ball" game

Figure 1.6   "Invaders from Space"

Figure 1.7   BBC computer

The modern miracle of electronics is that prices fall every year, and by 1980 prices were such that small "personal" computers could be purchased for the same as a single item of "hi-fi" equipment. Thus started the boom in demand which led in 1981 to the BBC producing a television series about computers and their uses ("The Computer Programme"), and commissioning Acorn Computers to build a low-priced, high-specification computer, to be called the BBC microcomputer (figure 1.7).

Many people buy a personal computer such as the BBC microcomputer with no intention of writing their own programs. They buy (or beg, borrow or steal!) programs written by others to play highly addictive games, or to use in education, or to convert their computer into a word-processor, or to carry out one of a multitude of different tasks. However, even the most addictive of games becomes stale in time, and someone else's view of the way to deal with a problem does not always accord with your own. So you need to learn how to write your own programs.

This book is intended to help you to learn just that. It uses a rather unusual approach however which, we feel, makes it much more suitable than the normal "text-book" approach.

We start from the premise that you have already used the computer to run other people's programs (even if these are only the programs on the Welcome tape supplied with your computer). These, especially if they are games, will probably use the special facilities of the computer (colour, sound, graphics, etc.) to provide visually interesting and stimulating results. It is therefore very undesirable for you to start by writing programs which solve trivial problems using white text on a black screen!

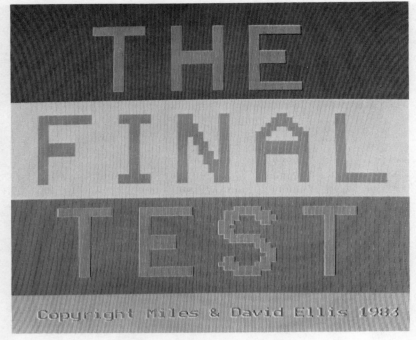

Figure 1.8   Opening title of game

At the end of this chapter we introduce a specially written program called The Final Test.

This is a game of the type known as Adventure games, in which you, the player, have to find your way through a computer-generated maze, overcoming various obstacles on the way, in order to achieve some final goal. In this particular case the task involves a multi-storeyed castle populated by dragons, evil spirits and other unpleasant creatures. Your objective is to find your way to the top of the tower, and to rescue the beautiful princess imprisoned there. The problem is that there are a great many doors and tunnels to go through, enemies to fight off (by both magical and physical means) and tests of initiative and speed of reaction to overcome.

This program is available in cassette form, although a full listing is also included in this book as Appendix A.

The game itself is an interesting and challenging one, but more important is the fact that it is written entirely in Basic. It can therefore be used as an example of how to carry out various types of operations on the computer, and equally importantly as a means whereby you can create your own personalised sophisticated game program at a very early stage in your programming career.

Of course there are plenty of other examples and programming experiments in the book, but the use of this program enables us to demonstrate and explain all the features of Basic in an easily understandable, and yet totally non-trivial, way. We hope and believe that you will find this approach easy and enjoyable to follow.

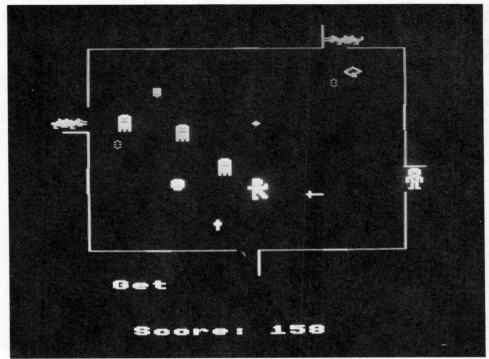

Figure 1.9   Screen during game (in Castle)

We should give one word of warning though. This book is intended to be read in the order in which it is written. The order in which items are introduced is very different from that employed in most books on programming because, as explained above, we feel that the conventional approach is not suitable for those who have already *used* computers but have not yet *programmed* them. Once you have reached the end of the book, you will find that the index will enable you to readily remind yourself of how some aspect of Basic works, but don't be tempted to use it to jump ahead to items in later chapters or you may find that you have missed some important point or experiment.

Incidentally, we have included a number of what we call "experiments" throughout the book for you to try. We have called them experiments rather than "exercises", "questions" or "problems" because that is what they are. We want you to *experiment* with the facilities of your computer – to make the dragons yellow instead of green, or to flash on and off the screen, or to be a different shape – to write a program to play a tune, or even to use the keys like the keys of a piano – to draw graphs in which colours are used to highlight particular aspects – to create abstract dynamic visual or aural effects – etc. In some cases we shall include an example of a typical result of the experiment (i.e. a program), in other cases we shall leave it to you to obtain a satisfactory conclusion by yourself. At the end of each chapter is a section called "Experimental Hints" which you may find useful to look at after you have completed a particular experiment, or group of experiments.

The remainder of this chapter explains a few basic principles concerning your computer and its language, and then describes how you can set up The Final Test so that you can play it and also (when you have had enough of that!) use it in conjunction with the rest of this book to learn how to write your own programs.

1.2 THE COMPUTER

When we refer to the BBC microcomputer we probably are thinking of a cream-coloured plastic box approximately 16 in × 12 in × 3 in high (40 cm × 30 cm × 7.5 cm), see figure 1.10.

In many ways we are correct, but at the same time we are partly wrong since this box can do absolutely *nothing* unless it is connected to some other pieces of equipment. In particular we must have some form of display (e.g. a television set) so that the computer can communicate with us. Figure 1.11 therefore is a more realistic view of the computer.

However, even now the picture is only partially complete because without some way of loading other people's programs and/or saving your own for another occasion the usefulness of the computer would be drastically reduced. Typically, therefore, we attach a cassette recorder to the computer for this purpose (see figure 1.12).

But even this isn't all it seems. Our original cream-coloured box actually consists of electronic and mechanical devices to carry out three very different functions, namely the input of information we wish to communicate to the computer, the (temporary) storage of that and other information, and the calculation of whatever results we require from the computer. These are performed, respectively, by the keyboard of the computer, the memory "chips" inside it and the microprocessor (or central processor unit, or CPU) which is also inside the case. Thus figure 1.13 gives a more accurate representation of our computer (or, perhaps, our computer *system*), and indicates that it consists essentially of five parts, of which three are contained within what we originally identified as the BBC microcomputer.

Figure 1.10   BBC computer

Figure 1.11 BBC computer with television

Figure 1.12 BBC computer with television and recorder

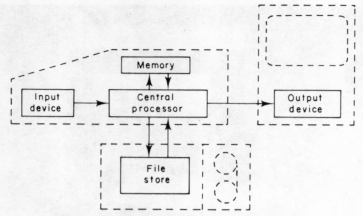

Figure 1.13   Diagram of computer system

These five parts, or functions, are common to virtually all computers whether large or small and it is therefore instructive to briefly summarise them.

The heart of the computer is the *central processor* and closely connected to this is the computer's *memory*. Every computer must have some form of *input device*, in this case the keyboard, and an *output device*, in this case a television set. (There may also be other input devices such as joy-sticks, light pens, etc. and other output devices such as printers or graph-plotters, but these do not alter the basic concept.) Finally there must be some type of *backing store* or *filestore* in which programs and data may be kept for use on a subsequent occasion. This will usually be a cassette recorder with a library of cassette tapes, but may also be one or more disc drives with a library of floppy discs.

There are, of course, a number of other bits and pieces of electronic, or other, hardware within the computer itself but we do not need to concern ourselves with these for most purposes. However, it is important to be aware of these five main parts of the computer system if you are to properly understand some aspects of programming the computer. Nevertheless, for many purposes we can think of the computer as a "black box" (or rather a cream one!) which will carry out any instructions that we give it, as long as these are properly expressed.

We have already referred to "the BBC microcomputer" on several occasions, and the time has come to introduce a shorter (and more friendly) name. Throughout the remainder of this book, therefore, we shall refer to the computer as "the Beeb" – a name which is widely used amongst those who use and/or own BBC microcomputers.

1.3   THE LANGUAGE

Computers cannot (yet) understand English (or any other conventional human language). In order that we can tell them what to do, we must therefore communicate with them in a language that they *can* understand. There are a great many computer languages in existence for different types of computers and different types of problems. The one that we shall be using is called BASIC (which stands for Beginner's All-purpose Symbolic Instruction Code) and is very widely used as the standard means of programming microcomputers (i.e. giving them instructions).

The electronic circuits which make up the central processing unit of any computer are arranged so that they recognise a number of *instructions* and then cause some appropriate action to take place (e.g. add two numbers, input a character from the keyboard, etc.). These instructions must be expressed in a special *machine-code* which, although ideal for a computer, is extremely difficult for a human to understand or to use. We, therefore, write instructions in a *programming language* such as Basic and arrange for them to be translated into a form that the computer can understand (i.e. machine code). On the BBC microcomputer this translation is carried out by a special program called the *Basic Interpreter* which is permanently installed in the computer. When you switch on your computer, this program starts immediately and displays the message "BASIC" to confirm that it is ready for use (see figure 1.14).

You can then type in your instructions using the Basic language. These can either be single *commands* such as

```
PRINT 2+2
```

or they can be sequences of statements which will subsequently be obeyed in sequence:

```
10 INPUT A,B,C
20 SUM = A+B+C
30 PRINT A,B,C,SUM
40 END
```

Figure 1.14   Screen at switch-on

Figure 1.15   "I found this vest on the pavement"

One major advantage of writing programs in a language such as Basic is that, in principle, the same program can be run on different types of computer without any difficulty because each computer's interpreter will translate the Basic program into the correct machine code form for that computer. This is exactly analogous to the words of an Englishman being translated (by an interpreter!) into French or German or Russian or Japanese as required by the listener.

Unfortunately there is one well-known problem with the English language – namely that many different versions (or *dialects*) exist in different parts of the world. For example if an Englishman says

"I found this vest lying on the pavement"

then an American will understand this to mean (in English English!) that a waistcoat has been found lying in the road. On the other hand if the American had said

"I found this vest lying on the pavement"

then the Englishman would have understood (in American English) that an undershirt had been found on the sidewalk!

The same problem exists with Basic, and different dialects exist for different types of computers. As with English, these dialects are the same in most essentials but may differ in some details. Also some dialects may contain words or expressions which do not exist in others, typically for special features such as graphics which vary widely from one machine to another, just as, for example, a "googly" (a cricketing term) is incomprehensible to most Americans and a "linebacker" (an American football term) is incomprehensible to most Britons.

The Beeb has a very powerful version of Basic which includes a number of advanced features which are not enjoyed by other dialects of Basic. This book will show you how to use these to create well-written, efficient and easily-understandable programs to solve a wide variety of problems. It will teach you BBC Basic and not just the common subset of Basic used in more general books, although Appendix D, which contains a summary of the various Basic statements, does identify those statements which are not generally available on other computers.

1.4 THE GAME

We mentioned earlier that this book uses a game (called The Final Test) both to add interest to your learning and to illustrate many of the features of Basic. This program is listed in full in Appendix A and is also available in cassette form. Since the program is very long we strongly recommend that you purchase the cassette so as to save yourself a very large amount of typing. If you *do* wish to type the program yourself then you should follow the instructions given in Appendix A (section A.1) to type the program and save it on a cassette tape (or disc if you have one). The remainder of this section assumes that you have the complete program already stored on a cassette.

The game actually consists of *four* programs called FINALTEST, CASTLE, CASTLE2 and Castle, which automatically load and run the next program in sequence. If your cassette recorder has remote control of the motor then you should load the tape and press PLAY. The tape will not move at this stage and you should now type

```
CHAIN "FINALTEST"
```

on the computer. This will start the motor of your recorder and load the first program. The motor will stop once the program is loaded but you should not alter the controls.

This first program describes the scenario in which the game takes place and then automatically "chains" the next program. This will cause the motor to be restarted and the usual searching and loading messages will appear in a small "window" at the bottom of the screen. The second program (CASTLE) is the start of the game proper and sets up various details of the game before loading the third program (CASTLE2), which sets up further details and provides some instructions should you want them. It then loads the last program (Castle), which is the actual game. (The fact that two programs are required to set up all the necessary game details is due to the (relatively) limited memory available when using graphics in more than four colours.)

If you do not have any remote control of your recorder then you should press STOP on the recorder as soon as each program is loaded. You can tell when this is because there will be a "beep" from the computer, and the red light at the bottom left-hand corner of the keyboard marked "cassette motor" will go out. When the next program is to be loaded you will see the word "Searching" appear near the bottom of the screen and the red light will go on; you should then press PLAY to start your cassette recorder once more.

The instructions about how to play the game are all included within it, so we shall say no more about that here except to say that the first program (FINALTEST) plays no part other than to give you, the player, some background information about the game. Once you have played the game once or twice, therefore, you may wish to skip this part of the game. If you type

```
CHAIN "CASTLE"
```

then the game will start from the second phase, leaving out the initial graphical and information phase. A new player should always start at the beginning though, so that he/she knows what the game is about.

The Final Test is, hopefully, an enjoyable game, but it also has a serious purpose. Throughout the remainder of this book we shall refer to it (or to parts of it) as examples of particular types of Basic statements and we shall also encourage you to modify it by means of a series of "experiments". However, in order to modify it you will need to know about two particular features of the Beeb.

The first of these concerns the listing of a program. If we wish, for example, to alter the Castle program, we may either play the game first, in which case the program will remain in the computer when the game is over, or we may type

```
LOAD "Castle"
```

which will load it, but not run it. In either case we may now type

```
LIST
```

in order to list the whole program. However it will be listed far too fast for you to read as it scrolls up the screen. There are three solutions to this problem.

The first is to buy a printer and to obtain a printed listing of the whole program. However, apart from being expensive this, as we shall see, does not fully solve the problem.

The second is to type

```
LIST n,m
```

where n and m are the line numbers of the first and last lines to be printed. Note that if we type

```
LIST ,m
```

then all lines up to, and including, line m will be listed, while typing

```
LIST n,
```

will cause all lines from line n onwards to be listed. Note the commas in the above commands; typing

```
LIST n
```

will cause only line n to be listed.

However, the most flexible way is to issue the above LIST commands in *page mode*. To do this we first press the keys marked CTRL and N together. (Actually, we don't really press them together – we first press CTRL and then hold it down while we press N.) Now the listing will stop every 20 lines or so and both the "caps lock" and "shift lock" lights will be illuminated. Pressing the SHIFT key will allow the next 20 or so lines to be printed. Thus, pressing CTRL and N, followed by typing

```
LIST 750,
```

will list about 20 lines, starting at line number 750.

Pressing the ESCape key (at the top left-hand corner of the keyboard) will abandon the listing.

Pressing CTRL+O (i.e. pressing the letter O while holding the CTRL key down) will cause normal (*scrolling mode*) listing to be resumed.

The second special feature concerns the editing features built-in to the computer. Towards the top right-hand corner of the keyboard are four pale grey keys marked ←, →, ↑ and ↓. If you press one of these keys you will see that a second cursor will appear on the screen and will move left, right, up or down as instructed by these special "cursor control" keys. Now press the key marked COPY which is situated near the bottom right-hand corner. You will find that the character indicated by the new, second, cursor is copied at the main cursor position, and both cursors are moved one character to the right. Thus, by use of these five keys, we may copy all or part of any line already displayed on the screen.

This can be useful in several ways but especially in correcting or modifying a program. For example figure 1.16 shows a listing of a very short program.

It is then possible to move the cursor to line 20, copy up to the word Miles, type in the word David, move the cursor to after the word Miles and copy the rest of the line. Figure 1.17 shows the state of the screen at various stages of this process.

The new line 20 now replaces the old one, and it has only been necessary to type the altered word; the rest of the line has been copied automatically.

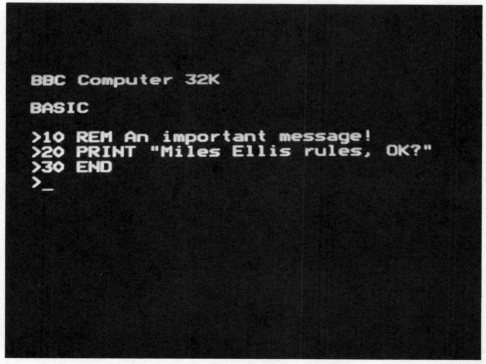

Figure 1.16   Program listing

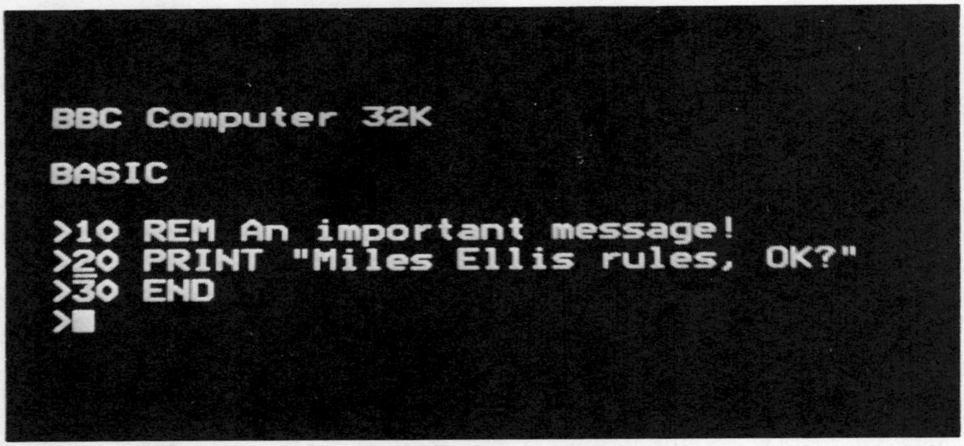

```
BBC Computer 32K

BASIC

>10 REM An important message!
>20 PRINT "Miles Ellis rules, OK?"
>30 END
>■
```

Figure 1.17a   ↑ to line 20

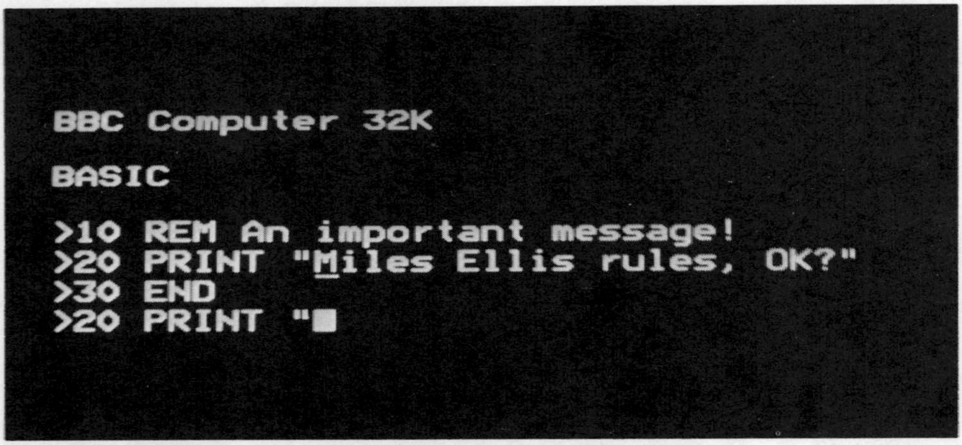

```
BBC Computer 32K

BASIC

>10 REM An important message!
>20 PRINT "Miles Ellis rules, OK?"
>30 END
>20 PRINT "■
```

Figure 1.17b   COPY to after "

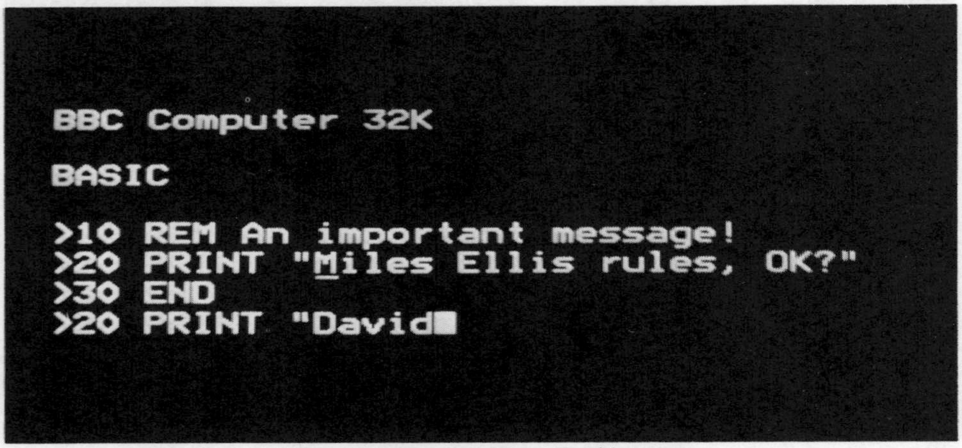

```
BBC Computer 32K

BASIC

>10 REM An important message!
>20 PRINT "Miles Ellis rules, OK?"
>30 END
>20 PRINT "David■
```

Figure 1.17c   Type David

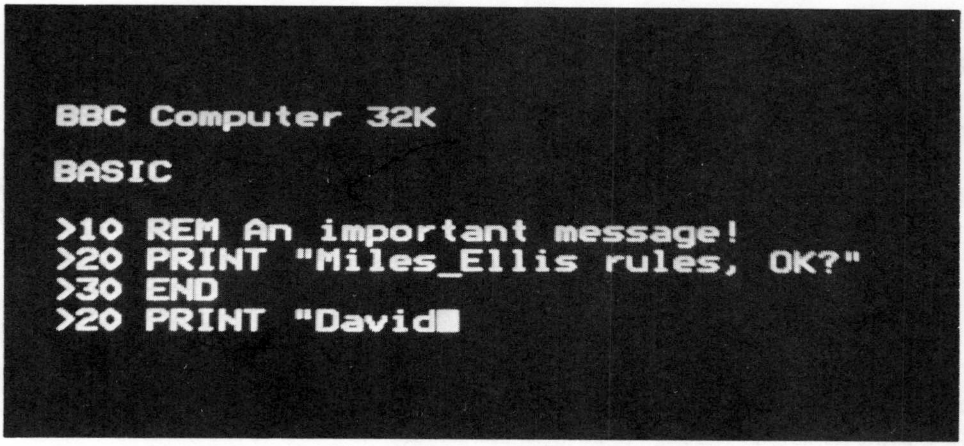

```
BBC Computer 32K

BASIC

>10 REM An important message!
>20 PRINT "Miles_Ellis rules, OK?"
>30 END
>20 PRINT "David█
```

Figure 1.17d   → to after Miles

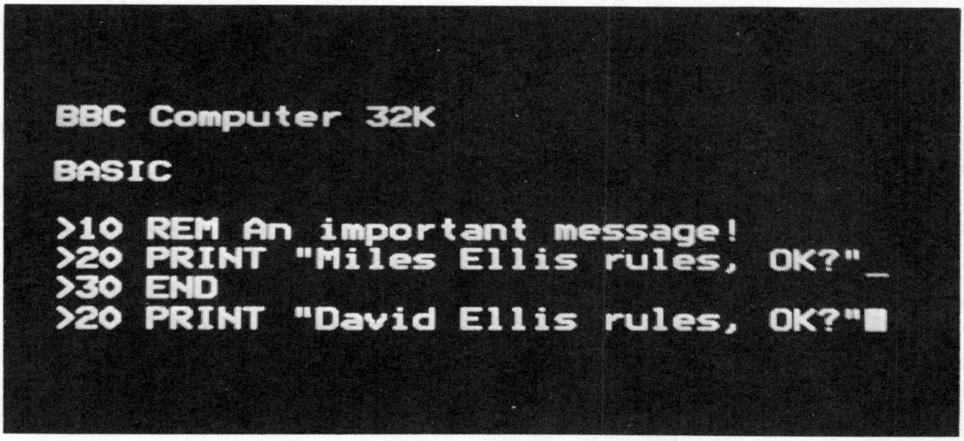

```
BBC Computer 32K

BASIC

>10 REM An important message!
>20 PRINT "Miles Ellis rules, OK?"_
>30 END
>20 PRINT "David Ellis rules, OK?"█
```

Figure 1.17e   COPY to end of line

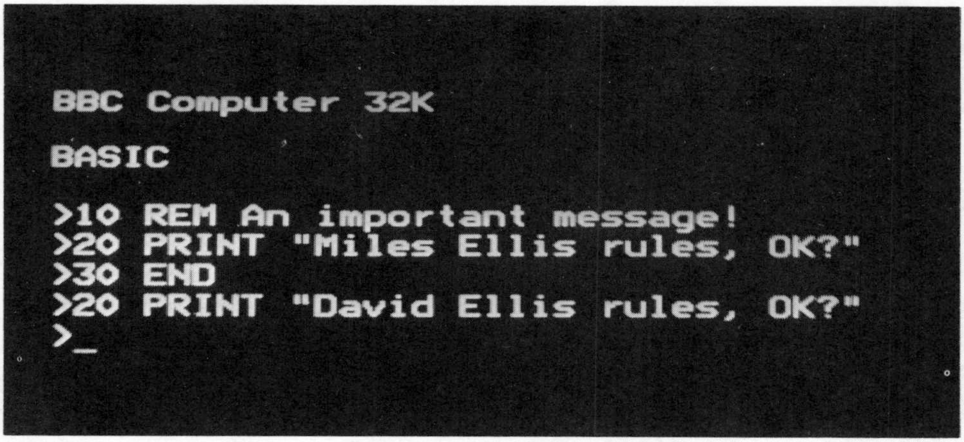

```
BBC Computer 32K

BASIC

>10 REM An important message!
>20 PRINT "Miles Ellis rules, OK?"
>30 END
>20 PRINT "David Ellis rules, OK?"
>_
```

Figure 1.17f   RETURN

Experiment 1.1

Run the game program either by typing CHAIN "FINALTEST" or CHAIN "CASTLE". At the completion of the game modify the program so that the player is drawn in green instead of white. This is achieved as follows:

1) When the game is finished and the screen has cleared press CTRL and N together, to enter page mode, and then type LIST.
2) Keep pressing the SHIFT key when the listing stops until line 460 is displayed; this line reads

```
460 DEF PROCman: VDU 18,3,E%,25,4,X%,Y%,A%,8,10,A%+1: ENDPROC
```

3) Press ESC
4) Use the cursor control keys to position the cursor at the start of line 460.
5) Use the COPY key to copy the line up to E%. Then type 2 and use the key to move the editing cursor two places to the right (i.e. omitting E%). Use the COPY key to copy the rest of the line. Finally press RETURN.
    The new line should read

```
460 DEF PROCman: VDU 18,3,2,25,4,X%,Y%,A%,8,10,A%+1: ENDPROC
```

6) Press the key marked f0 at the top of the keyboard. (This has been programmed by the CASTLE program to carry out certain initialisation and then to RUN the Castle program.) The program will run as before except that the man will be green, and if near to death he will not flash and flicker.

Experiment 1.2

Use the editing keys (←, →, ↑, ↓ and COPY) to make the man move silently. This is achieved by removing the expression

```
SOUND 0,-4,5,2:
```

from line 520 so that the line reads

```
520 PROCman: ENDPROC
```

Run the program as in experiment 1.1 (by pressing the f0 key) to check that you have altered the program properly.

Experiment 1.3

Alter the program so as to reverse the effects of experiments 1.1 and 1.2 and restore it to its original form. Run it as before to check that the alteration has worked.

1.5   A VERY IMPORTANT MESSAGE ABOUT SECURITY

None of the above experiments can in any way damage your copy of the programs which constitute The Final Test since the original programs are preserved on tape. Only if the tape is altered or destroyed will your master copy be affected. In order to avoid any risk of loss we advise you to keep two copies of your master tape. You can do this as follows:

1) Use your master tape to LOAD "FINALTEST". When the program is loaded press STOP on the cassette recorder (*do not rewind*), remove the cassette and insert a blank cassette. Ensure that the blank cassette is wound past the transparent (or coloured) plastic leader tape. Press RECORD and PLAY on the recorder and then type

   SAVE "FINALTEST"

   The computer will respond by printing

   RECORD then RETURN

   If for any reason you have not yet pressed RECORD and PLAY do so now, and then press the RETURN key on the computer.
       The program will now be recorded on the cassette tape. When recording is completed the computer will make a "beep" and turn off the motor of the recorder.
       It is usually advisable to check that the recording is satisfactory, and this is achieved by typing

   *LOAD "" 8000

   and then pressing REWIND on your recorder, followed by PLAY when the tape has rewound to the start of the recording. This will attempt to load the program in a part of the memory (from hexadecimal address 8000) which is occupied by the operating system. This part of the memory is *read-only memory* (ROM) and so the program cannot actually be loaded there. Nevertheless the computer will go through all the normal loading processes, and the screen will show the same information as is normally produced when loading a program. If, for any reason, the recording is faulty then this will be apparent during the "loading" process, and you should save the program again. (Because no loading actually took place, the program in memory is still exactly as it was.)

2) Once FINALTEST has been copied in this way the process should be repeated for the next program, i.e. CASTLE. The master tape should be correctly positioned for LOADing and the copy tape should also be correctly positioned for recording (i.e. after the end of the previous recording).

3) The process is repeated for CASTLE2 and again for Castle.

4) You now have two copies of the original program, so lock one of them away in a safe place in case a disaster should happen.

1.6   A WORD ABOUT USING DISCS

The foregoing description of the Beeb and the methods used to load and save programs has assumed that you are using cassette tape as the storage medium. The majority of BBC microcomputers only have this form of backing store and this book, therefore, always assumes that cassette tapes are being used when discussing the permanent storage of programs or other information. A substantial number of BBC microcomputers, however, have one or more disc drives in addition to a cassette recorder and we shall therefore briefly mention how these can be used with this book.

The first thing to note is that if your Beeb uses discs then it must be fitted with some extra electronic components, which are collectively referred to as the disc interface, or the Disc Filing System (DFS). This will either have been fitted during manufacture, or by your dealer as a subsequent upgrade. One very important effect of this enhancement is that the DFS requires some of the computer's memory for working space, thus reducing the memory available to your program by nearly 3000 bytes. This will not leave room for the programs which constitute The Final Test to be run.

The four programs in The Final Test must, therefore, always be run from tape, as already described; however, before doing this you must inform the Beeb that you wish to use cassette tapes instead of discs. This is achieved by typing the following two commands:

```
*TAPE
PAGE = &E00
```

which first causes the cassette tape filing system to be used, and then specifies that the extra DFS memory space referred to above is not required. Your Beeb will now behave exactly as though it was not fitted with any disc drives. Note, however, that if you press the BREAK key the computer will revert to its usual (disc) mode and you must type these commands again before using any cassette tapes.

You may, however, keep a security copy of the programs on disc as follows:

1) Hold down the CONTROL key and press BREAK; this will re-initialise the computer just as though it had just been switched on. Then type

```
*TAPE
```

but not the second command detailed above (PAGE=&E00). Now load the first program from tape by typing

```
LOAD "FINALTEST"
```

2) You can now save this on disc by typing

```
*DISC
SAVE "FINAL"
```

Note that disc file names are limited to seven characters, and also note that there is no need to check a disc recording.

3) Type

```
*TAPE
LOAD "CASTLE"
```

to load the second program, and so on.

Note that the Acorn DFS does not distinguish between capital and lower case letters in file names, and the last program (Castle) must therefore be given a different name (e.g. CASTLE3) to avoid confusion with CASTLE.

The above process may be reversed if you wish to copy your security copy from disc back to tape:

```
*DISC
LOAD "FINAL"
*TAPE
SAVE "FINALTEST"
```

etc.

The four utility programs listed in Appendix C (which are supplied on the same tape as The Final Test) may also be saved on disc. The first two (SLIST and COMPACTER) may be run directly from disc, but the others (ENVELOPE and SHAPES) are too large and must be run in tape mode as follows:

```
*DISC
LOAD "ENVELOP"
*TAPE
FOR I%=PAGE TO TOP STEP 4:!(&E00+I%-PAGE)=!I%:NEXT
PAGE=&E00
OLD
```

This will cause the program to be loaded from disc, and will then set tape mode. The program will then be moved to its correct place in memory before various pointers are reset. It can now be run as described in Chapter 16. A similar process can be used for SHAPES (see Chapter 12).

With these exceptions all the references in this book to the use of cassette tapes to save and load programs should work equally well with discs.

Experimental Hints

1.3   Appendix A.5 contains a full listing of Castle if you can't remember what lines 460 and 520 should be!

2

Some basic principles

2.1 DIRECT COMMANDS AND PROGRAM STATEMENTS

In the last chapter we showed some parts of Basic programs, and when carrying out the experiments in that chapter you should have listed (and altered!) a Basic program. Before we progress any further, however, we need to establish a number of basic concepts concerning the Basic language and Basic programs. The first of these is that Basic contains some 125 reserved words (or *keywords*) which have a particular meaning to the Basic system. We have already met LIST which lists all or part of a program, and we saw that it could take any of the forms

```
LIST
LIST m
LIST m,n
LIST m,
LIST ,n
```

where m and n are numbers which define the line or lines to be listed. In fact *all* Basic commands take the form

```
    KEYWORD
```
or
```
    KEYWORD text
```

where text is some appropriate combination of numbers, letters, special characters (e.g. punctuation marks) and, possibly, other keywords. For example, in chapter 1 we also met the commands

```
CHAIN "FINALTEST"
LOAD "CASTLE2"
SAVE "CASTLE"
```

Experiment 2.1

Type the following commands on your computer and observe what happens:

```
PRINT "HELLO"
PRINT 7
PRINT 7,5,7*5
SOUND 1,-15,52,40
SOUND 0,-15,5,15
MODE 5
COLOUR 130: COLOUR 1: CLS
PRINT "HELLO"
MODE 7
FOR I=0 TO 30: VDU 151,130+I MOD 7: NEXT
```

Note that you don't actually need to type everything. In chapter 1 we saw how to use the four cursor control keys and the COPY key to alter a program; we can use these at any time so that, for example, after typing the second line (and pressing RETURN) you can move the cursor up and COPY the line before adding the extra items (,5,7*5) at the end.

The first few commands cause one or more items to be listed on the screen before the next two commands produce noises – the first the note middle C (approximately!) and the second a "raspberry". The remaining commands put some colour on the screen as well as using much larger (wider) letters than usual.

We shall examine all these commands during this and the next few chapters; for the present it is merely necessary to note that they are obeyed immediately by the computer.

Experiment 2.2

Type NEW

Now type the same items as in experiment 2.1 but *start each line with a number* (different from and greater than the previous "line number").

e.g.
```
 1 PRINT "HELLO"
 2 PRINT 7
 5 PRINT 7,5,7*5
20 SOUND 1,-15,52,40
   etc.
```

Notice that now nothing appears to happen when you press RETURN at the end of each line. Don't worry, just type all the lines in.

Now type LIST
As you can see you have written a program!
Now type RUN
Did you see it? Type RUN again. And again.

These two experiments illustrate a number of important principles, the most important of which is that if a line begins with a number it is treated as a *program statement* (or sequence of statements) and is stored in the computer's memory to be obeyed later; if it does not begin with a number then it is treated as a *direct command* and is obeyed at once.

Notice also the speed at which the computer works. We know exactly what the program does because in experiment 2.1 we made the computer obey each line as a command. However when obeyed as a program the first five lines, which cause three lines of output to be displayed, are obeyed so quickly that we will be lucky to see them at all before the next line clears the screen. The two SOUND statements cause two different sounds to be produced but because the computer doesn't wait for a sound to finish before moving on to the next statement they are sounded almost together. The statements which cause a red HELLO on a green background also cause little more than a flash before the final stripes are produced – while the sounds produced earlier are still sounding.

We also met two important new commands – NEW and RUN. The command

NEW

tells the computer to forget any program it has stored in its memory as we are about to begin a *new* one. The command

RUN

tells the computer to obey the program *in the order of its line numbers*.

Experiment 2.3

Type NEW

and then type the same statements as before except that the first line should be given the number 100, the next 90 and so on.

```
e.g.    100 PRINT "HELLO"
         90 PRINT 7
         80 PRINT 7,5,7*5
        etc.
```

(If you still have the program from experiment 2.2 in the computer then you can type LIST before typing NEW. You can then use the editing keys to copy each statement after you have typed the line number.)

Now type RUN. What happens? and why does it happen?

Now LIST the program.

You will see that it is listed in the order of its line numbers and not in the order in which it was typed. Naturally it is also obeyed in this order and so the original program is now being run backwards!

(*Note:* Do not switch off the computer after experiment 2.3 as you will need this program for the next experiment.)

This experiment is of very great importance; for it paves the way for an understanding of the ease with which Basic programs may be altered and/or extended. As we have seen, lines which are preceded by a line number are stored in the computer's memory as part of a program. Furthermore, when the program is RUN these lines are obeyed in the order of their line numbers. It follows, therefore, that if we type in a new line then it will, in effect, be inserted at the appropriate place in the program. For example line 105 will be inserted between lines 100 and 110 in the program written for experiment 2.3. In order to allow room for subseqent insertions, therefore, most programmers initially number the lines of a program in tens (i.e. 10, 20, 30, . . .).

To simplify this process the Beeb has a special AUTO command, which can take any of three forms:

```
AUTO
AUTO m
AUTO m,n
```

This command *auto*matically generates the line number for the next line according to pre-defined rules. Thus the command

```
AUTO
```

causes the first line to be numbered 10, the next 20, and so on. If the keyword AUTO is followed by a single number then this is the number of the first line (instead of 10); thus

```
AUTO 75
```

causes the first line to be numbered 75, the next 85, then 95, etc.

Finally, if AUTO is followed by two numbers then the first is the number of the first line (as before) while the second is the increment (or step) between successive line numbers. Thus

```
AUTO 110,5
```

causes lines to be numbered 110, 115, 120, 125, . . .

When the AUTO command has been given, every time RETURN is pressed at the end of a line the computer generates a new line number. The question that then arises is how to get out of this cycle. The answer is to press the key marked ESC (for *escape*) which is situated on the left-hand side of the keyboard, near the top. This interrupts the computer and (in general) abandons the current process.

Experiment 2.4

Use AUTO to renumber the program written for experiment 2.3 so that the lines are in their original order. (See Experimental Hints if you need any help.)

Two other useful commands are RENUMBER and DELETE. The command

`RENUMBER m,n`

renumbers your program so that the first line is line number m, and subsequent lines have numbers increasing in steps of n. All references to line numbers in other Basic statements are altered, if necessary, at the same time. If m or n is omitted then the same assumptions are made as with AUTO. Thus

`RENUMBER`

will renumber a program so that it has lines 10, 20, 30, . . . while the command

`RENUMBER 65`

will change the line numbers to 65, 75, 85, etc. Finally, the command

`RENUMBER 20,4`

will cause the program to have its lines renumbered as 20, 24, 28, 32, etc.

The DELETE command is used, as one would expect, to delete a group of lines from a program and takes the form

`DELETE n1,n2`

This causes all lines with numbers between n1 and n2, inclusive, to be deleted; it is not necessary for any line to actually be numbered n1 or n2. Thus

`DELETE 0,150`

will delete all lines up to, and including, line 150.

A single line can be deleted by typing its line number, and then pressing RETURN *without any intervening spaces*, e.g.

`120` `RETURN`

2.2   SCREEN MODES AND THEIR EFFECT

In the last section we introduced the statements MODE 5 and MODE 7 in experiment 2.1, and we saw that the resulting output on the screen was very different. In fact the Beeb has *eight* different modes in which it can display information, as shown in figure 2.1.

On a model A computer, only modes 4–7 are normally available because the computer has only 16K bytes of memory (i.e. 16×1024 bytes). It is possible to increase the memory of a model A to 32K (which is the maximum possible and the same as the model B) in which case all eight modes are available.

Mode 7 is slightly different from the others in that it provides a low-resolution graphics capability using the same principles as the teletext graphics which can be seen on the BBC Ceefax service, the IBA Oracle service and the British Telecom Prestel service. The first

Mode	Colours Available	Resolution Text	Graphics	Memory Requirement
0	2	80 x 32	640 x 256	20 Kbytes
1	4	40 x 32	320 x 256	20 Kbytes
2	16	20 x 32	160 x 256	20 Kbytes
3	2	80 x 25	—	16 Kbytes
4	2	40 x 32	320 x 256	10 Kbytes
5	4	20 x 32	160 x 256	10 Kbytes
6	2	40 x 25	—	8 Kbytes
7	15	40 x 25	80 x 75	1 Kbyte

Figure 2.1   Screen modes and their effects

part of The Final Test uses mode 7 (teletext) graphics and illustrates that they can be used to produce quite effective results. The great advantage of mode 7 is that it uses very little memory (only 1K bytes). The way in which these graphics and the use of colour, double height letters, etc. are used is very different from the other modes and is described in chapter 13. When you first switch on your computer it is in mode 7, with text being displayed in white on a black background.

The other seven modes all operate in essentially the same way, the differences being the number of characters on a line, the number of colours available, and the horizontal resolution for graphical work. Modes 3 and 6 are slightly different in that they only have 25 lines to a screen instead of 32, and contain no graphical facilities at all.

Experiment 2.5

Type the following program (remembering to type NEW first if you already have a program in the computer):

```
10 VDU 19,0,4;0;0;15
20 PRINT TAB(0,0) "THIS IS THE TOP OF THE SCREEN"
30 PRINT TAB(5,12) "THIS IS LINE 12"
40 PRINT TAB(0,24) "THIS IS LINE 24";
50 END
```

Now type

```
MODE 0
RUN
```

In mode 0 there are 80 characters to each line and unless you have a high-quality television monitor you will probably find this almost (or completely!) unreadable.

Repeat this for the other modes

i.e.
```
      MODE 1
      RUN
```

etc.

Notice that in all except mode 7 the background is blue. This is because of the statement at line 10 which will be explained in detail in chapter 5. For the moment it is sufficient to say that it makes blue the background colour and then clears the screen (to blue).

You will probably find that modes 1, 4, 6 and 7 give the most easily readable display – they all put 40 characters on a line. Modes 3 and 6 are interesting because since only 25 lines are displayed (numbered from 0 to 24) there is a larger gap between lines than in the other modes, which have 32 lines displayed. A small black band is therefore left between each line which, especially in mode 6, can give a quite pleasing effect.

Modes 2 and 5 only display 20 characters per line which leads to very fat characters which you may find difficult to read. In particular, even quite short messages cannot fit onto one line and so "wrap-round" onto the next line.

Because mode 7 operates quite differently with regard to colour and graphics the statement at line 10 is ignored and the display is white on black.

Experiment 2.6

Type the following new program:

```
10 MOVE 320,832
20 DRAW 960,832
30 DRAW 960,192
40 DRAW 320,192
50 DRAW 320,832
60 DRAW 960,192
70 MOVE 320,192
80 DRAW 960,832
```

Run this program in modes 0, 1, 2, 4 and 5. What do you observe? (See Experimental Hints for some comments on this experiment.)

The choice of which mode to use depends upon a number of factors; in general, however, there is a conflict between the need for higher resolution graphics, a larger number of colours, and the availability of memory for programs and data. Thus, for example, the first program in The Final Test (FINALTEST) is in mode 7 since this uses teletext graphics, which is quite adequate for this purpose and leaves the maximum memory available for text and program. The second program (CASTLE) starts in mode 1 (with 40 characters per line) but changes to mode 2 towards the end in order to display the range of dragons, skeletons and spirits using the full range of colours. The remaining programs (CASTLE2 and Castle) are in mode 2 throughout.

2.3   PLANNING, DESIGNING AND STRUCTURING YOUR PROGRAMS

A computer program is a sequence of exact instructions to a computer which will cause it to do what we require. However, computers have no in-built intelligence, and the ambiguous or badly-expressed instructions which cause no problems to people will create terrible trouble for a computer (see figures 2.2 and 2.3).

Figure 2.2   "Give us a hand"

In the shampoo problem illustrated in figure 2.3 we have to be careful how we alter the instructions if they are to truly mean what they say. For example while clearly "rinse and repeat" will lead to what is called an infinite loop in computing terms because there is no indication of how many times to repeat the earlier instructions, the obvious alternative "rinse and repeat once" is no better! The reason that it is still wrong is that the instruction "repeat once" will itself be repeated!

In this case a solution in either of the forms shown in figure 2.4 would be quite unambiguous, although neither is a very natural way of expressing the required instructions.

When we write a program, therefore, it is important to plan what we want to do in advance and to avoid any ambiguity or impreciseness. This is most easily achieved by only dealing with one thing at a time and by first of all designing the overall plan and then gradually refining it. Often we can do this in English.

For example the main part of The Final Test is concerned with moving the player around a floor of the castle. It is possible to pick things up off the floor, to drop things already being carried, to open one or more of the doors, to fight off dragons or evil spirits and to enter a tunnel leading to another floor. The object is to reach the tower in which the

Figure 2.3   ". . . rinse and repeat"

a) Repeat the following twice
   Wet hair
   Apply shampoo
    .
    .

   Rinse

b)   Wet hair
   Apply shampoo
    .

Repeat above steps if not previously repeated

Figure 2.4   Some unambiguous shampoo instructions

princess is imprisoned. The evil spirits will appear if the player has remained motionless for more than a certain time, and will then follow him until a (magical) fight ensues. If the player goes down a tunnel to another floor then the process is repeated for that floor. The computer is told what is required by the player pressing the direction (editing) keys or typing a command. We can express this as follows:

Repeat the following until player reaches the tower

Wait for a key to be pressed
If it is a direction key then move the player
If it is the first letter of a valid command then read the rest of the command
If it is anything else then ignore it
If any spirits are present then move them and fight if appropriate
If the player has been still for too long then create a new spirit

Figure 2.5 shows lines 120 to 180 of Castle which follow this plan exactly. The major

```
120 TIME=0: REPEAT
129    REM Take action if a key has been pressed
130    C%=INKEY(0): IF C%>135 AND C%<140 THEN
          PROCmove
       ELSE
          IF C%<>-1 THEN
             PROCgetcom
139    REM Move spirits (if any present)
140    IF T%>0 THEN
          PROCmovespirit
149    REM Create a new spirit if maximum wait time exceeded
150    IF C%<>-1 THEN
          TIME=0
       ELSE
          IF TIME>W% THEN
             PROCgetspirit: TIME=0
159    REM If strength is exhausted then player must die!
160    IF S<.1 THEN
          RESTORE 1720: PROCtune: GOTO 1550
169    REM Calculate and print score
170    H%=(C+S)*(M+W+M%): VDU 4: PRINT TAB(4,31)"Score: ";
       H%;" ";: VDU 5
179    REM Repeat unless the tower floor has been reached
180    UNTIL Z%>F%
```

Figure 2.5   Main loop of Castle

part of the program consists of *procedures* (special parts of the program) which elaborate how the major functions (move the man, get a command, etc.) are to be carried out. Each of these major functions was in its turn planned in a simple way before being coded – often leaving the difficult bits to a still more detailed stage.

We shall discuss the use of procedures and how they can encourage well-planned, well-structured programs in chapter 4 when we shall start to see how a little bit of extra effort at the planning stage can save a lot of time later on. Before we do that though, we shall examine in some detail how to play tunes and make various pleasant and unpleasant noises with your computer.

Experimental Hints

2.3 You should have typed the following:

```
NEW
100 PRINT "HELLO"
 90 PRINT 7
 80 PRINT 7,5,7*5
 70 SOUND 1,-15,52,40
 60 SOUND 0,-15,5,15
 50 MODE 5
 40 COLOUR 130: COLOUR 1: CLS
 30 PRINT "HELLO"
 20 MODE 7
 10 FOR I=0 TO 30: VDU 151,130+I MOD 7: NEXT
```

2.4 List the program written in Experiment 2.3 and then type AUTO

The computer will display the first line number (10) and wait for you to type a statement. You should now use the ↑ (and possibly ← or →) key to move the cursor to the start of the line numbered 100 (after the 100!) and COPY it.

When you press RETURN the computer will respond by typing the next line number (20) and you can then COPY line 90, and so on until the original line 10 is copied as the new line 100.

Now press ESCape and then LIST the (altered) program.

Note that you were able to do this with this particular program because it only had ten lines. Why wouldn't the same technique work with a 15-line program? If you don't know then try it and see.

2.6 In all five modes you will get a square drawn on the screen. In modes 1 and 4 the top, bottom and sides will be drawn in lines of equal thickness; in modes 2 and 5, however, the sides are drawn with a much thicker line, while in mode 0 the sides are very thin.

This is because the horizontal plotting "resolution" is 2 units in mode 0, 4 units in modes 1 and 4, and only 8 units in modes 2 and 5. This is exactly analogous to the 80, 40 or 20 text characters per line in these modes. We shall investigate this phenomenon in more detail in chapter 5.

Sounding off

3.1 THE SOUND STATEMENT

The BBC microcomputer has a quite sophisticated facility for producing sound of both musical and non-musical varieties. There are, in fact, four separate sound "channels", three of which produce musical notes and the fourth "white noise" and any combination of these may be sounded together, thus enabling musical chords and other effects to be produced. In experiments 2.1 to 2.4 we used the SOUND command to produce both notes and other noises and we can now begin to explore how to use this very powerful feature of the computer in a predictable fashion.

The basic SOUND command takes the form

SOUND channel, amplitude, pitch, duration

where	channel	is a number in the range 0 to 3. (1 to 3 for musical notes.)
	amplitude	is a number in the range −15 to 0. (The reason for the negative values will become apparent later.)
	pitch	is a number in the range 0 to 255. (This is not the actual pitch (or frequency) but a value on which it will be based (see figure 3.1).)
	duration	is the length of the note in twentieths of a second, in the range 0 to 254, or 255 − which means for ever (or at least until ESCape is pressed).

Thus, for example, the command

SOUND 1,-15,52 40

will sound middle C on channel 1 for two seconds. Type it on your computer and check the sound. Now type

SOUND 1,-15,52,40: SOUND 1,-15,100,40

32

Octaves above middle C

Note	−2	−1	0	1	2	3	4
B	0	48	96	144	192	240	
A#/Bb		44	92	140	188	236	
A		40	88	136	184	232	
G#/Ab		36	84	132	180	228	
G		32	80	128	176	224	
F#/Gb		28	76	124	172	220	
F		24	72	120	168	216	
E		20	68	116	164	212	
D#/Eb		16	64	112	160	208	
D		12	60	108	156	204	252
C#/Db		8	56	104	152	200	248
C		4	52	100	148	196	244

Figure 3.1   Pitches and notes on the Beeb

This will sound middle C for two seconds as before, followed by a high C (one octave higher) – also for two seconds. Notice that the prompt character (>) indicating that the computer is ready for a new command appears well before the sound has finished.

You may notice that the values shown for the various notes in figure 3.1 are different from those given in the *User Guide*. There has been some dispute over exactly what values should be used, but detailed analysis with a special electronic frequency counter has shown that the values shown in figure 3.1 provide the most accurate musical notes. ["Extending the BBC's Sound Command – What the Manual Doesn't Tell You" by Dr. B. M. Landsberg, *Electronics & Computing*, February 1983.]

Experiment 3.1

Type the following program (after first clearing any current program by typing NEW):

```
10 SOUND 1,-15,52,20
20 SOUND 1,-15,60,20
30 SOUND 1,-15,68,20
40 SOUND 1,-15,72,20
50 SOUND 1,-15,80,20
60 SOUND 1,-15,88,20
70 SOUND 1,-15,96,20
80 SOUND 1,-15,100,20
90 PRINT "FINISHED"
```

(*Note:* You should be able to do this very quickly by use of AUTO and the editing keys.)
   This program will sound the C major scale and will then print "FINISHED".
   RUN the program. What do you notice when the program ends?

Experiment 3.2

When the program for experiment 3.1 ended, the notes continued for several seconds afterwards. We can investigate this phenomenon in more detail by modifying the program as follows:

```
10 SOUND 1,-15,52,20: PRINT "C"
20 SOUND 1,-15,60,20: PRINT "D"
etc.
```

This will PRINT on the screen the note which has just been sounded. Now RUN the program as before.

What do you notice? and what conclusions do you draw from this?

Experiment 3.3

Type in the following NEW program and RUN it:

```
 10 SOUND 1,-15,52,20
 20 SOUND 1,-15,60,20
 30 SOUND 1,-15,68,20
 40 SOUND 1,-15,72,20
 50 SOUND 1,-15,68,40
 60 SOUND 1,-15,52,40
 70 SOUND 2,-15,100,5
 80 SOUND 2,-15,108,5
 90 SOUND 2,-15,116,5
100 SOUND 2,-15,120,5
110 SOUND 2,-15,128,5
120 SOUND 2,-15,136,5
130 SOUND 2,-15,144,5
140 SOUND 2,-15,148,5
```

Now add an extra line

```
55 SOUND 1,-15,60,40
```

and RUN the program again.

What conclusions do you draw from this?

If nothing else, the above experiments will have shown you that when using SOUND statements things are not as simple as they may appear. In experiment 3.1 you will have noticed that the "music" continued for several seconds after the program ended. This also happened in experiment 3.2, but in addition you should have noticed that the first six notes

(C, D, E, F, G, A) were printed while the first note (C) was being sounded, and that thereafter the printed note remained five ahead of the sounded one.

Finally the third experiment produced two quite different effects as a result of the addition of only one extra line.

The program appears to be intended to play a slow rising and falling scale of C major (lines 10-60) followed by a faster scale one octave higher (lines 70-140). However, when it was run, the faster scale (1/4 second per note) started almost simultaneously with the slower one (1 second per note). The two scales were played together for two seconds after which time the upper scale was completed and the lower one continued with four more notes for a further six seconds.

However, when an extra note is added (line 55) which will, apparently, be sounded after the upper scale is finished, the effect is not what we would expect, as the start of the upper scale is delayed until the second note of the lower one.

The reason for these apparent contradictions is that, unlike other statements, a SOUND statement does not have to be completely executed before the next statement is obeyed. What happens is that a short *queue* is built up for each channel consisting of the note (if any) being played and up to five other notes which are waiting to be played. Once the note (or rather details about it) has been inserted in the queue the program continues and the appropriate sound(s) will be produced independently of the main body of the program.

Thus in experiment 3.1 the first note (middle C) is sounded and the next five (D, E, F, G and A) placed in the queue. As each note is completed the one at the head of the queue takes its place and the program creates the next one. When the program is stopped, the current note and the five in the queue will all be sounded (after the program itself has stopped). Experiment 3.2 merely confirms this by printing the note on the screen immediately after it has been inserted into the sound queue.

Experiment 3.3 is rather different as it uses two channels – one for a short slow scale starting at middle C, and one for a faster scale one octave higher. The program starts with six SOUND statements for channel 1 and so the first (C) is sounded, and the other five placed in the queue. The remaining statements, however, refer to channel 2 and so they are not delayed by the queue in channel 1. The high scale can therefore start at once. When an extra line (55) is added, however, which sounds a note on channel 1, the computer has to stop until the first note is completed and there is room in the queue. The higher scale, therefore, cannot begin in this case until the *second* note (D) of the lower one has started.

3.2   FIRST STEPS IN MUSIC

Figure 3.2 shows part of Elgar's "Pomp and Circumstance" which is better known as "Land of Hope and Glory". We can program the computer to play this quite easily. (For the benefit of those readers who do not read music we should mention that each line or vertical space corresponds to one note, with the lowest of the five continuous lines being the E above middle C. The length of each note is indicated by the way it is written.)

We shall define the lengths of the notes as follows:

♪	(quaver)	4	(i.e. $\frac{4}{20}$ or $\frac{1}{5}$ second)
♩	(crotchet)	8	(i.e. $\frac{2}{5}$ second)
♩	(minim)	16	(i.e. $\frac{4}{5}$ second)
○	(semibreve)	32	(i.e. $1\frac{3}{5}$ seconds)

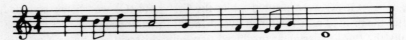

Figure 3.2   The melody of the opening bars of "Land of Hope and Glory"

and we can then write a suitable program:

```
 10 SOUND 1,-15,100,8
 20 SOUND 1,-15,100,8
 30 SOUND 1,-15,96,4
 40 SOUND 1,-15,100,4
 50 SOUND 1,-15,108,8
 60 SOUND 1,-15,88,16
 70 SOUND 1,-15,80,16
 80 SOUND 1,-15,72,8
 90 SOUND 1,-15,72,8
100 SOUND 1,-15,68,4
110 SOUND 1,-15,72,4
120 SOUND 1,-15,80,8
130 SOUND 1,-15,60,32
```

Experiment 3.4

Type the above program into your computer and run it. It will not sound quite right. Why not? See if you can alter the program so that all the notes sound correctly before you look in the Experimental Hints section.

The tune played by the above program sounds rather crude, and your computer is capable of more effective and realistic music than this. We shall examine this briefly later in this chapter and will discuss it in some detail in chapter 16. Before that stage is reached, however, we shall introduce a number of other aspects of Basic which will be necessary before any serious attempts can be made at music-making with the Beeb.

Experiment 3.5

Figure 3.3 shows a very well-known tune. Write a program to play it on your computer and test it. When it is working add the extra statement

```
GOTO number
```

at the end, where number is the line number of the first line of the program. This will cause the program to be repeated when it is finished; it will never end, therefore, and you must press the ESCape key to stop it. (This situation is known as an *infinite loop* and is normally to be avoided, for obvious reasons!)

In this form of the tune there is no pause before the tune is repeated. Add a one-bar pause (a silence of duration 32) to separate each repetition of the tune.

Figure 3.3   A traditional French tune – "Sur le pont d'Avignon"

Experiment 3.6

The program developed in experiment 3.5 played a tune which is often sung in a round –
that is with two or more groups slightly out of phase. Modify your program so that
channel 2 is used to play the same tune two bars behind the original music (on channel 1).
See Experimental Hints if you can't work out how to do this.

3.3   SOUND EFFECTS AND OTHER RANDOM NOISES

If the SOUND statement is used with a channel number in the range 1 to 3 then, as we
have seen, a musical note is produced. However if the channel number is set to zero then a
noise is produced which can be used to create various types of sound effects.

For channel 0 the pitch parameter is used to control the type of noise and should be in
the range 0 to 7.

Experiment 3.7

By using commands of the form

```
SOUND 0,-15,p,40
```

experiment with the various sounds available. You will find that values of p between 0 and
2 produce sounds which are similar to electric "buzzers" of high, medium and low fre-
quencies. If p is 3 or 7 then a "clicking" sound will be produced – we shall investigate this
later.

In fact, as can be seen in figure 3.4, values from 0 to 3 produce what is called *periodic
noise* which can be represented graphically as a *pulse wave* as shown in figure 3.5.

Value	Channel 0 sound effect
0	High frequency periodic noise
1	Medium frequency periodic noise
2	Low frequency periodic noise
3	Periodic noise of frequency related to the frequency on channel 1
4	High frequency "white noise"
5	Medium frequency "white noise"
6	Low frequency "white noise"
7	"White noise" of frequency related to the frequency on channel 1

Figure 3.4   Channel 0 sound effects

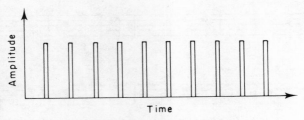

Figure 3.5   Graph of a pulse wave

Channels 1 to 3, on the other hand, produce a *square wave* (see figure 3.6) which does not have the harshness (or buzzer-like sound) of channel 0. A true musical note, however, takes the form of a continuous *sine wave* as shown superimposed over a square wave in figure 3.6.

If p=3 then the frequency of the periodic noise is determined by the frequency of channel 1, which is why only a clicking sound was produced in experiment 3.7 when channel 1 was not in use. Type the following command on your computer

```
SOUND 1,-1,52,40: SOUND 0,-15,3,40
```

This will cause the note middle C to be played on channel 1 at a very low volume (−1), while channel 0 produces a loud (−15) buzzing sound. Now type

```
SOUND 1,-1,100,40: SOUND 0,-15,3,40
```

This time the buzzing will be more high-pitched since the (quiet) note on channel 1 is one octave higher. In fact we don't actually need to sound the note on channel 1 at all! Type

```
SOUND 1,0,100,40: SOUND 0,-15,3,40
```

This will produce the same buzzing as before, although the volume on channel 1 is zero, i.e. channel 1 is completely silent. Experiment 3.8 illustrates one way in which this technique can be used with interesting effects.

Experiment 3.8

Type in the program for "Land of Hope and Glory" (see experiment 3.4) using channel 1 to produce the notes. (Remember to ensure that the pairs of notes on lines 10 and 20 and on lines 80 and 90 are separated by a brief pause.) Run the program to check that you have typed it properly.

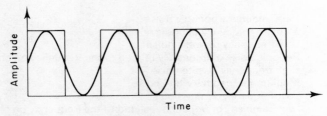

Figure 3.6   Graph of a square wave (sine wave superimposed)

Now change the volume to zero by replacing all the −15s by 0s. Run it again. You shouldn't hear anything.

Now add an extra line after the first line as follows

```
15 SOUND 0,-15,3,128
```

This will produce a "buzzing" whose frequency is determined by the note being played (at zero volume!) on channel 1. The duration of this buzzing is 128 twentieths of a second (i.e. four bars), which is exactly the same as the total duration of all the (silent) notes on channel 1. Now run the program. Did you like it?

Now change the extra line so that p is equal to 7 and run the program again. This time, although the tune is recognisable you will probably find the overall effect to be unsatisfactory and rather unpleasant.

In general you will probably find that using channel 0 with p set to 7 is of very limited use; however the other seven options are all useful in different circumstances and figure 3.7 shows some examples for you to try.

Notice also the use of channel 0 sound effects in The Final Test. In the initial program (FINALTEST) each step made by the man as he walks through the wood towards the castle is accompanied by the sound of a step produced by the SOUND statement

```
SOUND 0,-5,4,2
```

(see lines 1960, 2010, 2050). In the final program, however, each step inside the castle is accompanied by a quieter, lighter step:

```
SOUND 0,-4,5,2
```

(see line 520), while fights with dragons are accompanied by a succession of more complicated channel 0 sound effects (see line 980).

```
a)    SOUND 0,-15,3,254: FOR I=0 TO 100: SOUND 1,0,I,2: NEXT


b)    SOUND 0,-15,3,230: FOR I=255 TO 30 STEP -1:
      SOUND 1,0,I,1: NEXT


c)    SOUND 0,-15,7,80: FOR I=255 TO 100 STEP -2:
      SOUND 1,0,I,1: NEXT


d)    FOR I=1 TO 20: SOUND 0,-15,5,22-I: SOUND 0,0,5,3: NEXT:
      FOR I=1 TO 50: SOUND 0,-15,5,2: SOUND 0,0,5,3: NEXT


e)    FOR I=1 TO 30: SOUND 0,-15,1,1: SOUND 0,-15,2,1: NEXT


f)    FOR I=1 TO 30: SOUND 0,-15,5,1: SOUND 0,-15,2,1: NEXT
```

Figure 3.7   Sound effect programs

3.4 CHANGING THE SOUND OF YOUR COMPUTER

The SOUND commands discussed so far provide a wide range of musical notes and effects and enable you to create tunes, noises, etc. to your own specification. However, although more powerful than most other computers, this is only the beginning of the sound capability of the Beeb. We shall discuss this in some detail in chapter 16, but it is appropriate to introduce one fundamental concept at this stage.

When the computer obeys the statement

```
SOUND c,-a,p,d
```

it produces a note (or sound) of duration d on channel c, whose amplitude (or volume) is determined by −a, and whose frequency is determined by p. However, real musical instruments do not produce notes whose volume is constant throughout their life, and this is one of the reasons why tunes played on a computer usually sound very artificial. In real music a note will rapidly build up to its full volume, then fall slightly, remain there (perhaps) for some time, and then gradually die away (see figure 3.8).

This outline of the amplitude of the notes is called the *amplitude envelope*, and every type of instrument has a quite different envelope. BBC Basic has a special ENVELOPE statement which enables you to define your own envelopes and thus alter the type of sound produced by your computer. It is possible to define up to four different ENVELOPES at any one time and they are referred to in a SOUND statement by using a positive value (in the range 1 to 4) in place of the amplitude in the SOUND statement.

Experiment 3.9

Type the following commands:

```
ENVELOPE 1,10,0,0,0,0,0,0,3,-1,0,-3,126,76
ENVELOPE 2,25,0,0,0,0,0,0,10,-4,-1,-10,126,90
ENVELOPE 3,3,0,0,0,0,0,0,1,-30,0,-5,126,66
ENVELOPE 4,10,0,0,0,0,0,0,1,4,0,0,50,126
```

(As you can see ENVELOPE is a complicated statement!)

Now type

```
SOUND 1,1,80,250
```

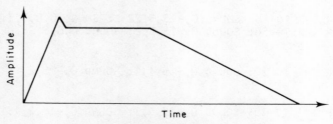

Figure 3.8   A four-part amplitude envelope

You will find that the single note (G) starts very quietly and gradually gets louder, reaching full volume after about four seconds, whereupon it starts to fade even more slowly. It will actually fade very slowly for about five seconds, then remain the same for 3.5 seconds and then die away more rapidly over a further 2.5 seconds. The whole process will therefore last some 15 seconds.

Now repeat the SOUND statement for envelope 2:

```
SOUND 1,2,80,250
```

This will rise rapidly to full volume (in about 3 seconds) and then drop slightly over the next two seconds. The volume will then gradually fade over the next seven seconds after which the rate of decay will accelerate.

Repeat this experiment for envelopes 3 and 4. What do you observe? (*Note* that you will need to ESCape from using envelope 4.)

The ENVELOPE statement actually consists of four parts which define the number of the envelope, the time intervals to be used in specifying the envelope, the pitch envelope and the amplitude envelope. The four envelopes in experiment 3.9 all affected the amplitude (or volume) of the note created by the SOUND command. The next experiment shows how the frequency can be altered as well.

Experiment 3.10

Type the following envelopes:

```
ENVELOPE 1,25,4,-4,4,12,24,12,126,0,0,0,126,126
ENVELOPE 2,1,1,-1,1,1,2,1,126,0,0,0,126,126
ENVELOPE 3,50,4,-8,4,1,1,1,14,-50,0,-4,126,76
ENVELOPE 4,1,3,-6,3,1,1,1,1,0,0,-1,126,126
```

and use them with statements of the form

```
SOUND 1,1,100,250
```

As you can see, some quite complicated combinations of frequency and amplitude variation are possible. We shall explain how to define your own envelopes in chapter 16, but you can still use certain pre-defined envelopes in any programs you write without needing to fully understand how they work. Figure 3.9 shows a short program which produces some interesting effects, while figure 3.10 gives envelopes which can be used to alter the normal sound of notes on channels 1 to 3 so that they resemble certain musical instruments (if you have a good imagination!).

Experiment 3.11

Use the envelopes shown in figure 3.10 to play "Land of Hope and Glory" in the style of a piano, then in the style of an organ, and finally in the style of a harpsichord. Next modify the program so that the same tune is played as a duet played by a piano and an accordion.

```
10 REM This program demonstrates some unusual sound effects
20 ENVELOPE 1,2,5,-5,5,10,20,10,1,0,0,-1,126,126
30 ENVELOPE 2,10,20,-30,25,10,10,15,4,-1,0,-1,126,80
40 ENVELOPE 3,8,-125,100,75,100,100,100,1,0,0,-1,126,126
50 ENVELOPE 4,6,1,2,-1,60,40,30,4,-1,0,-1,0,0
60 CLS: SOUND 1,1,120,120:
   PRINT TAB(11,12)"A passing police car"
70 PROCwait(8)
80 CLS: SOUND 0,1,4,200: PRINT TAB(12,12)"Passing Martians!"
90 PROCwait(15)
100 CLS: SOUND 1,2,130,250: PRINT TAB(15,12)"Crazy scales"
110 PROCwait(20)
120 CLS: SOUND 1,3,0,250: PRINT TAB(12,12)"More crazy scales!"
130 PROCwait(25)
140 CLS: SOUND 1,4,0,30: SOUND 0,-15,3,255: PROCwait(1):
    PRINT TAB(18,12)"Going?"
150 SOUND 1,4,0,30: PROCwait(1.5): PRINT TAB(18,13)"Going?"
160 SOUND 1,4,0,150: PROCwait(6): PRINT TAB(19,14)"Gone!"
170 PROCwait(15)
180 ENVELOPE 4,10,120,100,110,80,80,80,1,-1,-1,-1,126,125
190 CLS: SOUND 16,0,0,0: SOUND 0,4,2,255:
    PRINT TAB(16,12)"Look out!"
200 PROCwait(30): CLS
210 END
220 DEF PROCwait(time)
230 T%=TIME+100*time
240 REPEAT
       UNTIL TIME>T%
250 ENDPROC
```

Figure 3.9   Sound effects using envelopes

Piano:	ENVELOPE 1,1,0,0,0,0,0,0,126,-10,0,-4,126,100
Organ:	ENVELOPE 2,5,0,0,0,0,0,0,40,20,0,-4,100,126
Harpsichord:	ENVELOPE 3,1,0,0,0,0,0,0,126,-126,-4,-4,126,100
Xylophone:	ENVELOPE 4,2,0,0,0,0,0,0,126,-7,-7,-20,126,80
Accordion:	ENVELOPE 4,1,1,-1,0,1,1,0,10,5,0,-2,100,126

Figure 3.10   Musical instrument envelopes

Finally modify the program written in experiment 3.6 so that the first part is played by an organ and the second by a xylophone.

Experimental Hints

3.1   You should have noticed that the last line (which prints FINISHED) is apparently obeyed before lines 40–80, as the scale continues for some time after FINISHED is displayed.

3.2 The letters C, D, E, F, G, A are printed immediately, and the remaining letters one at a time as the note changes. Notes continue to be sounded long after the final letter (C) has been displayed. It should be apparent that there is some form of *queue* for the SOUND notes.

3.3 This experiment should confirm the existence of a five note queue. The detailed explanation will be found in the main text if you haven't already worked it out for yourself.

3.4 The repeated notes on lines 10, 20 and 80, 90 are sounded as a single, long, note. To correct this you must insert a short silent note, i.e.

```
10 SOUND 1,-15,100,8
15 SOUND 1,0,100,1
20 SOUND 1,-15,100,7
```

3.6 You need to insert a two bar silence at the head of the channel 2 queue. You can then repeat every SOUND statement on both channels:

```
 5 SOUND 2,0,0,64
10 SOUND 1,-15,100,8
15 SOUND 2,-15,100,8
etc.
```

3.9 Envelope 3 will rise to full volume over about 4 seconds, drop abruptly to a lower level, and stay there for another 8 seconds or so. It will then fade rapidly away in about half a second.

Envelope 4 will increase very slowly for about 5 seconds, and then more rapidly over the next 2 seconds to reach maximum volume. It will remain at this level until you press ESCape.

Using the right procedures

4.1 PROGRAM STRUCTURE AND PROCEDURES

In chapter 2 we described the main part of The Final Test as consisting of several fundamental steps which are repeated until the player reaches the tower (or until he is killed) (see
figure 4.1).

Although we have not yet introduced any of the Basic commands required to program
this, it is quite obvious that the difficult parts will be moving the player (including checks
for walls and doors), dealing with commands to collect or drop objects, or to open doors,
and creating moving and fighting spirits. We can therefore leave these for the moment and
write a more concise form of the plan in figure 4.1 as follows:

```
Repeat
    If a cursor control key has been pressed then MOVE
    or if another key has been pressed then READ COMMAND
    If there are any spirits present then MOVE SPIRIT(S)
    If more than "n" seconds since last move then CREATE SPIRIT
Until tower is reached (or player dies)
```

BBC Basic provides us with a very powerful feature for developing our programs in this
way known as a *procedure*, which allows a sequence of statements to be grouped together
with a name and then obeyed simply by referring to them by name. Such a name must

```
Repeat the following until player reaches the tower
    Wait for a key to be pressed
    If it is a direction key then move the player
    If it is the first letter of a valid command then read the rest of the command
    If it is anything else then ignore it

    If any spirits are present then move them and fight if appropriate

    If the player has been still for too long then create a new spirit
```

Figure 4.1   Structure plan of main loop of Castle

```
120 TIME=0:
    REPEAT

129    REMark - KeyValue is 136 to 139 for cursor keys
                KeyValue is -1 if no key has been pressed

130    KeyValue=INKEY(0):
       IF KeyValue>135 AND KeyValue<140 THEN PROCmove
       ELSE IF KeyValue<>-1 THEN PROCgetcom

140    IF NumSpirits>0 THEN PROCmovespirit

150    IF TIME>MaxWait THEN PROCgetspirit

180 UNTIL FloorNum>TopFloor
```

Figure 4.2   Simplified main loop of Castle

begin with the letters PROC (short for procedure) and so we could define four procedures for our four main actions called PROCmove, PROCgetcom, PROCmovespirit and PROCgetspirit.

Notice, incidentally, that although Basic keywords must be in capital letters, other, user-defined, names may be in lower case. Figure 4.2 shows how our plan would be written in Basic and although the meaning of some of the statements will not be clear the overall structure can be easily seen, with the four procedures being provided later in the program.

4.2   DEFINING A PROCEDURE

A procedure starts with a special definition statement of the form

```
DEF PROCname
```

and ends with

```
ENDPROC
```

As we have already seen it can then be used simply by writing

```
PROCname
```

as a Basic statement.

We could therefore write a procedure to play middle C on sound channel 1 like this:

```
DEF PROCmidC
SOUND 1,-15,52,20
ENDPROC
```

Rather more ambitiously we could write a procedure to play "Land of Hope and Glory":

```
100 DEF PROCtune
110 SOUND 1,-15,100,8
115 SOUND 1,0,100,1
120 SOUND 1,-15,100,7
130 SOUND 1,-15,96,4
140 SOUND 1,-15,100,4
150 SOUND 1,-15,108,8
160 SOUND 1,-15,88,16
170 SOUND 1,-15,80,16
180 SOUND 1,-15,72,8
185 SOUND 1,0,100,1
190 SOUND 1,-15,72,7
200 SOUND 1,-15,68,4
210 SOUND 1,-15,72,4
220 SOUND 1,-15,80,8
230 SOUND 1,-15,60,32
240 ENDPROC
```

Experiment 4.1

Write a procedure to play the following tune:

Use the procedure to play the tune three times with a one bar rest between each playing (32 time units). Did you recognise the tune? Did your program fail at the very end? If it did you will see why in the next section.

Experiment 4.1 illustrates a very important aspect of program development – namely the need to think before you write anything down. Most people will write a single procedure containing a total of 32 SOUND statements which will play the required notes. However, a moment's thought will show that each phrase is repeated twice – the four phrases consisting of 4, 3, 6 and 3 notes respectively. If each phrase is made into a procedure then the main procedure need only consist of eight procedure calls (see figure 4.3).

Furthermore, if we wish, we may write a further procedure which causes a one bar rest:

```
500 DEF PROConebarrest
510 SOUND 1,0,0,32
520 ENDPROC
```

```
100 DEF PROCtune
110 PROCphrase1: PROCphrase1
120 PROCphrase2: PROCphrase2
130 PROCphrase3: PROCphrase3
140 PROCphrase4: PROCphrase4
150 ENDPROC
```

Figure 4.3   Five procedures to play "Frère Jacques"

and our program then becomes extremely easy to read:

```
10 PROCtune
20 PROConebarrest
30 PROCtune
40 PROConebarrest
50 PROCtune
60 END
```

Note the use of a new Basic keyword

```
END
```

This means exactly what it says and tells the computer that this is the END of the program. We have not needed it before since if there are no more program statements the computer knows that it has reached the end. In this case, however, there are more statements, but these are procedure definitions and not part of the main program. If the END is omitted then after the main program has finished the computer will start to obey the first procedure. However, as it has not been called properly the program will fail when the ENDPROC is reached as there is nowhere for the processing to return to. This error probably occurred in your solution to experiment 4.1.

These procedures, however, are not especially useful since they always produce exactly the same result. A far more useful form of procedure is one which can be varied each time it is used. This is achieved by use of one or more procedure *parameters*. Consider the following procedure:

```
100 DEF PROCC(vol)
110 SOUND 1,vol,52,20
120 ENDPROC
```

This includes the parameter name vol in parentheses after the procedure name (PROCC), and then uses this in place of −15 in the SOUND statement. If we now write

```
PROCC(-15)
```

then the procedure will sound middle C at maximum volume (−15), whereas

```
PROCC(-10)
```

will sound it rather more quietly, and

```
PROCC(-1)
```

will sound it at minimum volume.
    We can extend this to all the parameters of the SOUND statement:

```
100 DEF PROCC(channel,vol,octave,length)
110 SOUND channel,vol,52+48*octave,4*length
120 ENDPROC
```

This will sound the note C on channel channel at volume vol for length beats. The note played will be octave octaves above middle C. Notice that multiplication in Basic is indicated by an asterisk (*) and that the expression "52+48*octave" therefore defines a pitch corresponding to 100 if octave is 1, to 148 if it is 2, etc., as required. Similarly 4*length defines the duration of the note where one "beat" is four twentieths of a second.

Experiment 4.2

Write a set of procedures to play all 13 notes from C to B on any channel, at any volume, in any possible octave, for any duration. Use these procedures to play the following tune:

Music for "Three Blind Mice" | *Note:* A dot after a note increases its length by one half; thus if $\lesssim$ has a length of two beats then $\lesssim$· has a length of three beats.

Experiment 4.3

Extend the program you wrote for experiment 4.2 so that a second "voice" starts the tune when the first "voice" reaches the point marked "NEXT VOICE". When you have done this add a third "voice" when the second one reaches the marked point. (See Experimental Hints when you have completed this experiment.)

Experiment 4.4

In chapter 3 we saw how the ENVELOPE statement could be used to change the sound of notes produced by SOUND statements. write a series of procedures called PROCpiano,

PROCorgan, etc. which set up appropriate envelopes, and use them in programs to play some of the tunes already introduced in the style of different instruments.

4.3   USING THE RED KEYS TO SAVE TYPING

In all of the above programs you will have found that the same keywords (e.g. DEF, PROC, ENDPROC, SOUND) kept being repeated and, although using the COPY key can speed things up, it is still annoying to keep repeating the same sequences. We can use the ten red keys at the top of the keyboard (marked f0 to f9) to considerably simplify matters.

These keys are called function keys and can be programmed with any required sequence of characters. They are programmed by typing

```
*KEYn
```

where n is the number of the key, followed by the characters which the key is to represent. For example we can type

```
*KEY0 DEF PROC
*KEY1 PROC
*KEY2 ENDPROC
*KEY3 SOUND 1,-15,
```

which will define the four keys with the character sequences shown. We could then write a short program by typing the following

```
AUTO RET
f1 C RET
f1 D RET
f1 E RET
END
f0 C RET
f3 52,20 RET
f2 RET
f0 D RET
f3 60,20 RET
f2 RET
f0 E RET
f3 68,20 RET
f2 RET
```

although what appears on the screen will be as shown in figure 4.4.

Notice that after pressing the f2 key (ENDPROC) we always follow it by pressing

```
>AUTO
   10 PROCC
   20 PROCD
   30 PROCE
   40 END
   50 DEF PROCC
   60 SOUND 1,-15,52,20
   70 ENDPROC
   80 DEF PROCD
   90 SOUND 1,-15,60,20
  100 ENDPROC
  110 DEF PROCE
  120 SOUND 1,-15,68,20
  130 ENDPROC
```

Figure 4.4   Program produced by function keys

RETURN. We can, in fact, involve the RETURN in the function key definition by typing the two characters |M – although notice that in mode 7 (the normal default screen mode) this will be shown on the screen as ‖M. If we redefine key 2 by typing

```
*KEY2 ENDPROC|M
```

then we shall see that it is not necessary to press RETURN after pressing f2.

Experiment 4.5

Program function keys 8 and 9 so that one of them will list your current program and the other will run it.

In chapter 2 we saw that the listing of a large program was simplified by use of "page mode", which causes the listing to stop every 15–20 lines. The computer was put into page mode by pressing the CTRL and N keys together, and we can put this sequence into a function key definition by typing |N, thus

```
*KEY8 |N LIST|M
```

We see from this that the character | in a function key definition means "CTRL together with the next character". We would therefore expect pressing CTRL and M together to have the same effect as pressing RETURN. Try it and see for yourself.

When we are running a program we usually do not want it in page mode, and we can revert to the normal scrolling of text by pressing CTRL and the letter O together. We could improve our RUN key definition therefore by typing

```
*KEY9 |O RUN|M
```

The function keys have a wide range of uses and can be programmed both directly and by a program. For example the CASTLE program defines key f0 with the following sequence:

```
MODE 2: VDU15,23;8202;0;0;0;: RUN|M
```

which puts the computer into screen mode 2 (with 16 columns), switches off paging (VDU15 is an alternative to |O), switches off the flashing cursor, and then runs the current program. The subsequent programs (CASTLE2 and Castle) are then run, if necessary, by pressing f0 instead of by typing RUN, thus ensuring that certain initial conditions are set up.

Experiment 4.6

Define function keys f0 to f7 so that they play the scale of C, i.e. f0 plays C, f1 plays D, etc. Choose your own volume and note duration. Then use the keys to play a simple tune, such as one of those in figure 4.5.
    What problems (if any) do you have with this "electronic piano"?

In the last experiment, because of the queueing of notes, the notes did not normally sound at the same time as the keys were pressed. We can get round this by causing each key to terminate the current note before producing its own. Chapter 16 will explain a lot more about the SOUND and ENVELOPE commands, but for the present we shall simply state that the command

```
SOUND 17,0,0,1
```

will stop the note on channel 1, and similarly

```
SOUND 16,0,0,1
SOUND 18,0,0,1
SOUND 19,0,0,1
```

Figure 4.5   Two tunes

will stop the sounds on channels 0, 2 and 3 respectively.

Thus if we type

```
*KEY0 SOUND 17,0,0,1|M SOUND 1,-15,52,4|M
```

we shall find that pressing f0 will stop any existing note on channel 1 and then play the note middle C for one beat.

If we replace the duration of the note (4) by the number 255 (or −1) then we will find that the note never stops! This is because a duration of 255 (or −1) has a special meaning – namely that the duration is infinite. If all the keys first stop any existing note, however, we have an easy way of providing variable length notes.

Experiment 4.7

Reprogram the function keys along the lines discussed above and then play the following tune:

What happened at the end? (See Experimental Hints if you have any problems.)

4.4   THE BREAK KEY

Next to the f9 key is a key marked BREAK. Normally this should never be pressed as it clears a large part of the memory and "forgets" your current program. If you do press it, perhaps by accident, you can recover your program by typing

```
OLD
```

as long as you have not typed any new statements already.

Fortunately, however, we can program the BREAK key in a similar fashion to the ten function keys so that it produces the defined string of characters immediately after the "break". For this purpose we refer to it as key 10 and can thus type

```
*KEY10 OLD|M
```

Once this has been done there is no risk of losing a program through accidentally pressing the BREAK key. It is, of course, possible to program the BREAK key in this way from within a program and The Final Test programs are all protected against accidental loss in this way.

4.5   ADDING COMMENTS TO YOUR PROGRAMS

Although we can still only write quite simple programs which play tunes or produce various sounds on the computer, it is not always obvious (especially with SOUND and ENVELOPE statements) exactly what is supposed to happen. Basic therefore provides a means for us to add comments or remarks to our programs. These will be ignored by the computer, but will provide us with extra information. They consist of the keyword REM followed by the text of the remark (or comment). Thus we could write

```
 10 REM A program to play "Frere Jacques"
 20 PROCbar1: PROCbar1
 30 PROCbar2: PROCbar2
 40 PROCbar3: PROCbar3
 50 PROCbar4: PROCbar4
 60 END
 70 DEF PROCbar1
 80 REM Procedure for 1st repeated bar
 90 SOUND 1,-15,100,8
100 SOUND 1,-15,108,8
110 SOUND 1,-15,116,8
120 SOUND 1,-15,100,8
130 ENDPROC
140 DEF PROCbar2
150 REM Procedure for 2nd repeated bar
etc.
```

Notice that we are not limited to capitals for our comments and, indeed, they are more readable if typed in lower case in the conventional way. (To change the computer from always using capitals you should press the key marked CAPS LOCK near the bottom left-hand corner of the keyboard. The CAPS LOCK light will go out and the keyboard will function like an ordinary typewriter in lower case, with the SHIFT key being held down to produce capitals. Pressing CAPS LOCK again will reverse the process.)

Comments should be used sparingly since they occupy valuable memory space within the computer, but it is a good idea to include them at the start of a procedure or at any other place in your program whose purpose is not obvious.

Experimental Hints

4.3   It is clear that a two bar silence is required before the second "voice" starts on channel 2, and a further two bar silence (four bars in all) before channel 3 starts. However, it is not possible to have a procedure (e.g. PROCtune) which has the channel number as a parameter and then plays the whole tune. This is because there are considerably more than six notes in the tune, and so no exit will be made from the procedure until the tune is almost complete.

  The following approach *will* work however:

```
10 PROCG(1,-15,0,8)
11 PROCG(2,0,0,8)
12 PROCG(3,0,0,8)
20 PROCF(1,-15,0,8)
21 PROCF(2,0,0,8)
```

At the appropriate point the PROC calls for channel 2 will have a non-zero volume and will start to play the correct notes; later still, those for channel 3 will join in. Judicious use of the COPY facility will mean that most of the new lines (for channels 2 and 3) can be produced from the earlier program with very little effort.

  Use of AUTO can make it even easier, e.g.

```
AUTO 11
```

to produce lines 11, 21, 31, etc.

4.6   The notes will usually not sound as you press the keys because of the queueing of the notes.

4.7   The last note will never stop! (Until you press ESCape that is.)

5

Seeing is believing

5.1 CHOOSING YOUR OWN COLOURS

In chapter 2 we discussed the concept of different screen "modes" and, in particular, emphasised the difference between mode 7 and the other modes, which are numbered from 0 to 6. In this chapter we shall explain how to obtain coloured backgrounds, coloured text and coloured drawing in modes 0 to 6. The use of colour and graphics in mode 7 is discussed in chapter 13.

As we mentioned in chapter 2, the choice of mode is determined by balancing the importance of colour, resolution and, perhaps, memory requirement. Figure 5.1 shows the differences in these areas and, in particular, the very large memory requirement of modes 0 to 2.

Nevertheless, we shall start our examination of this subject with mode 2, since this is the only mode in which all possible colour combinations are available.

According to the *BBC User Guide* mode 2 has 16 colours, and from a theoretical point of view this is so. However, as figure 5.2 shows, this is not really the way that we understand it, since two of these colours are black and white, and eight of them are flashing (or alternating) pairs of colours.

In particular, it is normally difficult to tell the difference between, for example, colour 11 which is flashing yellow/blue and colour 12 which is flashing blue/yellow! (It should be noted, however, that it is possible to alter the times for which the two colours are displayed

Mode	Colours Available	Resolution Text	Graphics	Memory Requirement
0	2	80 x 32	640 x 256	20 Kbytes
1	4	40 x 32	320 x 256	20 Kbytes
2	16	20 x 32	160 x 256	20 Kbytes
3	2	80 x 25	—	16 Kbytes
4	2	40 x 32	320 x 256	10 Kbytes
5	4	20 x 32	160 x 256	10 Kbytes
5	2	40 x 25	—	8 Kbytes
7	15	40 x 25	80 x 75	1 Kbyte

Figure 5.1   Table of screen modes

```
0   black
1   red
2   green
3   yellow
4   blue
5   magenta
6   cyan
7   white
8   flashing black/white
9   flashing red/cyan
10  flashing green/magenta
11  flashing yellow/blue
12  flashing blue/yellow
13  flashing magenta/green
14  flashing cyan/red
15  flashing white/black
```

Figure 5.2   Normal colour assignments in mode 2

so that one is shown for longer that the other; the difference between these two colour combinations is then readily apparent.)

We can specify the colour in which text is to be written by the command

```
COLOUR c
```

where c is the required colour, in the range 0–15 for mode 2. Thus if we type

```
COLOUR 1
```

we shall have red characters on a black background for all future text displayed either by the computer or as a result of being typed on the keyboard.

We can also change the background on which the character is displayed by a similar command except that 128 is added to the number of the colour. Thus

```
COLOUR 130
```

causes a green background (130 = 128+2) to be used.

Experiment 5.1

Type the following commands on your computer

```
MODE 2
COLOUR 129
COLOUR 0
COLOUR 130
COLOUR 3
COLOUR 132
COLOUR 6
```

```
COLOUR 133
COLOUR 11
COLOUR 140
COLOUR 7
COLOUR 132
```

Note that the computer is now ready to display white letters on a blue background.

Experiment 5.1 shows how you can readily change the colours being used, but the result is less than satisfactory due to the fact that the major part of the screen is still black and the new background only affects the area immediately around any characters which are typed. In order to produce a more pleasing presentation we need a new command

```
CLS
```

which clears the screen to the current background colour. Notice incidentally that the whole television screen is not used and that there is a small margin at the top and bottom with larger ones at the sides.

Experiment 5.2

Type the following commands:

```
MODE 2
COLOUR 129
CLS
COLOUR 0
COLOUR 130
COLOUR 3
CLS
COLOUR 132
COLOUR 6
COLOUR 11
COLOUR 12
COLOUR 7
CLS
```

Mode 2 thus provides a choice of 16 "colours" but at the cost of large characters, medium resolution for graphics (as we shall see) and a large memory requirement.

Mode 1, on the other hand, provides a much more readable 40 characters to a line and good graphics resolution, although it also has a large memory requirement. In exchange for this the number of available colours is reduced to 4 (see figure 5.3).

```
0    black
1    red
2    yellow
3    white
```

Figure 5.3   Normal colour assignments in modes 1 and 5

These same four colours are also available in mode 5 which has the same large characters and medium resolution as mode 2, but has a much smaller memory requirement.

Note that in modes 1, 2 and 5 the default (or initial) colour choices are white text on a black background. Because different modes have different ranges of colours, the foreground (text) and background colours are always reset to these default values when you change mode, and you must yourself set them to any other colours you may require.

Experiment 5.3

Type the following commands

```
MODE 2
COLOUR 130
COLOUR 3
PRINT "Yellow on Green"
MODE 1
COLOUR 130
COLOUR 3
PRINT "White on Yellow"
MODE 5
COLOUR 129
COLOUR 2
PRINT "Yellow on Red"
```

You will have noticed that in modes 1 and 5 only two "proper" colours (red and yellow) are available in addition to black and white. In modes 0, 3, 4 and 6 the situation is even worse as these modes only have two colours – black and white.

Mode 0 gives 80 characters to a line and the highest resolution graphics available, while mode 3 gives only 25 lines of 80 characters per line. Mode 4 gives 40 characters to a line, but less memory is required than for modes 0–3, while mode 6 gives 25 lines of 40 characters and no graphics (see figure 5.1). Unless you have a high-definition television *monitor* you will probably have difficulty reading the text in modes 0 and 3; nevertheless, for some purposes they are very useful if a suitable display is available.

We now come, for the first time, to a very powerful command – VDU. This is a

```
0    black
1    white
```

Figure 5.4   Normal colour assignments in modes 0, 3, 4 and 6

command which allows you to alter any or all of the normal display parameters, for example the colours being used, the area of the screen being used, the way in which draw-ings are produced, etc. We shall look at it in more detail in subsequent chapters but at present we shall concern ourselves only with the way in which we can use it to alter the normal meaning of colours. In this mode of use the statement takes the form

```
VDU 19,lc,ac;0;
```

Notice in particular the two semi-colons before and after the final zero; *these are vital.*
    This statement causes the *logical colour* lc to represent the *actual colour* ac. Thus

```
VDU 19,0,4;0;
```

in mode 1 will cause the logical colour 0 (which is usually black) to represent the actual colour 4 (which is blue, as for mode 2). The normal mode 2 colours are the 16 actual colours used in this statement.
    This means, therefore, that modes 1, 2 and 5 may use *any* four colours, and that modes 0, 3, 4 and 6 may use *any* two colours from the 16 colours available in mode 2.

Experiment 5.4

Type the following program

```
10 MODE 1
20 COLOUR 1
30 PRINT "This is colour 1 on colour 0"
40 COLOUR 2
50 PRINT "This is colour 2 on colour 0"
60 COLOUR 3
70 PRINT "This is colour 3 on colour 0"
80 END
```

Now RUN the program. Is the result what you expected?
    Now type

```
VDU 19,0,6;0;
```

Notice the difference between the effect of this statement and of changing the background colour in earlier experiments. In this case the background is still colour 0; however colour 0 is instantaneously changed to cyan (light blue) instead of black.
    Now type

```
VDU 19,3,3;0;
```

What has happened? and why? (See Experimental Hints if you don't understand.)
    Finally type

```
VDU 19,2,6;0;
```

```
10 MODE 6
20 PRINT
30 PRINT "This program produces a variety"
40 PRINT "of different coloured displays."
50 PRINT
60 PRINT "The use of MODE 6 gives a narrow"
70 PRINT "black band between each pair of lines."
80 PRINT
90 FOR I=1 TO 6
100 INPUT "Press RETURN for new background" X$
110 VDU 19,0,I;0;
120 NEXT
130 INPUT "Press RETURN for black text on white" X$
140 VDU 19,0,7;0;: VDU 19,1,0;0;
150 FOR I=1 TO 6
160 INPUT "Press RETURN for new foreground" X$
170 VDU 19,1,I;0;
180 NEXT
190 INPUT "Press RETURN to restore white text on black" X$
140 VDU 19,0,0;0;: VDU 19,1,7;0;
```

Figure 5.5   Program to produce mode 6 listings

The second line of text has disappeared because both logical colours 0 and 2 have been set to actual colour 6. Typing

VDU 19,0,7;0;

will set the background to white (actual colour 7) and enable all three lines (in red, cyan and yellow) to be seen once again.

The use of this VDU statement enables the two colour modes to use two colours other than black and white in a similar way. As we saw in chapter 2, modes 3 and 6 leave a thin black gap between the lines which, although not visible when a black background is in use, can be quite pleasing when a coloured one is created by using the VDU 19 statement. The program in figure 5.5 produces several lines of text and then cycles through various combinations of background and foreground colours. In the BBC television series "The Computer Programme" and "Making the Most of the Micro" many of the program listings are in mode 6 with white letters on a blue background, i.e.

MODE 6
VDU 19,0,4;0;
LIST

5.2   DRAWING WITH LINES

In modes 0, 1, 2, 4 and 5 we can draw lines as well as write text. However, for reasons which will become apparent in chapter 11 we use different statements to define the colours we wish to use for foreground and background, and to clear the background. The colours are specified by the command

```
GCOL n,c
```

where c is the colour required (as with the COLOUR statement) and n is a number which for the present will normally be zero. Thus

```
GCOL 0,134
GCOL 0,1
```

will define the graphics background to be logical colour 6 ($134 = 128 + 6$) and the graphics foreground to be logical colour 1. In mode 2, unless the default colours have been altered, this will lead to red lines on a pale blue (cyan) background. The screen is cleared to the graphics background colour by the command

```
CLG
```

For graphical purposes the screen is considered as consisting of a large number of dots or *pixels* (short for picture elements) which are set to one of the available colours. Regardless of the mode being used these pixels are considered to be on a grid consisting of 1280 points across the screen (the x-direction) and 1024 from top-to-bottom (the y-direction) (see figure 5.6).

However, not all the points on this grid are individually addressable, and pixels actually consist of small rectangles of grid points. In mode 0 these rectangles are four "points" high and two wide, thus giving a resolution of 640 pixels across the screen and 256 down it. In modes 1 and 4 they are four "points" high and four wide, thus giving a resolution of 320×256, while in modes 2 and 5 they are four "points" high and eight wide, giving a resolution of 160×256. Thus the vertical resolution is always the same while the horizontal resolution varies considerably, see figure 5.7.

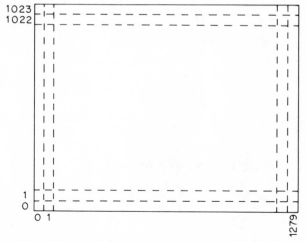

Figure 5.6   The graphical co-ordinate system used in modes 0 to 6

Mode	Resolution	Pixel Size
0	640 x 256	2 x 4
1 or 4	320 x 256	4 x 4
2 or 5	160 x 256	8 x 4

Figure 5.7   Graphical pixels in different modes

There are a great many ways of drawing lines on the screen but we shall only consider the simplest ones at this stage. The basic principle is that an invisible *graphic cursor* is moved about the screen and either leaves a line as it moves, or does not leave any line.

The command

```
DRAW x,y
```

moves the cursor from its present position to the point defined as having grid co-ordinates x across the screen and y up it, drawing a straight line as it moves.

The command

```
MOVE x,y
```

on the other hand, also moves the cursor from its present position to the point (x,y) but without drawing a line.

The graphic cursor, which is invisible and does not flash like the text cursor, is initially positioned at the point (0,0), i.e. at the lower left-hand corner of the screen.

Experiment 5.5

Type the following program;

```
 10 MODE 1
 20 GCOL 0,1
 30 MOVE 320,832
 40 DRAW 960,832
 50 DRAW 960,192
 60 DRAW 320,192
 70 DRAW 320,832
 80 GCOL 0,2
 90 DRAW 960,192
100 MOVE 320,192
110 DRAW 960,832
```

Now run it. Observe carefully how the screen appears.

Now type

```
10 MODE 5
RUN
```

What differences do you observe? Why?

Now type

```
10 MODE 2
RUN
```

Is this what you expected?

Now type

```
10 MODE 4
RUN
```

Do you understand what has happened? Mode 4 only allows two colours (0 and 1). If a colour greater than 1 is specified then that number modulo 2 is used, i.e. the remainder after dividing by 2. In this case colour 2 is specified at line 80 for the diagonals and this is therefore interpreted as colour 0, which is the background colour, and so they are not visible.

Now type

```
80 GCOL 0,5
RUN
```

Colour 5 is treated as colour 1 and so all is well.

Now type

```
10 MODE 0
RUN
```

Observe the fine horizontal resolution which leads to very narrow vertical lines.

Experiment 5.6

Type the following program and run it.

```
 10 MODE 1
 20 GCOL 0,2
 30 PROCman(200,200)
 40 PROCwoman(300,700)
 50 PROCwoman(600,300)
 60 PROCman(800,600)
 70 PROCwoman(900,100)
 80 PROCman(1100,500)
 90 END
100 DEF PROCman(x,y)
110 MOVE x-80,y
120 DRAW x-60,y: DRAW x,y+90: DRAW x+60,y: DRAW x+80,y
130 MOVE x,y+90: DRAW x,y+160
140 MOVE x-90,y+150: DRAW x+90,y+150
```

```
150 PROChead(x,y+160)
160 ENDPROC
170 DEF PROChead(x,y)
180 MOVE x,y: DRAW x-30,y+12: DRAW x-30,y+42: DRAW x,y+54:
    DRAW x+30,y+42: DRAW x+30,y+12: DRAW x,y
190 MOVE x-18,y+36: DRAW x-6,y+36: MOVE x+6,y+36: DRAW x+18,y+36
200 MOVE x,y+30: DRAW x,y+18
210 MOVE x-12,y+12: DRAW x+12,y+12
220 ENDPROC
230 DEF PROCwoman
240 PROCman(x,y)
250 MOVE x-30,y+40: DRAW x+30,y+40
260 ENDPROC
```

Notice the use of a procedure to draw the figures with their position defined by arguments to the procedure.

Experiment with this program to alter the colours and positions of the figures. Can you think of a way of arranging for different figures to be in different colours?

5.3   COLOURING SOLID AREAS

The CASTLE program uses a technique, very similar to that used in experiment 5.6, to draw the various dragons, skeletons and spirits after the "blinding flash". (The latter, incidentally, is achieved by a rapid sequence of VDU 19 statements which set the background alternately to white and red – see line 180.) The dragons, skeletons and spirits, however, are composed of solid areas of colour and not of lines as in experiment 5.6. This is achieved by use of the PLOT statement, which takes the form

```
PLOT k,x,y
```

where x and y have the same meaning as for MOVE and DRAW, and k indicates which of a wide range of plotting operations is required. We shall discuss the more general use of PLOT in chapter 11, but it is perhaps worth noting that

```
PLOT 4,x,y
```

and

```
MOVE x,y
```

are identical in their effect, and that

```
PLOT 5,x,y
```

and

```
DRAW x,y
```

are also identical in their effect.

However, the statement

```
PLOT 85,x,y
```

is very different, and fills in a triangle formed by the last two points specified in any PLOT, MOVE or DRAW statement and the point (x,y). Thus the statements

```
MOVE 100,100
MOVE 400,200
PLOT 85,250,600
```

will fill in a triangle defined by the points (100,100), (400,200) and (250,600). A further statement

```
PLOT 85,900,750
```

will fill in another triangle, this time defined by the points (400,200), (250,600) and (900,750) (see figure 5.8).

This provides a powerful way for rapidly filling in an area of any shape by breaking it up into a series of triangles, e.g.

```
10 MODE 1
20 GCOL 0,1
30 MOVE 320,832
40 MOVE 960,832
50 PLOT 85,320,192
60 PLOT 85,960,192
```

will fill the square drawn in experiment 5.5. Notice that care must be taken to visit the

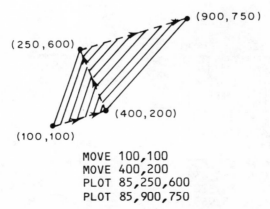

```
MOVE 100,100
MOVE 400,200
PLOT 85,250,600
PLOT 85,900,750
```

Figure 5.8   An example of triangle drawing

corners in the best order; if line 50 had read PLOT 85,960,192 then it would not have been possible to complete the square with the next PLOT statement (see figure 5.9).

The procedures PROCdragon (lines 1020–1090), PROCspirit (lines 1100–1140) and PROCskeleton (lines 1150–1220) build up their respective shapes in exactly this way. They all use one extra statement, however, which we have not yet met:

```
VDU 29,x;y;
```

which moves the *origin* to the point (x,y), so that all subsequent plotting statements are relative to this point. Notice the semi-colons after the values x and y; these are essential if the statement is to work correctly (as were the semi-colons in the VDU19 statement used to alter logical colours). Without this statement all the points specified in the procedures would have had to have x and y added to their respective co-ordinates, e.g.

```
1170 MOVE 30+x,90+y: MOVE x,80+y: PLOT 85,60+x,80+y:
```

At the end of the procedure the statement

```
VDU 29,0;0;
```

moves the origin back to its original position, i.e. the point (0,0). *Note* that the co-ordinates of the origin in a VDU20 statement are always in terms of the original origin, and not of any new one which may be in force.

Notice also that, as elsewhere in The Final Test, a number of statements have been written on a single line, separated by colons, thus

```
1160 GCOL 0,7: VDU 29,x;y;
```

is the same as

```
1160 GCOL 0,7
1165 VDU 29,x;y;
```

but takes up less space both on the screen and in the computer's memory.

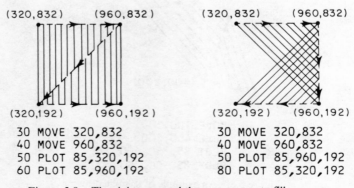

30	MOVE 320,832	30	MOVE 320,832
40	MOVE 960,832	40	MOVE 960,832
50	PLOT 85,320,192	50	PLOT 85,960,192
60	PLOT 85,960,192	80	PLOT 85,320,192

Figure 5.9   The right way and the wrong way to fill a square

PROCskeleton uses GCOL 0,7 to cause the skeleton to be drawn in colour 7 (i.e. white in mode 2). PROCspirit, however, defines the colour by the statement

```
GCOL 1,14
```

which causes it to be drawn in flashing cyan/red in such a way that it does not necessarily totally obliterate any items it is plotted on top of. Similarly PROCdragon uses the statement

```
GCOL 1,c
```

to draw the dragon in colour (c) specified as an argument to the procedure (either 1 or 2 to give red or green dragons). The dragons are also drawn in a way which allows them not to obliterate any item underneath them, as is the case with the text and the uppermost red dragon.

We shall discuss this and other forms of the GCOL statement in chapter 11; for the present you should normally use GCOL 0,c if you wish to have predictable results.

Experiment 5.7

Use some squared paper to imitate, by hand, plotting carried out by the three procedures PROCdragon, PROCspirit and PROCskeleton. Then use a similar technique to write a program to produce a drawing on the screen similar to that shown in figure 5.10. Choose your own colour scheme.

Experiment 5.8

The opening titles produced when the program CASTLE is run without the preceding FINALTEST program are created by use of a number of quite sophisticated colour combinations which will be analysed in chapter 11. The actual title "THE FINAL TEST" is drawn using the triangle technique, however, in the procedure PROCtitle by lines 770–810. To simplify matters a special procedure PROCline is used (see lines 990–1010) which draws a solid rectangle. A call to

```
PROCline(x,y,u1,v1,u2,v2)
```

will draw a "line" as shown in figure 5.11.

Figure 5.10   Computer Art?

68

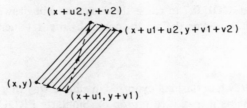

Figure 5.11   PROCline(x,y,u1,v1,u2,v2)

A special case is when v1 and u2 are zero, when the rectangle becomes either a vertical or a horizontal line (see figure 5.12).

Alter this procedure so that, for example, the program is called "CASTLE OF DOOM". Ensure that your title uses only three lines and that these are positioned at the same height as in the original, or strange things may happen when you come to run it.

Lines 770–810 use a number of features that we have not yet met, and you should write your version using only the simple statements already discussed. Delete all of these lines, but start your new line 770 with

GCOL 0,15

and end the last line of your title with

PROCwait(2): RESTORE 1280: PROCtune

as in line 810. (This will play the second part of "Greensleeves".) You should also delete lines 1300–1400 which will no longer be needed.

Test this procedure as a replacement for the one supplied, and when it is working SAVE the complete program as the first step in your own personalised version of the game.

Experimental Hints

5.4   The program runs in mode 1, in which the logical colour assignments are as follows:

0   black
1   red
2   yellow
3   white

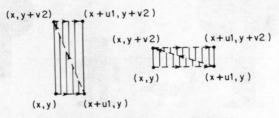

Figure 5.12   PROCline(x,y,u1,0,0,v2)

In a VDU 19 statement the actual colours are those used in mode 2 and therefore a statement such as

VDU 19,3,3;0;

assigns *actual* colour 3 (which is yellow) to *logical* colour 3. The third line of text (which uses colour 3) therefore changes from white to yellow.

5.5   In mode 1 a red square is drawn with yellow diagonals.

In mode 5 the colours are the same, but the width of the vertical lines (and, more obviously, the diagonals) is increased. This is the same as in experiment 2.6, and is due to the different resolutions.

In mode 2 the diagonals become green because this is the colour assigned by default to logical colour 2 in mode 2.

In mode 4 the lines are once again of the same width, although as this is a two colour mode the diagonals cannot use colour 2 but will use colour 0 instead, and disappear!

In mode 0 the vertical lines are very narrow, and will not show properly on most domestic television receivers. They will be perfectly clear on a monitor, however.

6

Variety is the spice of life

6.1   REPEATING OURSELVES

All the programs that we have written so far have consisted of a sequence of statements which are obeyed in turn until the end of the program is reached. If we want to repeat the same sequence of statements several times then we have to repeat the statements – although we have seen how using a procedure can simplify this somewhat. The need to repeat a sequence of statements, however, is so fundamental that Basic, in common with all other programming languages, provides a special statement (or rather pair of statements) to simplify the process. The first of these statements takes the form

```
FOR count=first TO last
```

where   count   is a name consisting of letters and digits, of which the first must be a
letter. It will be   used to identify some location in the computer's
memory which will be used to count how many times the statements
have been obeyed.
first   is the value at which counting is to start.
last   is the value at which counting is to end.

e.g.   FOR I=1 TO 10
```
FOR count=18 TO 27
FOR counter=0 TO 9
FOR J4a=-4 TO 5
```

Note that both capitals and lower-case letters may be used although, as we shall see later in this chapter, there are a few minor restrictions on the names that may be chosen.

All of the above statements will cause the statements following to be repeated ten times (1 = 1, 2, 3, . . ., 9, 10; count = 18, 19, 20,. . . 26, 27; counter = 0, 1, 2, . . ., 8, 9; J4a = −4, −3, −2, −1, 0, 1, 2, 3, 4, 5). One problem that remains, however, is defining which statements are to be obeyed.

70

In English we can write

Repeat the following ten times
   First statement
   Second statement
   Third statement
Carry out some other activity

and the layout of the writing makes it quite clear what is to be repeated. However, spaces used for indentation of lines are ignored by the Basic interpreter, as are blank lines, and so we need a different method of identifying which statements are to be repeated. This method is to add another statement consisting of the word

`NEXT`

although, if we wish, we may write

`NEXT count`

where count is the same name as that used in the FOR statement.

The use of the name of the FOR counter in the NEXT statement helps with the readability of the program but also slows down the program and so is not normally to be recommended.

Experiment 6.1

Write a program to play "Frère Jacques" (see experiment 4.1) ten times with a one bar rest between each playing. Use a FOR statement for this experiment!

6.2 KEEPING THINGS FOR LATER IN VARIABLES

The FOR statement introduced above used a *name* to identify some location in the memory which the computer then used to count how many times it had repeated the sequence of statements between the FOR and the NEXT. A named location such as this is called a *variable* and is the key to most aspects of computer programming. For the moment we shall assume that we are only concerned with numbers – we shall discuss how strings of characters may be stored in the computer's memory in chapter 9.

Essentially we can consider the computer's memory to consist of thousands of "boxes", each of which can contain a single number (see figure 6.1).

Thus when we write

`FOR I=1 TO 10`

we are telling the computer to give the name I to one of these boxes and to store the value 1 in it. Each time the NEXT (or NEXT I) statement is obeyed, the computer has a look at this box and if the value in it is less than 10 it adds 1 to the value stored and repeats the sequence of statements following the FOR statement. After it has obeyed these statements

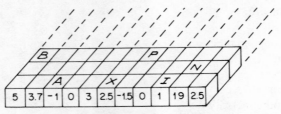

Figure 6.1   A representation of the computer's memory

ten times the value in the **I** "box" will be 10 and so it will not repeat them again but will proceed to the next statement (i.e. the one after the NEXT statement).
    Similarly

```
FOR count=18 TO 27
```

will cause a box to be given the name count and the initial value 18. On the tenth time through the loop (as such a sequence of statements is usually called) the count box will contain 27 and so the loop will not be repeated.
    We can store values in a variable ourselves (though not while it is being used as a counter in a FOR loop) by means of the statement

```
LET name=value
```

which *assigns* the value specified to the variable whose name is specified (i.e. the box called name has the number value stored in it). Thus

```
LET cost=7.4
```

will store the value 7.4 in the variable cost, and

```
LET colour=5
```

will store the value 5 in the variable colour.
    In practice the word LET is optional and so we may write

```
cost=7.4
colour=5
```

as long as we remember that we are not saying that "cost is equal to 7.4" or "colour is equal to 5" but rather "Let the variable cost be assigned the value 7.4" or "Let the variable colour be assigned the value 5". This is rather a mouthful to say and so when necessary the statement

```
X=63
```

is read as "X *becomes* 63".

Once we have assigned a value to a variable we may simply write the name of the variable in any place where we could have written a number, and the current value of the variable will be used when the program statement is obeyed. Thus we may write

```
100 pitch=100
110 SOUND 1,-15,pitch,20
```

and the SOUND statement will play the note having a pitch of 100 (i.e. C, one octave above middle C). *Note* that this is very similar to the way in which procedure parameters work (see section 4.2), and in fact a procedure parameter is simply a special type of variable whose value is assigned to it when the procedure is *called* (or *referenced*):

```
 50 PROCnote(100)
    .
    .
    .
100 DEF PROCnote(pitch)
110 SOUND 1,-15,pitch,20
120 ENDPROC
```

The use of variables enormously increases the power of a computer, as is demonstrated in a very graphic manner in the next few experiments.

Experiment 6.2

A very useful feature of Basic is its ability to provide *random numbers* for use in games or for other purposes. We shall examine this in more detail in chapter 8, but for the present we shall state that if we write

```
RND(n)
```

where n is a whole number greater than 1, then a random number in the range 1 to n will be provided in place of the *function call*. Thus if we write

```
X=RND(20)
```

some whole number in the range 1 to 20 will be assigned to the variable X. We can use this to create some interesting random, abstract shapes on our screen.
Type in the following program, and RUN it.

```
10 MODE 2
20 MOVE 0,0
30 MOVE 1279,1023
40 FOR I=1 TO 100
50    X=RND(1280)-1
```

```
 60    Y=RND(1024)-1
 70    C=RND(8)-1
 80    GCOL 0,C
 90    PLOT 85,X,Y
100    NEXT
```

Do you understand what has been happening?

The statements on lines 20 and 30 move the graphic cursor to the bottom left and top right corners before the main loop begins. Line 50 sets X to a random number in the range 0 to 1279, which is the valid range of x co-ordinates for graphical work, and line 60 sets Y to a random number in the range 0 to 1023. Line 70 then sets C to a random number in the range 0 to 7. (*Note* the subtraction of 1 from the random number provided in each of the above cases. RND(1023) would give a number in the range 1 to 1023; RND(1024) gives a number in the range 1 to 1024 which leads to a range from 0 to 1023 after one has been subtracted.)

Line 80 then sets the graphical foreground colour to the random colour chosen in line 70. The PLOT statement at line 90 then fills a triangle with that colour – the triangle being defined by the last two points defined and the random point created by lines 50 and 60.

A total of 100 such random triangles are drawn.

Experiment 6.3

It is not necessary to store the random values in variables before they can be used; it is equally acceptable to write GCOL 0,RND(8)–1.

Modify the program in experiment 6.2 so that it uses no variables apart from the one used to control the FOR loop, and also so that it uses all 16 colours (i.e. the flashing as well as the non-flashing ones). RUN this program.

Experiment 6.4

Alter the GCOL statement in the program you have just written so that it is GCOL 3, . . . instead of GCOL 0, . . . and RUN the program.

We shall see in chapter 11 why you get these very different effects, but if you wish to experiment further try using other values for the first value in a GCOL statement, i.e. GCOL 1, . . . or even GCOL RND(n), . . .

Experiment 6.5

The following program uses two FOR loops, one *nested* inside the other. This means that the inner loop is repeated the required number of times *for every pass* through the outer loop. In order to clarify the structure, the loops have been indented and the loop variable names included in the NEXT statements. *Note* that we have not yet met the statement on line 120 but its purpose in this program should be perfectly obvious; we shall discuss it in some detail in chapter 10.

```
10 REM Use screen mode with most colour
20 MODE 2
30 REM Clear screen to magenta background
40 GCOL 0,133
50 CLG
60 REM Initialise drawing colour
70 col = 0
80 REM Main loop defines 10 sets of boxes
90 FOR set=0 TO 9
100    REM Update drawing colour
110    col=col+1
120    IF col>7 THEN col=0
130    REM Draw boxes for this set
140    FOR box=0 TO 13
150       REM Calculate coordinates of 1st corner
160       corner=100*set+7*box
170       REM Alter foreground colour
180       GCOL 0,col
190       REM Move to first corner
200       MOVE corner,corner
210       REM Draw box
220       DRAW 1279-corner,corner
230       DRAW 1279-corner,1023-corner
240       DRAW corner,1023-corner
250       DRAW corner,corner
260       NEXT box
270    NEXT set
280 REM All boxes drawn so repeat using different colours
290 GO TO 90
```

Type this program into your computer and then RUN it. Do you like the results produced? An even more interesting set of patterns can be obtained by altering line 180 to read GCOL 3,col.

Note that this program is based on one used in the videotape programming course *Getting Down to Basic*, written by Miles Ellis and published by Guild Learning (Peterborough, 1982), which is in turn based on a program presented by N. Cryer and P. Cryer (*BASIC Programming on the BBC Microcomputer*, Prentice-Hall, London, 1982).

6.3   VARIABLE NAMES

We stated earlier that there were a few minor restrictions on the names that may be chosen for variable names. The rules relating to variable names are, in fact, quite simple and are:

1. A variable name may consist of any number of letters, digits and underline characters.
2. The first character of a variable name must be a letter.
3. A variable name must not begin with a Basic keyword.

Thus the following names are all valid:

```
A
Acorn
BBC
xyz
My_name
Last_set_of_data
X17
Ab234xyPQ_74_roger
```

Notice that although we cannot have a space in a name we can have an underline character to visually space out parts of a long name.
    The following names are *not allowed:*

```
My name              contains a space
P17/4                contains an illegal character (/)
1st set of data      begins with a digit
PROCESS              begins with a keyword (PROC)
TOMORROW             begins with a keyword (TO)
```

There is a complete list of Basic keywords in Appendix D, and also in the *User Guide* (pages 483–484 in the first edition, 1982). However, one way of avoiding the risk of inadvertently starting a variable name with a Basic keyword is to use lower case for variable names – which also helps with the readability of your programs. Thus

```
process
Process
tomorrow
Tomorrow
```

are all valid names since Basic keywords (e.g. PROC and TO) must be in capitals.

6.4   VARIABLES IN PROCEDURES

Normally, once a value has been assigned to a variable then that variable may be used anywhere else in the program, including any procedures. However, this can cause problems when writing procedures since it is necessary to ensure that any variables used do not conflict with those used elsewhere. The solution to this problem is to specify that some (or all) of the variables used in a procedure are *local* to that procedure by means of a statement of the form

```
LOCAL name1,name2,...
```

Local variables are only defined from the time when the LOCAL statement is obeyed until the ENDPROC statement is obeyed at the end of the procedure. They are thus a form of temporary storage which can be used within the procedure without the risk of confusion with variables used elsewhere (see figure 6.2).

Experiment 6.6

Type in the following program and RUN it.

```
 10 FOR I=1 TO 2
 20    PRINT I
 30    PROCsound
 40    NEXT
 50 END
 60 DEF PROCsound
 70 LOCAL I
 80 FOR I=0 TO 63
 90    SOUND 1,-15,4*I,1
100    NEXT
110 ENDPROC
```

The program should print the value 1 on the screen (line 20) and then call the procedure PROCsound to produce a rapid "glissando" from a very low to a very high note. The FOR loop on lines 10–40 will then repeat causing a 2 to be printed, followed by another glissando.

Now delete line 70 by typing

70

and RUN the program again. Do you understand why the result is different?

In the second case, the statement which makes I a *local* variable has been deleted and so the *global* variable I is used. When the procedure is entered, this is first set to 0 and then

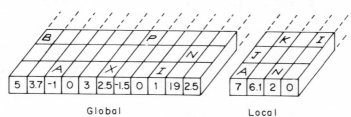

Figure 6.2   A representation of global and local memory

successively incremented in the FOR loop on lines 80–100 until it reaches the value 63, whereupon the loop is terminated and the ENDPROC obeyed. Since in this case the *same* variable name is used in the main program and in the procedure, the variable I which is controlling the main loop on lines 10–40 has the value 63 which is greater than 2 and so the loop is not repeated.

You can confirm this as follows:

i)   Add an extra line

```
35 PRINT I
```

which will print the value of I on return from the procedure, and RUN the program again.

ii) Replace the line

```
70 LOCAL I
```

and RUN it again. This time the value printed by line 35 is the same as that printed by line 20, thus confirming that altering the *local* variable I has no effect on the *global* variable I.

We have already seen that a procedure may have one or more parameters, and such parameters are, in fact, merely local variables which are assigned a value during the process of "calling" the procedure. The following procedure is very similar to the one used in experiment 6.6 but has two parameters which are used to define the range of notes to be played:

```
 60 DEF PROCsound (N1,N2)
 70 LOCAL I
 80 FOR I=N1 TO N2
 90    SOUND 1,-15,4*I,1
100    NEXT
110 ENDPROC
```

This procedure therefore has three local variables defined within it – the two parameters N1 and N2 and the variable I

It is important to remember that procedure parameters are local variables which have a value assigned to them during the call to the procedure. Because they are local variables they cannot be used to pass any information back to the calling program. Experiment 6.7 demonstrates this.

Experiment 6.7

Type the following program into your computer and RUN it.

```
10 I=1: J=2: K=3
20 PRINT I,J,K
```

```
 30 PROCdemo(I,J,K)
 40 PRINT I,J,K
 50 END
 60 DEF PROCdemo(A,B,C)
 70 PRINT A,B,C
 80 A=4: B=5: C=6
 90 PRINT A,B,C
100 ENDPROC
```

The program first sets the (global) variables I,J,K to the values 1, 2, 3 and prints them. It then calls the procedure PROCdemo with these variables as arguments. In the procedure the *local* variables A,B,C (which are the parameters to the procedure) will be assigned the values of I,J,K and these (i.e. 1, 2, 3) are then printed. The procedure then assigns new values to A,B,C and prints them before returning from the procedure. The main program then prints the values of I,J,K to confirm that they have not been altered. The results displayed will therefore be:

1	2	3
1	2	3
4	5	6
1	2	3

In this experiment the names of the parameters (A,B,C) were different from the names of the arguments used in the call. However, the result would have been the same if the same names had been used.

Alter lines 60–90 of the above program to use I,J,K instead of A,B,C and RUN the program again.

Notice that the results are the same, thus confirming that the I,J,K used as arguments in the procedure call are not altered by the procedure even though the corresponding parameters are also called I,J,K.

Now alter the program once again by typing in the following two lines:

```
60 DEF PROCdemo(A,B,C)
65 I=A: J=B: K=C
```

RUN the program and observe the result. This time the original (global) variables have been altered because the only local variables in the procedure are the parameters A,B,C and the assignments at line 65 copy their values to the global variables I,J,K which are then altered at line 80.

Finally add a further line

```
61 LOCAL I,J,K
```

and RUN the program again. All the variables referred to in the procedure are now local and so the global I,J,K are, once again, unaltered.

Because of the importance of local and global variables it is essential that you don't confuse the two. One way, which is used in The Final Test programs is to write all local variable names in lower case but to begin all global variables with a capital letter. It is then easy to tell at a glance what sort of variable we are using. Look at the listing of the programs in Appendix A to see for yourself how effective this is.

Experimental Hints

```
6.1   10 FOR I=1 TO 10
      20    PROCtune
      30    PROConebarrest
      40    NEXT
      50 END
      60 DEF PROCtune
          .
          .
          .
```

```
6.3   10 MODE 2
      20 MOVE 0,0
      30 MOVE 1279,1023
      40 FOR I=1 TO 100
      50    GCOL 0,RND(16)-1
      60    PLOT 85,RND(1280)-1,RND(1024)-1
      70    NEXT
```

Communication is the name of the game

7.1 GIVING INFORMATION TO THE USER

It is frequently necessary for a program to provide information for the user (or programmer). This is usually in one of three forms – sound, pictures or printed text. Sound and pictures are, of course, very useful in special contexts, but the only general form of communication from the computer to us is by printed text on the screen. We have used the PRINT statement in a number of programs so far without really explaining how it works, and we are now ready to examine it in some detail:

PRINT list of items

Essentially it consists of the word PRINT, followed by a list of items that are to be printed. Thus if we write

```
PRINT 1,2,3
```

we shall get the following displayed on the screen

```
1          2          3
```

Notice the wide spacing. This is because the screen is considered to be divided into *fields* of ten characters, and when a comma is used to separate numbers then the numbers are printed in consecutive fields. Notice also that numbers will be printed at the right of the field.

In modes 0 and 3 there are eight fields of ten characters, in modes 1, 4, 6 and 7 there are four fields, and in modes 2 and 5 there are only two fields (see figure 7.1).

As well as numbers we can also print text by enclosing the word(s) to be printed between quotation marks:

```
PRINT "The cat sat on the mat"
```

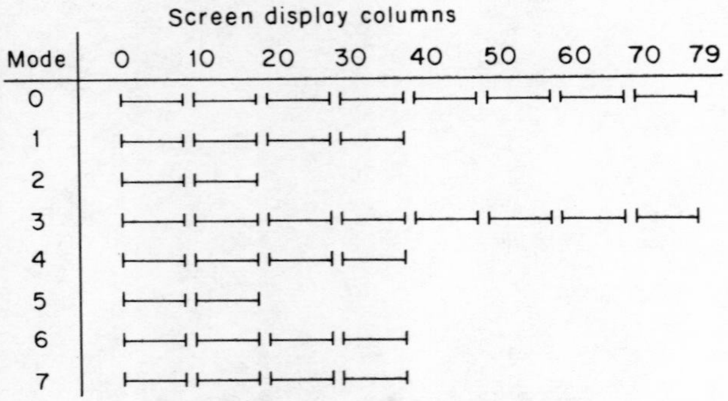

Screen display columns

Figure 7.1   Default printer fields

Character strings (the formal way of defining text) are always printed at the left of the field and so the following program will produce the results shown in figure 7.2:

```
10 PRINT 1,2,3,4
20 PRINT "First","Second","Third","Fourth"
```

The wide spacing caused by these fields is not always what we require, especially when text and numbers are combined. If we use a semi-colon (;) instead of a comma to separate items in a list then the next item is printed immediately after the last one. Figure 7.3 shows the result produced by running the following program:

```
10 I=1: J=2: K=3
20 PRINT I,J,K
30 PRINT "I=",I,"J=",J,"K=",K
40 PRINT "I=";I;"J=";J;"K=";K
50 PRINT "I=";I;" J=";J;" K=";K
60 PRINT "I=";I,"J=";J,"K=";K
```

You will see that the results produced by line 30 have continued onto the next line since there are six items to be printed and only four fields to a line (in the default mode 7). Also notice that the layout is very uneven due to the fact that the text ("I=", etc.) is printed at the left of a field while the numbers are printed at the right.

The results produced by line 40, which uses semi-colons as terminators, are too "squashed up" due to the complete absence of any spaces and so the next PRINT statement, on line 50, inserts a space before the strings "J=" and "K=". Finally, line 60 uses both semi-colons and commas so that each number is printed immediately after its identifying text, but the next piece of text starts at the beginning of the next field.

```
        1          2          3          4
First      Second     Third      Fourth
>
```

Figure 7.2   Results of above program

```
            1              2        3
  I=                      1J=                    2
  K=                      3
  I=1J=2K=3
  I=1  J=2  K=3
  I=1          J=2        K=3
  >
```

Figure 7.3   Results of above program

Experiment 7.1

Write a program to print the "seven times table". The table should be displayed on a pale blue (cyan) background with dark blue text. It should have a title followed by twelve lines of the form

```
8 times 7 is 56
```

Note that multiplication is carried out by using an asterisk (*) as a multiplication sign, thus:

```
I=J*K
```

(See Experimental Hints if you *really* can't work out how to do this.)

7.2   GIVING INFORMATION TO THE COMPUTER

Just as the computer normally displays (i.e. PRINTs) any information which is to be given to the user, so the user normally types (and thus also displays for him/herself) any information which is to be provided for the computer.

We have seen how we can type Basic commands or program statements, but we have not yet seen how we can type information for use by a program when it is running. This process is in fact initiated by the program, which will request some information from the user by means of a statement of the form

INPUT "text" list of variable names

This will print the "text" on the screen and then wait for you to type appropriate information, which is stored in the variables whose names are listed in the statement. Thus the statement

```
50 INPUT "Give number of cases" N
```

will print the message

```
Give number of cases
```

on the screen and then wait for you to type a number. When you have typed the number (followed, of course, by pressing RETURN) the value of the number will be stored in the variable N.

Experiment 7.2

Modify the program that you wrote for experiment 7.1 so that it asks which table is to be produced and then prints that table on a clear screen using yellow text on a red background.

In the examples above, the INPUT keyword is followed by some text (in quotation marks) and a variable name. If we wish we may separate the text from the variable name by a comma, in which case the text is followed by a question mark (known in this case as a prompt). Thus

```
50 INPUT "How many cases",N
```

will print the message

```
How many cases?
```

and then wait for a number to be typed.

We can also use an INPUT statement to obtain several values by giving a list of variable names separated by commas:

```
70 INPUT "Give age, weight and height" AGE,WT,HT
```

In this case three numbers will be required, and these may be typed with commas between them, or with RETURN pressed after each one. In the latter case, a prompt (?) will be given to remind you that more data is still needed.

Finally there may be occasions when you wish to instruct the computer to input some information from the keyboard without printing any message first. The statement

```
90 INPUT X
```

will merely print the usual prompt character (?) and then wait for a number to be typed, while

```
100 INPUT P,Q,R
```

will print a ? and then expect three numbers; if RETURN is pressed before three numbers have been input then a further ? will be printed.

The following program uses several different types of INPUT statement; the results produced by running it can be seen in figure 7.4.

```
10 PRINT "This program works out your budget"
20 PRINT
30 PRINT "It will ask for your salary and regular"
```

```
40 PRINT "expenses and will calculate how much"
50 PRINT "you can spend each week"
60 PRINT: PRINT
70 INPUT "Please give your weekly earnings " Wage
80 INPUT "How many regular weekly expenses do you have", N
90 PRINT "Please give your ";N;" weekly expenses"
100 Total=0
110 FOR I=1 TO N
120    INPUT Cost
130    Total=Total+Cost
140    NEXT
150 Spare=Wage-Total
160 INPUT "What will your annual holiday cost",Hol
170 Hcost=Hol/52
180 PRINT "You must save $";Hcost;" each week";
190 PRINT " for your holiday"
200 PRINT "You will then have $";Spare-Hcost;
210 PRINT " to spend"
```

Notice that the PRINT statements on lines 20 and 60 have no items to be printed; in this form they merely cause a blank line to be produced. Also notice that in line 170 an oblique stroke (or "slash") is used to indicate division; we shall be discussing arithmetic on the Beeb in more detail in the next chapter. There are also two points to note about the PRINT statement. The first (see lines 180 and 200) is that if the last item is followed by a semi-colon (or a comma) then a new line is not taken and the next information sent to the

```
This program works out your budget

It will ask for your salary and regular
expenses and will calculate how much
you can spend each week


Please give your weekly earnings after tax 160
How many regular weekly expenses do you have?5
Please give your 5 weekly expenses
?17
?23
?6
?12
?33
How much will your annual holiday cost?800
You should save $15.3846154 each week for your holiday
You will then have $53.6153846 left to spend
>
```

Figure 7.4   Results of above program

screen will be put on the same line. The statements

```
180 PRINT "You must save $";Hcost;" each week";
190 PRINT " for your holiday"
```

are, therefore, the same as

```
180 PRINT "You must save $";Hcost;" each week";" for your holiday"
```

which is the same as

```
180 PRINT "You must save $";Hcost;" each week for your holiday"
```

The second point is that it is permissible to calculate a value to be printed in the PRINT statement itself (see line 200).

Normally the three alternative forms of the INPUT statement discussed above are sufficient to meet any particular requirement. Sometimes, however, you may want to input some information without printing either a message or a ? prompt; in this situation you can use a statement of the form

```
30 INPUT "" N
```

which prints a *null string* (i.e. nothing) before waiting for the input data. Usually the only situation in which this is required is when some text has already been produced by a PRINT statement such as

```
110 PRINT "Number of cases = ";
120 INPUT "" N
```

which is identical in its effect to

```
110 INPUT "Number of cases = " N
```

In a simple case such as this it is obviously more sensible to use the latter method; however, in chapter 10 we shall see that it is possible to instruct the computer to take one of several alternative courses of action and it may then be appropriate to separate the printing of a message (or one of several messages) from the subsequent input.

Experiment 7.3

Write a program which will calculate some simple health statistics based on a set of figures giving the age, height and weight of a number of hospital out-patients. The program should explain what data is required and then ask for the number of patients. It should then request the age, height and weight for each patient. Finally it should print the average height of the patients (the sum, or total of all the heights divided by the number of patients), the average weight of the patients and the average age of the patients. The results should appear exactly like those shown in figure 7.5.

```
This program calculates various averages
concerning a set of hospital outpatients

How many patients are there?5

Patient number 1
Age = 43
Height = 1.86
Weight = 63.5

Patient number 2
Age = 56
Height = 1.75
Weight = 48.25

Patient number 3
Age = 77
Height = 1.64
Weight = 47.0

Patient number 4
Age = 21
Height = 2.03
Weight = 78.5

Patient number 5
Age = 41
Height = 1.81
Weight = 62.5

Average height is 1.818

Average weight is 59.95

Average age of patients is 47.6
>
```

Figure 7.5   Results for experiment 7.3

7.3   A WORD ABOUT CHARACTER STRINGS

In chapter 6 we said that the variables that we were using could only be used to store numbers. We frequently need to store names or other character strings, however, and for this purpose we need a different kind of variable whose name has a $ as its last character:

name$ A$ Leader_of_the_pack$

We shall discuss the use of character variables in some detail in chapter 9, but it is appropriate at this stage to explain how to INPUT and PRINT character information. This, as we would expect, is carried out exactly as for numbers except that, during printing, any character (text) results are printed at the left of the ten-character field instead of at the right, as shown in figure 7.6.

```
>INPUT A$,B$,C$
?First
?Second,Third
>PRINT A$,B$,C$
First      Second      Third
>
```

Figure 7.6   Example of character input and output

Experiment 7.4

Modify the program that you wrote for experiment 7.3 so that, as well as the age, height and weight, it asks for the patient's name.

Experiment 7.5

Modify the program written in the last experiment so that explanatory information and requests for data are displayed in green, data typed by you is in yellow, and the final results are in red. (Hint: you should use mode 1.)

7.4   TEXT AND GRAPHIC WINDOWS

Experiment 7.6

Type in the following program:

```
10 REM This program draws triangles
20 MODE 1
30 CLG
40 PRINT "Give co-ordinates of first point"
50 INPUT "X= (in range 0-1279)",X
60 INPUT "Y= (in range 0-1023)",Y
70 MOVE X,Y
80 PRINT "Now second point"
90 INPUT "X= "X
100 INPUT "Y= "Y
110 MOVE X,Y
120 FOR I=1 TO 12
130    INPUT "Colour of next triangle = "C
140    GCOL 0,C
150    INPUT "X-coordinate of vertex = "X
160    INPUT "Y-coordinate = "Y
170    PLOT 85,X,Y
180    NEXT
```

Now RUN this program to produce 12 triangles. What do you observe?

Add an extra line:

25 GCOL 0,134

and RUN the program again. What do you observe this time?

In both the above programs there have been two major problems. The first is that because the triangles are using the same screen as the text they may cover the text, making it difficult to see what is happening. In a similar way, the text displayed or input will be printed on top of any triangles, making an untidy and difficult to read display.

The second problem is that towards the end (on the ninth and subsequent sets of data) the text "scrolls" because it has reached the bottom of the screen. Unfortunately this means that the graphical display also scrolls! In the second version of the program this effect is emphasised by having a cyan graphic background which is also scrolled, since the graphic background is only set by a CLG statement.

This conflict between text and graphics is a common one and can be dealt with by defining a *text window* and/or a *graphic window*. The command

VDU 28,leftX,bottomY,rightX,topY

is used to define a text window in which all subsequent text will be displayed. The four values after the VDU 28 represent the left-hand edge, bottom edge, right-hand edge and top edge of the window, measured in character positions. Thus in mode 1, which allows 32 lines of 40 characters, the values for leftX and rightX must be in the range 0–39, and those for bottomY and topY must be in the range 0–31.

We can use this to avoid the scrolling problems in experiment 7.6 by restricting the text to a band of (say) 3 lines at the top or bottom of the screen.

Experiment 7.7

Modify the program written for experiment 7.6 by adding the extra line

35 VDU 28,0,2,39,0

Now RUN the program. Is this what you expected?

Alter the program so that the window is at the bottom and RUN it again.

Figure 7.7 shows the general position of a text window and the VDU statement needed to define it. In different modes, of course, the maximum screen size (in terms of characters) will be different but the principles will be the same.

The Final Test makes quite extensive use of text windows in several different ways. For example when one program is loading its successor, a text window is defined for the messages produced while the tape is being read so that the existing screen display is left unaltered (see FINALTEST line 2160, CASTLE line 240 and CASTLE2 line 1100 – although all of these are part of more complicated VDU statements).

A text window is also used in the main game program "Castle" whenever any text is to be displayed (see line 1470) so that it is kept separate from the plan of the castle floor.

A text window can be defined in any mode although, as already mentioned, the limits are different in different modes.

90

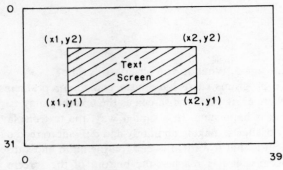

Figure 7.7   VDU 28,x1,y1,x2,y2 (in mode 1)

Experiment 7.8

RUN the program you wrote for experiment 7.7 again with the following values for the first five sets of co-ordinates (choose your own colours):

X	Y
0	0
1279	0
0	1023
960	1200
1500	0

What do you observe? Can you explain the effects that you have created? (See Experimental Hints if you can't.)

The last experiment (and perhaps the previous one) will have shown you that defining a text window is not necessarily a complete solution to the problem of overlapping text and graphics; it may sometimes also be necessary to define a graphics window. This is achieved in a very similar fashion to the text window by the command

```
VDU 24,leftX;bottomY;rightX;topY;
```

Notice the semi-colons after the four co-ordinate values.

A graphics window can only be defined in modes 0, 1, 2, 4 and 5 since modes 3 and 6 are text only modes and mode 7 is the special (teletext) mode with a quite different type of graphics. The four edges are defined in terms of the graphics co-ordinates discussed in chapter 5, which are, of course the same for all modes. The left and right edges may therefore have values in the range 0–1279 and the top and bottom edges in the range 0–1023 (see figure 7.8).

Since all the graphic modes provide 32 lines of text we can readily see that one line of text corresponds to 32 vertical graphical units. We can then define adjacent text and graphic windows.

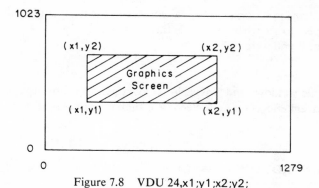

Figure 7.8   VDU 24,x1;y1;x2;y2;

Experiment 7.9

Modify the program written in experiment 7.7 so that the text is confined to the top four lines of the screen and the triangles to the rest of the screen. Test this program with data which causes triangles to go off all four sides of the screen.

Now alter your program so that the text is confined to the *bottom* four lines.

Experiment 7.10

Look at the following program and see if you can understand what it does. When you have decided (and not before!) type it into your computer and RUN it.

```
10 MODE 2
20 FOR I=0 TO 7
30    VDU 24,160*I;0;1279;1023;
40    GCOL 0,I+128
50    CLG
60    NEXT
```

Were you right?
  Now add the following lines

```
11 VDU 19,1,0;0;
12 VDU 19,2,0;0;
13 VDU 19,3,0;0;
14 VDU 19,4,0;0;
15 VDU 19,5,0;0;
16 VDU 19,6,0;0;
17 VDU 19,7,0;0;
70 VDU 20
```

The VDU 20 statement restores all logical colours to the normal (default) actual colours. What do you expect to see when you RUN this program?

RUN it and see if you were right.

This use of graphic windows and "invisible" colours indicates how it is possible to produce quite dramatic visual effects on your Beeb. We shall investigate this in more detail in later chapters.

7.5   MORE CONTROL OVER LAYOUT

Up to this point we have had very little control over where information is printed on the screen other than by use of ; or , in a PRINT statement. Frequently, however, we wish to position some text and/or numbers at an *exact* position on the screen, rather than at the edge of a particular print field. To do this we use a TAB command as part of a PRINT statement.

The command

```
TAB(x,y)
```

in a PRINT statement moves the text cursor to character position x on line y. (Remember, in this context, that the left-most character position is numbered 0 and that the top line is numbered 0.)

Thus if we write

```
PRINT TAB(20,12);"*"
```

an asterisk (*) will be printed in character position 20 of line 12. In modes 1, 3, 4, 6 and 7 (which have 40 characters per line) this will be almost in the centre of the screen. It is not possible (using this method) to place it exactly in the centre, since the centre is between characters 19 and 20.

Notice the semi-colon after the TAB command, which ensures that the next item (i.e. the *) is printed without any intervening spaces. In fact we can omit this and simply write

```
PRINT TAB(20,12)"*"
```

since the BBC Basic interpreter assumes that if you have used the TAB command to position the cursor then that is where the next item should start, and the closing bracket identifies the end of the TAB command. (This may seem obvious but a lot of computers do require the ; if they are to work properly, or even at all!)

All the programs in The Final Test use the TAB command extensively to control the layout of printed text. This is usually in a special procedure called PROCtell or PROCsay which also uses another very useful feature (DATA) to simplify the handling of large amounts of text; we shall discuss this in the next section.

Experiment 7.11

Write a program which prints your name in the middle of line 5 of the screen, then leaves

James East

Home address:

    123 Westborne Road
    Northtown
    South Yorkshire NW9 9SE

School address:
    Upper Green Middle School
    Lower Drive
    Northtown
    South Yorkshire NW8 8ES

Figure 7.9   A name and addresses

four blank lines followed by both home and work/college/school addresses laid out in a similar way to figure 7.9.

Experiment 7.12

Write a program which asks for two numbers x and y and then prints an asterisk (or other character) at character x of line y. The program should then loop back and ask for another pair of numbers. Use the program to draw a simple shape. (*Note* that you will need to ESCape to leave this infinite loop and end the program.) Make sure that your input data does not spoil the picture! (See Experimental Hints if you have any problems.)

There is an alternative form of the TAB command which only has a single value enclosed in parentheses:

TAB(x)

This causes spaces to be printed until the cursor reaches character position x on the current line, or on the next line if the cursor was already past column x. Thus the following program will print two columns — the first containing a single digit in column 10 and the second containing a row of Xs starting in column 15:

```
10 FOR I=1 TO 9
20    PRINT TAB(10) I;
30    FOR J=1 TO I
40       PRINT TAB(J+14) "X";
50    NEXT
60 NEXT
```

In this program the inner loop (lines 30–50) prints a succession of Xs in successive character positions from 15 onwards. Each PRINT statement is followed by a semi-colon. When the inner loop is completed, processing returns to line 20 of the outer loop and

PRINTs the next value of I in column 10. However, since the cursor is at column 16 or beyond, the computer automatically starts a new line before moving to column 10 – which is what is required.

Notice the semi-colon after the TAB in line 20. This is required because otherwise the value of I will be printed at the right of the next field. Try it both ways and see for yourself.

Both forms of the TAB command can also be used in an INPUT statement both with and without any text prompt:

```
10 CLS
20 INPUT TAB(4,7) "Next value " X
30 INPUT TAB(6) "And the next ... " Y
40 INPUT TAB(10,12) A
50 INPUT TAB(6) B
```

An INPUT statement containing a TAB command is particularly useful when running a program which uses graphics, as it enables question and answer to be placed at a well-defined part of the screen. For example in experiment 7.12 it was necessary to prevent the text produced during input from overwriting the drawing.

The easiest solution to this problem is as follows:

```
10 CLS
20 INPUT TAB(5,23) "X=" X: INPUT TAB(15,23) "Y=" Y
30 PRINT TAB(X,Y) "*";
40 PRINT TAB(7,23) "            ";TAB(17,23) "            "
50 GOTO 20
```

This program always prints the two prompts "X=" and "Y=" in the same place on the screen and then uses a PRINT statement to erase the values supplied once the point has been plotted. *Note* that line 23 has been used and not line 24 (the bottom line in mode 7) in order to avoid any risk of scrolling taking place.

The above program prints two strings consisting solely of spaces in order to blank out the previous input values. The need to print a row of spaces is a common one both for this reason and also for layout purposes, and a special facility exists to simplify the process. In a PRINT statement (or an INPUT statement) the expression

```
SPC(n)
```

causes n spaces to be printed. Thus line 40 in the above program could be written

```
40 PRINT TAB(7,23) SPC(8);TAB(17,23) SPC(8)
```

Note also that once TAB with two values has been moved to position the cursor on a line then TAB with one argument may not work correctly on that line because of the different methods used. Thus we should never write

```
40 PRINT TAB(7,23) SPC(8);TAB(17) SPC(8)
```

as it could give the wrong result.

Separator		Meaning
,	(comma)	print next item in the next print field
;	(semicolon)	print next item at next character position
'	(apostrophe)	print next item on next line

Figure 7.10   PRINT list separators

Finally we should note that there is often a requirement to simply start printing on a new line. We can, of course, do this by writing

```
50 PRINT "First Line"
60 PRINT "Second Line"
```

but we may also include an apostrophe (') in the list of items to be printed to cause subsequent items to be printed on the next line:

```
50 PRINT "First Line"'"Second Line"
```

This is a separator of the same nature as a comma or a semi-colon, and figure 7.10 summarises the three possible options.

7.6 READING DATA

As we have seen, the INPUT statement accepts data which is typed at the keyboard and stores it in specified variables. Basic also contains a facility for storing data within the program itself and then transferring it to specified variables on request. The data is stored in DATA statements which take the form

```
DATA value1,value2,...
```

and is transferred by means of a READ statement which is essentially like an INPUT statement without any text prompt:

```
READ name1,name2,...
```

The values specified in DATA statements may be either numbers or text; in the latter case the text may be enclosed in quotation marks (as in a PRINT or INPUT statement) or it may be written without quotation marks. If a text value contains a comma then it *must* be enclosed in quotation marks as otherwise the comma would be treated as the end of the string:

```
150 DATA 1,2,3,4
160 DATA Tom,Dick,Harry
170 DATA "Tom, Dick and Harry"
```

The way that DATA statements are used is quite interesting as, in effect, *all* the DATA statements in the program are combined (in line number order) to produce one long list of data items. Unless otherwise instructed, the first READ statement that is obeyed will start to read data from the beginning of the list, and every subsequent READ statement to be obeyed will continue reading from the point at which the previous one stopped. The following program uses this technique to print several lines of text at various places on the screen:

```
 10 CLS
 20 READ num
 30 FOR I=1 TO num
 40    READ x,y,text$
 50    PRINT TAB(x,y) text$;
 60    NEXT
 70 END
 80 DATA 4
 90 DATA 6,0,This is the top line
100 DATA 6,24,This is the bottom line
110 DATA 6,12,This is the middle line
120 DATA 0,4,X  This shows the width of the screen  X
```

The statement at line 20 will read the first DATA item (from line 80) and the statement at line 30 will then cause a loop to be repeated that many times. The loop itself first reads two numbers (x and y) and a text string (text$), and then prints the text at a point specified by x and y. The data provided in lines 80–120 will cause the top, middle and bottom lines to be so labelled, and the effective width of the screen to be indicated. If we were to add a new line

```
 5 DATA 1,12,6,This is line 6!
```

then the program would only produce a single line of output.

Considerably greater flexibility is given to the READ statement when it is used in conjunction with the RESTORE statement, which overrides any default position in the "list" of DATA items and instructs the computer which DATA statement is to be used with the next READ. It takes one of the forms

```
RESTORE
```

or

```
RESTORE linenum
```

In the first case the next READ will revert to the beginning of the data (i.e. to the first item in the first DATA statement). The second case, on the other hand, specifies a line number and the next READ starts with the first item in the DATA statement on that line.

All four programs which comprise The Final Test make extensive use of this facility. In each program there is a procedure called either PROCtell or PROCsay which repeatedly reads data and then prints it in a very similar way to that used above. Before the procedure is called, the RESTORE statement is used to select which of the various messages is to be printed. For example in the program Castle an attempt to go through a door may fail because a skeleton with too much magic is present, or because a dragon defeats you in a fight, or because Morgan le Fey is there and you have not accumulated enough courage, strength, magic and weapons. In each case a message will be printed by PROCsay after either

	RESTORE 1710	(line 1030 – skeleton)
	RESTORE 1700	(line 1040 – Morgan le Fey)
or	RESTORE 1690	(line 1050 – dragon)

This method not only saves a significant amount of space, which may be important in a large program, but also makes it easier to correct or improve your program by keeping all the display text away from the rest of the program.

The other main use of READ and DATA is associated with setting up initial values; we shall investigate that in more detail in chapter 14.

Experiment 7.13

Both FINALTEST and CASTLE use a procedure called PROCtune to play the opening music ("Greensleeves"). The procedure operates by READing a number of pairs of values from DATA statements. The first number in each pair gives the pitch and the second gives the duration of the note; the procedure arranges for a zero duration to give a very brief pause. A single negative number (pitch) terminates the data.

The tune is played in two parts; the first part starting at line 2310 in FINALTEST and the second part at line 2330.

Write a set of DATA statements to replace "Greensleeves" by your own choice of opening music.

7.7   MORE WAYS OF GETTING INFORMATION

The normal method of inputting information from the keyboard is by use of the INPUT statement. As we have seen, this allows you to type any required data on request from the computer. It also allows you to use the DELETE key to cancel any incorrectly typed characters. Only when the RETURN key is pressed is the information actually looked at by the computer.

Sometimes, however, it is useful to be able to make the computer react as soon as a key is pressed without waiting for the RETURN key to be pressed; games programs are an obvious example, but there are many others. The functions GET, GET$, INKEY and INKEY$ are provided for this purpose. If we write

```
50 X=GET
```

then when the program reaches line 50 it will wait for a key to be pressed. As soon as this happens the internal (or ASCII) code for that key is placed in the variable X and the program continues. (*Note* that this means that you cannot use the DELETE key to correct any mistake!) Figure 7.11 shows the ASCII codes for all the characters that you can type on your Beeb keyboard.

	0	1	2	3	4	5	6	7	8	9
30		space	!	"	#	$	%	&	'	
40	(	)	*	+	,	−	.	/	0	1
50	2	3	4	5	6	7	8	9	:	;
60	<	=	>	?	@	A	B	C	D	E
70	F	G	H	I	J	K	L	M	N	O
80	P	Q	R	S	T	U	V	W	X	Y
90	Z	[	\	]	^	_	£	a	b	c
100	d	e	f	g	h	i	j	k	l	m
110	n	o	p	q	r	s	t	u	v	w
120	x	y	z	{			}	˜	delete		

Figure 7.11   ASCII codes

An alternative way of doing this is to use GET$ which provides the actual character pressed instead of its numeric code. In this case a character variable must be used to store the value input from the keyboard:

```
50 X$=GET$
```

In general these two types of statements are only useful in conjunction with the Basic decision making commands which allow the program to take one of several courses of action depending upon the key pressed; we shall discuss this aspect of programming in chapter 10. It is worth mentioning at this point that GET$ is used extensively in The Final Test so that only one letter is required in response to most queries, the program then providing the rest of the word.

One very important point about GET and GET$ is that the character "typed" is not automatically printed on the screen. If you wish it to appear there then you must arrange for it to be printed yourself:

```
50 X$=GET$: PRINT X$
```

The other two functions (INKEY and INKEY$) operate in a very similar way to GET and GET$ except that they only wait for a limited amount of time. The function reference

```
INKEY(n)
```

will wait for n hundredths of a second before proceeding. If a key is pressed in that time then the ASCII value of the key is provided, exactly as with GET. However, if no key is pressed then the value −1 is returned and the program continues. GET, on the other hand, will wait (for ever if necessary!) until a key is pressed.

INKEY$ is similar except that if no key is pressed in the time allowed then a *null string* is returned − i.e. a string containing no characters at all.

These two functions are very useful in situations where the program is controlled by keys pressed at random intervals by the user, as it can continually cycle (or loop) while testing if a key has been pressed.

An important point about all forms of input (INPUT, GET, GET$, INKEY and INKEY$) is that you can type ahead of the computer. When you press a key then the code for that key is placed in a special part of the memory (called the *keyboard buffer*) which can hold up to 256 such character codes. When any form of input statement is obeyed it first looks to see if there are any characters waiting in the buffer. If there are none then the program waits until a key is pressed (to place a character code in the buffer) or until the time allowed has elapsed.

The main loop of Castle utilises this fact in the statement

```
130 C%=INKEY(O): IF . . . . .
```

which doesn't wait at all for a key to be pressed, but will read from the buffer if a key was pressed since the last time through this part of the loop. This means that the program reacts almost instantly to a key being pressed but doesn't wait if one hasn't been pressed.

We shall investigate the uses of GET, GET$, INKEY and INKEY$ in chapter 10, but one use of GET or GET$ is illustrated in experiment 7.14.

Experiment 7.14

There is a special *pseudo-variable* called TIME which can be used to measure time intervals. It can be set to any required value by a simple assignment statement:

```
TIME = 0
```

or its current value may be stored in a variable:

```
Time = TIME
```

At all other times, however, its value is constantly being incremented so as to record the passage of time in hundredths of a second (i.e. one is added to its value every hundredth of a second).

Write a reaction timer which measures the time between the program printing a "GO" message and the player pressing a key.

(*Note:* the special command

```
*FX 15,1
```

on a line by itself will empty the keyboard buffer and prevent cheating!)

See Experimental Hints if you have trouble with this experiment.

Experiment 7.15

Use the RND function introduced in chapter 6 to modify the program written for experiment 7.14 so that there is a variable delay before the "GO" message is printed.

Experimental Hints

7.1 Mode 4 is a suitable mode as it gives us 40 characters per line and allows us to specify the required colours easily. Mode 6 would also do, but we cannot get a solid background because, as we described earlier, each line is separated from the next by a narrow black band.

```
10 MODE 4
19 REM Choose cyan background and blue text
20 VDU 19,0,6;0;: VDU 19,1,4;0;
30 PRINT "Seven times table"
40 PRINT
50 FOR I=1 TO 12
60   PRINT I;" times 7 is ";I*7
70   NEXT
```

Alternatively, we could replace line 60 by

```
55   J=7*I
60   PRINT I;" times 7 is ";J
```

7.3   A suitable program is as follows:

```
10 PRINT "This program calculates various averages"
20 PRINT "concerning a set of hospital outpatients"
30 PRINT
40 INPUT "How many patients are there",N
50 AgeSum=0: HtSum=0: WtSum=0
60 FOR I=1 TO N
70    PRINT: PRINT "Patient number ";I
80    INPUT "Age = "Age
90    AgeSum=AgeSum+Age
100   INPUT "Height = "Ht
110   HtSum=HtSum+Ht
120   INPUT "Weight = "Wt
130   WtSum=WtSum+Wt
140   NEXT
150 PRINT: PRINT "Average height is ";HtSum/N
160 PRINT: PRINT "Average weight is ";WtSum/N
170 PRINT: PRINT "Average age of patients is ";AgeSum/N
```

7.8   You should have noticed two things.

Firstly, the triangles drawn will happily "wipe out" text, even when the text is restricted to a text window. You may also have noticed this in the last experiment.

Secondly, if co-ordinates are specified which are outside the screen limits (e.g. in the fourth and fifth sets of data) then no error results – the plotting is carried out as though only a part of the (infinite) plotting space was actually displayed. Thus plotting is only displayed if it lies in a predefined window (x in the range 0–1279, y in the range 0–1023).

7.12   The key to this program is always to request the data in the same place on the screen:

```
10 CLS
20 PRINT TAB(0,0) "X coordinate (0-39)";: INPUT X
30 PRINT TAB(0,1) "Y coordinate (2-23)";: INPUT Y
40 PRINT TAB(X,Y) "*"
50 REM Delete previous coordinates
60 PRINT TAB(19,0) "        "
70 PRINT TAB(19,1) "        "
80 GOTO 20
```

7.14
```
 10 CLS
 20 PRINT TAB(0,5) "Press Space Bar when 'GO' appears"
 30 REM Produce a delay
 40 FOR I=1 TO 2000
 50    NEXT
 60 *FX 15,1
 70 PRINT TAB(20,10) "GO"
 80 TIME=0
 90 A$=GET$
100 Time=TIME
110 PRINT TAB(0,15) "You took ";Time/100;" seconds"
```

7.15 Change line 40 to, for example,

```
40 FOR I=1 TO 2000+RND(1000)
```

8

Adding it all up

8.1 SIMPLE ARITHMETIC

People often think that computers are mainly concerned with arithmetic and mathematics and yet this is chapter 8 and we have hardly discussed arithmetic at all! There is, in fact, very little to say, as can be seen from the fact that this is one of the shorter chapters in this book.

We have already seen that we can write

```
10 LET A=B+C+17.4
```

or simply

```
10 A=B+C+17.4
```

to add values together, and we have seen that an asterisk is used for multiplication:

```
20 X=Y*Z
```

A computer keyboard does not contain a division sign either and so we use an oblique stroke, or "slash", for this purpose. Thus the statement

```
30 P=Q/R
```

takes the value stored in Q, divides it by the value stored in R, and stores the result in P.

Note that if you press the key marked ˜ when in mode 7 you will get a division sign (÷) displayed; this is a feature of the mode 7 (teletext) character set, however, and is not interpreted as a division sign by the Basic interpreter.

We can, of course, build as complicated an arithmetic expression as we like, e.g.

```
40 A=1.5*B-X/Y+P-Q*R/S+T
```

Once we start to do this, however, we must be careful that we know in which order the various arithmetic operations will be carried out. For example what will be printed by the following program?

```
10 X=4+5*6
20 PRINT X
```

Will it be 54 (i.e. 9*6) or 34 (i.e. 4+30)?

Experiment 8.1

Write a series of short programs (such as the one above) to discover (or confirm, if you think you know) in what order the various arithmetic operations (+, −, * and /) are carried out.

There is also a fifth arithmetic operator in Basic (and all other programming languages) which is concerned with *exponentiation*, or raising one number to the power of another. In ordinary arithmetic we write

$$5^2$$

to mean "five raised to the power of two" (or "five squared"), in other words "five times five", and

$$7^3$$

to mean "seven to the power of three" (or "seven cubed"), that is "seven times seven times seven".

We can't do this in Basic because we can't write the power as a superscript, raised above the line. Instead we write

```
5^2 or 7^3
```

where ^ is an *exponentiation operator*. Thus the statement

```
50 A=B^C
```

causes the value stored in B to be raised to the power of the value stored in C, with the result being stored in A.

Exponentiation has a higher priority than any of the other arithmetic operators.

Sometimes the order in which Basic will evaluate an expression (i.e. exponentiation, followed by multiplication or division, followed by addition or subtraction) is not suitable and we wish to alter it. We may, therefore, enclose any part of the expression in *parentheses* (i.e. round brackets), in which case the sub-expression in parentheses is evaluated first. Thus the following program will set A to 54 and B to 34 before printing both values:

```
10 A=(4+5)*6
20 B=4+5*6
30 PRINT "(4+5)*6=";A'"4+5*6=";B
```

Experiment 8.2

Work out what values will be stored in each of the variables A to H by the following program.

```
10 A=2*3^3-2^4/2
20 B=(2*3)^3-2^(4/2)
30 C=2*3^(3-2)^4/2
40 D=C/3/3/3
50 E=2^D+D^2
60 F=E*D+B/4-(A+2*D)
70 G=1/D+E/D
80 H=F/E-D*G/E
```

Now type the program into your computer, with appropriate PRINT statements and RUN it to check your results.

Are they what you expected? And what about the last one? See Experimental Hints for a further explanation.

8.2   STANDARD FUNCTIONS

The five operators introduced above, together with parentheses where necessary, are all that is required to evaluate the most complicated arithmetic expressions. However, there

ABS(X)	absolute (or positive) value of X
ACS(X)	arc-cosine of X (i.e. the angle (in radians) whose cosine is X)
ASN(X)	arc-sine of X
ATN(X)	arc-tangent of X
COS(X)	cosine of X (cosX), where X is in radians
DEG(X)	X radians expressed in degrees
EXP(X)	exponential of X (e^X)
INT(X)	integer (or whole number) part of X
LN(X)	natural logarithm of X ($\log_e X$)
LOG(X)	common logarithm of X ($\log_{10} X$)
RAD(X)	X degrees expressed in radians
SGN(X)	the sign of X (+1 if X>0, 0 if X=0, −1 if X<0)
SIN(X)	sine of X (sinX)
SQR(X)	square root of X ($\sqrt{X}$)
TAN(X)	tangent of X (tanX)

Figure 8.1   Mathematical functions available in Basic

are a substantial number of common mathematical functions such as logarithms, trigonometrical functions, square roots, etc. which are often required but would be difficult, if not impossible, for all save the most mathematically minded to calculate. (If we were using these in a hand calculation we would refer to a book of tables.) Basic therefore provides a set of such functions as part of the language, for use whenever required.

Figure 8.1 shows the mathematical functions available, all of which can be used in expressions such as

```
10 A=B+SQR(C)
```

or

```
70 X1=(-B+SQR(B^2-4*A*C))/(2*A)
```

One point that should be emphasised is that the trigonometric functions use radians and not degrees (there are 2π radians in a circle, or 360 degrees). If you are involved with any trigonometrical calculation but wish to work in degrees then you must use the functions RAD and DEG to convert from one to the other:

```
110 REM Xdeg is in degrees
120 Xrad=RAD(Xdeg)
130 CosX=COS(Xrad)
140 Yrad=ATN(TanY)
150 Ydeg=DEG(Yrad)
```

Since a function reference can be used in an arithmetic expression just like a variable it can have another function reference as an argument. The above example could, therefore, be written

```
120 CosX=COS(RAD(Xdeg))
130 Ydeg=DEG(ATN(TanY))
```

In this connection it is also worth noting that the value of π is part of Basic. The special named constant PI has the value 3.141 592 65 and can be used anywhere that a constant could have been written. Thus the area of a circle could be calculated as follows:

```
10 INPUT "Radius of circle ",Area
20 Area=PI*R^2
30 PRINT "The circle's area is ";Area
```

8.3 RANDOM NUMBERS

A rather special function which can be very useful in a wide variety of situations is RND, which produces a "random" number which can then be used in a game, or in testing a program, or in simulating some activity, etc. It was briefly mentioned in chapter 6, but will now be described in detail, as it can be used in a variety of different ways.

The normal usage is by writing

```
RND(N)
```

where N is a whole number greater than 1 (and less than 2 147 483 648). This will create a random whole number which lies between 1 and N, or which may equal 1 or N. Thus the statement

```
10 Month=RND(12)
```

will set the variable Month to a random whole number in the range 1 to 12, inclusive.

Experiment 8.3

If you have been using your computer, switch it off and then switch it on again. Now type in the following program:

```
10 FOR I=1,20
20    PRINT RND(1000)
30    NEXT
```

and RUN it. The numbers printed should be a fairly random selection in the range 1–1000.
  Now switch off your computer and repeat the experiment. What do you observe?
  Now RUN it again (without switching off). What do you observe this time?
  Now add an extra line

```
5 X=RND(-50)
```

and RUN the program. Then RUN it again. What do you observe now?

The above experiment will have shown you that the computer's "random numbers" are not totally random, since in some situations the same sequences re-occur. In fact a "random number generator" cannot generate truly random numbers but uses a sophisticated mathematical function to produce a sequence of numbers which have no obvious connection with each other and which, in addition, are evenly distributed over the range required. Such a sequence thus consists of "pseudo-random" numbers.

Because the sequence is mathematically generated it will always produce the same sequence if it is started at the same place. By switching off the computer before writing and running the short program we ensured that the sequence was started at the same place on the first two occasions. When the program was run a second time without switching off and on again, however, the random number generator was not restarted and so a new set of numbers was produced.

Often when testing a program it is useful to ensure that the same sequence is always used and we can ensure this by calling RND with a negative argument, as this resets the random number generator to a number based on the argument. The extra line 5 will therefore ensure that the program *always* produces the same sequence of numbers.

We can also use this to ensure a completely random starting position by writing

```
5 X=RND(-TIME)
```

since TIME contains the time that has elapsed since it was last reset (in hundredths of a second) and will therefore almost certainly be different every time the program is run. Line 390 of the CASTLE2 program contains a statement of this form to ensure that a different set of random numbers is used each time the program is run. Since the position of objects in the castle, the type and strength of dragons and skeletons, the passages between doors and the results of battles are all influenced by random numbers, this ensures that every game is different.

Experiment 8.4

Modify the CASTLE2 program so that the same scenario is always produced. Save this version on a separate tape — you will find it useful when altering the main game later. (This was the method used when developing the program — you can't be certain that an error has been corrected unless you can repeat the same game.)

If we write RND(1) then the random number produced is one that lies between 0 and 0.999 999, which is not generally as useful as a whole random number, while RND(0) repeats the last number provided by RND(1).

Finally, if we write RND without any argument or parentheses then a whole number is returned in the range −2 147 483 648 to +2 147 483 647!

Figure 8.2 summarises these alternatives.

8.4   DEFINING YOUR OWN FUNCTIONS

In chapter 4 we saw how we could write our own procedures, and in chapter 6 we saw how we could use global variables to return information from the procedure to the part of the program which called it.

A function is a special type of procedure which returns a single value (known as the *function value*) in such a way that it can be used directly, as with a standard function such

N	RND(N)
$1 < N < 2147483647$	random whole number R, $1 \leqslant R \geqslant N$
1	random number R, $0 \leqslant R \geqslant 0.999999$
0	last value provided by RND(1)
$N < 0$	N
	but also resets random number generator to a value based on N
In addition	
RND	returns a random number R, $-2147483648 \leqslant R \leqslant 2147483647$

Figure 8.2   RND options

as ABS, SQR or RND. A function name takes the form

```
FNname
```

and is used just like a standard function:

```
10 X=FNname(A,B)
```

or

```
70 A=B+FNname(X,Y)*P+SQR(FNname(U,V))
```

A function definition starts with the statement

```
DEF FNname(p1,p2,...)
```

in a very similar way to a procedure definition. The major difference is that the function is ended by a statement of the form

```
=value
```

which returns *value* as the function value. There is no ENDPROC statement.

Thus a (trivial) function to add three numbers could be written as follows:

```
150 DEF FNsum(A,B,C)
160 LOCAL total
170 total=A+B+C
180 =total
```

or simply as

```
150 DEF FNsum(A,B,C)
160 =A+B+C
```

In this case we can even further simplify the function definition to a single statement:

```
150 DEF FNsum(A,B,C)=A+B+C
```

Experiment 8.5

Write a function which returns successive numbers from a sequence stored in one or more DATA statements. Use this in a program to find the average of a set of numbers, where the set of numbers is preceded by the number of numbers in the set.

For example if the data was

```
8,9,7,12,25,1,17,41,13
```

then the result would be 15.625 (125/8)

When the program is working correctly, alter the function so that the data is provided from the keyboard instead of from DATA statements.

A function can always be replaced by a procedure which returns its value through a global variable, but in certain situations a function is a more satisfactory solution because it fits in with the general program flow more easily.

8.5 INTEGERS

Up to this point we have talked about "numbers". In fact there are two quite different sorts of numbers in computing – whole numbers and those which can have fractional (or decimal) parts. Unless otherwise specified all numbers in Basic are real numbers and may contain a fractional part if necessary.

Real numbers on the Beeb can be used to store any number between

200 000 000 000 000 000 000 000 000 000 000 000 000 (or 2×10^{38})

and

0.000 000 000 000 000 000 000 000 000 000 000 000 002 (or 2×10^{-39}),

or negative numbers in the same range, or zero. Because of the method used to store these numbers they are only kept to an accuracy of nine significant figures, but this is quite enough for most purposes.

Sometimes, however, we know that a variable can only take values which use whole numbers and so we may specify that it is an *integer* variable. We do this by following the name by a percentage sign (%):

```
Name%    X%      number%
```

An integer variable can store a whole number between −2 147 483 648 and +2 147 483 647 with complete accuracy.

Integer arithmetic is considerably faster than real arithmetic as you can confirm for yourself by the following experiment.

Experiment 8.6

Write a program to calculate the speed of real and integer arithmetic. You can do this by repeating the same operation a large number of times, thus

```
10 TIME=0
20 FOR I=1 TO 1000
30    NEXT
40 Looptime=TIME
50 A=4: B=6
60 TIME=0
70 FOR I=1 TO 1000
80    X=A+B
```

```
 90   NEXT
100 Time=TIME
110 PRINT "Real addition takes ";(Time-Looptime)/100000;" secs"
```
.
.
.

Note the use of the initial (dummy) loop to measure the time taken to obey the FOR and NEXT statements. Since TIME counts in hundredths of a second the final value must be divided by 1000 (the number of times the statement was obeyed) and 100 (to convert to seconds).

Do you notice anything unusual about the division times?

When using integers for addition, subtraction and multiplication no problems arise, but for division it is different. For example what should be printed by the following?

```
10 A%=4: B%=17
20 C%=B%/A%
30 PRINT C%
```

Clearly the "correct" answer is 17/4 or $4\frac{1}{4}$ or 4.25, but since C% is an integer only a whole number may be stored, i.e. 4. But what about this?

```
10 A%=4: B%=17
20 PRINT B%/A%
```

In this case the result printed will be 4.25! Try it on your computer if you don't believe us.

How do we explain this apparent contradiction?

The answer is that / is a *real* operator and so the values in A% and B% are converted to *real* form before the calculation is carried out. In the first case this result is then stored in an *integer* variable (C%) and so it is converted into an integer, losing the fractional part in the process. In the second case the result is printed without the need for any conversion. Obviously all this conversion takes time and should be avoided if possible.

Basic provides two extra operators for use with whole numbers – DIV and MOD.

DIV is the integer equivalent of / and if we write

```
20 C%=B% DIV A%
```

then the division is carried out with whole numbers and any remainder is ignored.

MOD is a related operator that provides the remainder. Thus

```
25 R%=B% MOD A%
```

stores the remainder, after dividing B% by A%, in the variable R%.

Experiment 8.7

Alter the program you wrote for experiment 8.6 to time DIV and MOD as well.

DIV and MOD can also be used with real operands, in which case the operands are converted to integers before the division takes place. In general this is a dangerous thing to do unless you are very clear about the exact effect you require. For example

12.1/4.9

is equal to 2.469 387 8, whereas

12.1 DIV 4.9

is equal to 3!
   Furthermore

12.1 MOD 4.9

is equal to 0!
   These rather surprising results are due to the fact that 12.1 and 4.9 are converted to integers by truncation before division takes place (i.e. to 12 and 4).
   Note that DIV and MOD should be preceded by a space to avoid the possibility of their being mixed up with a variable name. For example

70 X=ADIVB

will attempt to store the contents of the variable ADIVB in X, and will (presumably) fail with the message

No such variable at line 70

If we write

70 X=A DIV B

or even

70 X=A DIVB

then all will be well.
   As we have seen, integer arithmetic is faster than real arithmetic and is carried out with complete accuracy within the range of whole numbers which can be stored as integers. Real arithmetic, on the other hand, is slower and is only accurate to nine figures (although this is more than enough for most purposes). If you are dealing with arithmetic problems which either concern only whole numbers or which can readily be altered to use whole numbers (i.e. by working in pence instead of pounds, in millimetres instead of metres, or in grams instead of kilograms) then it is worth considering the use of integers; but beware of

division! In other cases, or where there is not much calculation, it is usually easier to use the (normal) real variables.

8.6 RESIDENT INTEGER VARIABLES

There are 26 special integer variables with names A%, B%, C%, ..., Y%, Z% which are stored in a special part of the computer's memory and have a number of special characteristics.

They are called the resident integer variables because, unlike all other variables, they are not cleared and reset when a program is loaded or RUN. This means that they can be used to preserve information between successive executions of a program or even to pass information between programs. The Final Test uses some of the resident integers to pass the player's name to later programs and to determine whether or not to produce a title sequence in CASTLE.

Because these 26 variables are stored in a fixed place the Basic interpreter can also access them more quickly than it can access other variables. Where speed is important, therefore, a slight improvement can always be achieved by using the resident integer variables whenever possible. However, because they have such simple names their use makes a program slightly less easy to follow.

In the final part of The Final Test (Castle) all 26 resident integer variables are used for particular purposes as shown in figure 8.3.

A%	ASCII code of current man (first) character (248, 250, 252 or 254)
B%	current man direction (−1 = right, +1 = left)
C%	code of last key pressed, or −1
D%	new man direction
E%	man colour (normally 7)
F%	top floor of castle (3, 5 or 7)
G%	game level (1, 2 or 3)
H%	current score
I% J% K% L%	loop variables, etc.
M%	number of items currently held
N%	total number of items in castle
O%	"feather factor" (1 or 2)
P%	player's skill (1 to 8)
Q%	spirit indicator
R%	next spirit to be moved
S%	maximum number of spirits allowed (0 or G%)
T%	number of spirits present on current floor
U% V%	proposed new player coordinates
W%	maximum wait before a spirit appears
X% Y%	current player coordinates
Z%	current floor level (0 to 7, or −1 for dungeon)

Figure 8.3   Table of resident integer uses in Castle

Experimental Hints

8.1 The priority order is * or /, followed by + or −
Thus the expression

```
4+5*6
```

is first evaluated to 4+30, and then to 34.

8.2 A is 2*27−16/2 = 54−8 = 46

B is 6^3−2^2 = 216−4 = 212

C is 2*3^1^4/2 = 2*3^4/2 = 2*81/2 = 81

D is 81/3/3/3 = 27/3/3 = 9/3 = 3

E is 2^3+3^2 = 8+9 = 17

F is 17*3+212/4−(46+2*3) = 51+53−52 = 52

G is 1/3+17/3 = 0.333333333+5.66666667 = 6

H is 52/17−3*6/17 = 3.05882353−18/7 = 3.05882353−1.05882353 = 2

Note that in the last two cases the computer's ability to carry out accurate arithmetic is tested. Line 70 leads to one divided by three plus seventeen divided by three, which is clearly equal to six, while line 80 reduces to fifty-two divided by seventeen minus eighteen divided by seventeen, which is equally clearly equal to two! However, in calculating such real expressions the computer cannot store the resulting values with 100% accuracy. Nevertheless, the Beeb is remarkably accurate in its arithmetic calculations, and the resulting inaccuracies are too small to be detected in the first nine significant digits!

8.5 A suitable function is

```
500 DEF FNav
510 LOCAL sum,n,x,i
520 sum=0
530 READ n
540 FOR i=1 TO n
550    READ x: sum=sum+x
560    NEXT
570 =sum/n
```

For keyboard input lines 530 and 550 require the READ statements to be replaced by (informative) INPUT statements.

8.6 Division for integers will be the same as for reals (or even longer!).

Some characters to play with

9.1 CHARACTER STRINGS AND THEIR STORAGE

We have already seen that a variable name ending with a $ is used to store character strings. Before we see how we can manipulate character strings, however, we must understand one or two basic principles about the way in which they are stored in the computer's memory.

A character is stored in coded form as a number between 0 and 255; however, the numbers 0–31 have special meanings, as we shall see later, and the numbers 128–255 are normally undefined. In practice, therefore, we need only consider the values 32–127 in most cases, and figure 9.1 shows the characters which correspond to these codes.

The most important implication of this, however, concerns the amount of storage required for a character string. A computer's memory is usually measured in terms of *bytes*, where one byte consists of 8 *bits*, and where a bit takes the value 0 or 1. A single byte may be used to store an integer in the range 0–255 using the binary notation. (If you don't understand what binary is it doesn't matter at all – suffice to say that each bit (or binary digit) represents a power of two, just as each digit in a decimal number represents a power of ten.) It is not a coincidence that 0–255 is the range of numbers that can be used to represent a character!

	0	1	2	3	4	5	6	7	8	9
30		space	!	''	#	$	%	&	'	
40	(	)	*	+	,	–	.	/	0	1
50	2	3	4	5	6	7	8	9	:	;
60	<	=	>	?	@	A	B	C	D	E
70	F	G	H	I	J	K	L	M	N	O
80	P	Q	R	S	T	U	V	W	X	Y
90	Z	[	\	]	^	_	£	a	b	c
100	d	e	f	g	h	i	j	k	l	m
110	n	o	p	q	r	s	t	u	v	w
120	x	y	z	{			}	~	delete		

Figure 9.1   ASCII codes 32–127

114

Thus one byte can be used to store one character in coded form, five bytes to store five characters, and so on.

This is very different from numbers where four bytes are used to store any integer number from $-2\,147\,483\,648$ to $+2\,147\,483\,647$, and five bytes are used to store any real number from $-2*10^{38}$ to $+2*10^{38}$ (to an accuracy of nine significant figures).

We can begin to see the implications of this by considering the following program extract:

```
170   A=2.5
180   A%=7
190   A$="FRED"
200   A=3.5
210   A%=10
220   A$="DAVID"
```

At line 170 the value 2.5 is stored in a variable called A. This is a real name and so five bytes are allocated. At line 200 the value 3.5 is assigned to A and so this number replaces 2.5 in the five bytes allocated to A.

At line 180 the value 7 is stored in a variable called A%. This is an integer name and so four bytes are allocated. At line 210 the value 10 is assigned to A% and so this number replaces 7 in the four bytes allocated to A%.

At line 190 the string "FRED" is stored in a variable called A$. This is a character name and four bytes are allocated — one for each character of the string. At line 220 the string "DAVID" is assigned to A$; however this will require five bytes and only four were allocated to A$. A new block of five bytes is therefore allocated to A$ and the original four are deleted from the list of variable storage allocations. In general these four bytes are now wasted space and cannot be utilised again until the program has finished. (With later versions of the Basic interpreter this is not always the case, but it is wise to assume that it will be.)

On the other hand, if line 190 had been

```
190   A$="RICHARD"
```

then seven bytes would have been allocated to the variable A$ and when line 220 was obeyed the first five of these could have been used for "DAVID" and it would not have been necessary to allocate a new storage area. If a further line

```
230   A$="WILLIAM"
```

were then to be obeyed there would still be no problem because the original statement at line 190 had caused seven bytes to be allocated, and even though only five are required at line 220 all seven are available if necessary for any subsequent assignment, such as that at line 230.

Experiment 9.1

We can add two strings together (or *concatenate* them) by using a + sign. The following program therefore repeatedly adds one * to the strings stored in A$ and B$.

```
10 MODE 1
20 A$=""
30 FOR I=1 TO 250
40   A$=A$+"*"
50   B$="B"+A$
60   C$="C"+A$
70   D$="D"+A$
80   PRINT I;" asterisks in A$, etc."
90   NEXT
```

Type this program into your computer and RUN it.
Did the result surprise you?

Experiment 9.1 shows how easy it is for a program to inadvertently waste a very large amount of memory due to the Beeb's method of allocating storage for character variables. We can therefore make a rule that

all character variables should initially be assigned a string which is at least as long as any that will subsequently be assigned.

If this is done then obviously the initial space allocated will be suitable for all strings subsequently assigned to the variable.
There is a very useful function that simplifies this initial assignment:

```
STRING$(n,string)
```

produces as its result a character string consisting of n copies of the string string. Thus

```
STRING$(4,"+-+-")
```

will produce the string "+-+-+-+-+-+-+-", which can be very useful for decorative features, and

```
STRING$(25," ")
```

will produce a string consisting of 25 spaces, which can be assigned to a character variable to cause the allocation of sufficient memory for strings of up to 25 characters.

Experiment 9.2

Add the line

```
15 A$=STRING$(250," "): B$=A$: C$=A$: D$=A$
```

to the program in experiment 9.1 and RUN it. This time there are no problems. (Note that line 20 sets A$ to a null string ready to have asterisks added to it; if this was not done then the asterisk would be added to a string of 200 spaces and the program would fail even more quickly than before!)

9.2   MANIPULATING CHARACTERS

In the last section we saw that it is possible to add, or concatenate, two strings by use of a
+ sign:

```
10   A$="FRED"
20   B$="DIE"
30   C$=A$+B$
40   D$=A$+"DIE"
50   E$="FRED"+B$
60   F$="FRED"+"DIE"
```

Thus in the above example the variables C$, D$, E$ and F$ will all contain the string
"FREDDIE".
  We also saw that we can use the function STRING$ to create a string consisting of mul-
tiple repetitions of a single string.
  We can also extract *sub-strings* from a character string by use of the three functions
LEFT$, RIGHT$ and MID$:
  LEFT$(string,n) creates a new string consisting of the first n characters of string. Thus

```
130 L$=LEFT$("FREDDIE",4)
```

will store the string "FRED" in the variable L$.

RIGHT$(string,n) on the other hand, creates a new string consisting of the last n
characters of string. Thus

```
140 R$=RIGHT$("FREDDIE",3)
```

will store the string "DIE" in the variable R$.
  MID$(string,p,n) is a more general function and creates a new string of n characters,
starting at character p of string. Thus

```
150 M$=MID$("FREDDIE",2,3)
```

will store the string "RED" in M$. It is also possible to omit the third argument n, in
which case the new string consists of the remainder of string, starting at character p.
Thus

```
160 M$=MID$("FREDDIE",3)
```

will store the string "EDDIE" in M$.

Another useful function in character manipulation is LEN which returns the length of the
character string supplied as its argument. Thus after obeying line 160 above, the statement

```
170 N=LEN(M$)
```

will set N to 5, i.e. the length of the string "EDDIE" which was most recently assigned to
M$. We can also see that the function references

```
MID$(S$,P)
```

and

```
MID$(S$,P,LEN(S$)-P+1)
```

are identical in their effect, since LEN(S$)-P+1 is the number of characters in S$ from
character P to the end of the string.

Experiment 9.3

Write a program which inputs a word or sentence and prints it back to front (i.e. MILES
ELLIS should be printed as SILLE SELIM). RUN it on your computer to make sure that
it works properly.

9.3   MORE CHARACTER FUNCTIONS

We saw in section 9.1 that every character has a numeric code associated with it. There are
occasions when it is useful to know this code and the function ASC will provide it for us.
(ASC is short for ASCII, the name of the code used on most computers, including the
Beeb.) Thus

```
50 N=ASC("H")
```

will store the value 72 in N (see figure 9.1), and

```
60 n=ASC("h")
```

will store 104 in n.
  If the argument contains more than one character then the value returned is the code for
the first character of the string. Thus

```
70 M=ASC("Donkey")
```

will store the value 68 (the code for D) in the variable M.
  The reverse conversion is carried out by the function CHR$, which returns the single
character whose code is supplied as an argument to the function. Thus

```
80 A$=CHR$(75)
```

will store the character "K" in the variable A$ and

```
90 B$=CHR$(42)
```

will store "*" in B$.

If the argument is greater than 255 then the remainder after dividing by 256 is used as the argument, thus

```
100 C$=CHR$(333)
```

will cause the character "M" to be stored in C$ (333 MOD 256 is 77; CHR$(77) is "M").

Experiment 9.4

Write a program to produce a table of characters corresponding to codes 32 to 127 and compare the results it produces with figure 9.1. Do you notice any differences?

Run the program in mode 6 as well as mode 7. Compare both with figure 9.1. What conclusions do you draw?

Two other useful functions are STR$ and VAL which are used to convert numbers into character strings and vice-versa. The function reference

```
STR$(num)
```

will provide as its value a string containing the character representation of the number num. The number will be converted into characters in exactly the same way as when PRINTing a number, and so the two PRINT statements in the following program will produce identical output:

```
10 INPUT "Please type a number " N
20 N$=STR$(N)
30 PRINT "Your number was ";N
40 PRINT "Your number was ";N$
```

The function VAL is the opposite of STR$ and returns the number corresponding to the character string provided as its argument. This character string should start with a + or a − sign, a space, or a digit; if it starts with any other character then zero will be returned. The three PRINT statements in the following program will therefore produce identical output:

```
10 A$="2": B$="-5": C$="+3": D$="ZERO"
20 A=VAL(A$): B=VAL(B$)
30 C=VAL(C$): D=VAL(D$)
40 PRINT A$;B$;C$;"=";D
50 PRINT A;B;"+";C;"=";0
60 PRINT A$+B$+C$;"=";A+B+C
```

A more useful function than VAL is EVAL which takes a complete expression as its argument and evaluates the expression before returning its value. Thus we may write

```
70 N=EVAL("X+SIN(PI*T)-A MOD B")
```

which is the same as writing

```
70 N=X+SIN(PI*T)-A MOD B
```

The main use of this function is to allow expressions, or non-numeric values, to be INPUT from the keyboard. For example the following program will allow a very flexible form of input:

```
10 INPUT "Please type a number or expression "A$
20 N=EVAL(A$)
30 PRINT "The value you typed was ";N
```

When this program is run any of the following would be valid replies:

```
1.234
3+6/4
SIN(RAD(63))
&ABCD
```

The first (1.234) is a simple number.

The second (3+6/4) is a simple arithmetic expression which will be evaluated to 4.5.

The third is a nested function reference which will first convert 63 degrees to radians and then find the sine of that angle; the result will be 0.891 006 524.

The last is a *hexadecimal* number (i.e. a number to base 16). The computer uses hexadecimal numbers internally and, if required, a program may use them. A hexadecimal number uses the letters A to F as well as the digits 0 to 9 and is preceded by an ampersand. The number &ABCD will be evaluated to 43 981 (10*4096 + 11*256 + 12*16 +13).

Experiment 9.5

Write a program to "solve sums" and test it with a variety of different types of sums.

Experimental Hints

```
9.3   10 REM Input sentence
      20 PRINT "Please type a short sentence"
      30 INPUT A$
      40 REM Now print it in reverse
      50 PRINT: PRINT "The reverse of this is:"
      60 N=LEN(A$)
      70 FOR I=N TO 1 STEP -1
      80   PRINT MID$(A$,I,1);
      90   NEXT
     100 PRINT
```

9.4   In mode 7 the characters for 91–93 and 123–126 are not the standard ASCII representations; in all other modes they are standard.

    The only characters that will normally be affected in a Basic program are ˜ (to indicate hexadecimal printing) which will appear as ÷ in mode 7, and | (to indicate a control character in a function key definition) which will appear as ‖.

A bit more flexibility

10.1 DECISION TIME

We have now met most of the fundamental features of Basic and are able to write programs which can input numbers and/or text from the keyboard, print numbers and/or text using a layout determined by ourselves, calculate with both real and integer numbers, manipulate character strings, draw simple pictures in colour using either lines or solid blocks of colour, and make a variety of both musical and non-musical sounds. We have learned how to use FOR and NEXT statements to create loops, and we have seen how any or all of these may be incorporated in procedures or functions in order to simplify programs and to clarify their structure.

However, one very important aspect of programming still remains unexplored – the ability of a program to follow one of several alternative courses of action, depending upon some condition, which can be tested at the moment when the decision needs to be made, as to which course of action to take. An example of this is the section of code in Castle which tests to see which key has been pressed – if any. This reads as follows:

```
130 C%=INKEY(0): IF C%>135 AND C%<140 THEN
     PROCmove
   ELSE
     IF C%<>-1 THEN
        PROCgetcom
```

Notice that this line has been listed in a *structured* manner, as is the complete program listing in Appendix A. This is because this form of listing emphasises the structure of the statement better than does a straight listing:

```
   130 C%=INKEY(0):IF C%>135 AND C%<140 THEN PROCmove ELSE IF C%<>-1
 THEN PROCgetcom
```

It is clear that the line contains two separate statements, separated by a colon. The first

```
C%=INKEY(0)
```

uses the INKEY function to obtain the code of any key that has been pressed. Because the value in parentheses is zero the function will not wait, but will return −1 if no key has been pressed.

The next statement starts with the expression

```
IF C%>135 AND C%<140 THEN PROCmove
```

which means exactly what it says – "If the value in C% (i.e. the code for the key pressed) is greater than 135 and less than 140 then obey the procedure PROCmove". Since C% is an integer variable, the only values which satisfy this test are 136, 137, 138 and 139, which are the codes produced by the four cursor control keys ←, →, ↑ and ↓. Thus this part of the statement says that if one of the cursor control keys has been pressed then PROCmove should be obeyed (to move the man character).

The statement then continues

```
ELSE IF C%<>-1 THEN PROCgetcom
```

which is slightly more confusing since it is not obvious what < > means. In fact it means "less than or greater than", in other words "not equal to". This second part of the statement thus means " . . . otherwise (i.e. if C% is 135 or less, or is 140 or more) if C% is not equal to −1 then obey the procedure PROCgetcom (to get the command, e.g. OPEN DOOR)". Now −1 is the value returned if no key was pressed so the full statement now means that

"if one of the cursor control keys was pressed then
    obey the procedure PROCmove
otherwise
    if any other key was pressed then
        obey the procedure PROCgetcom"

Essentially, that is all there is to making decisions in Basic programs. However, before we can use them in our programs we need to examine their syntax in rather more detail.

The first thing to remember is that IF. . .THEN. . .ELSE is a single statement and must, therefore, occupy only a single line of the program – that is a program line, not necessarily a single printed line. It is quite unlike a FOR. . .NEXT loop which can last for as many lines as are required.

We can consider the IF statement in two basic forms:

IF condition THEN statement(s)

which states that if the condition is true then the statement(s) following must be obeyed; if the condition is not true then the statement(s) following will not be obeyed. Alternatively we may write

IF condition THEN statement(s) ELSE statement(s)

which states that if the condition is not true then the statement(s) after the keyword ELSE must be obeyed.

It is important to realise that either sequence of statements may contain a further IF statement; this was the case in the example from Castle above. Thus we may write

```
IF c1 THEN s1: s2 ELSE s3: IF c2 THEN s4 ELSE s5
```

which means that if c1 is true then s1 and s2 will be obeyed. If c1 is false (i.e not true) then s3 will be obeyed, *and then* if c2 is true s4 will be obeyed, while if it is false s5 will be obeyed. The structure is made clearer by the form of listing used earlier:

```
IF c1 THEN
   s1: s2
ELSE
   s3: IF c2 THEN
      s4
   ELSE
      s5
```

There is one rather unfortunate discrepency in the BBC Basic interpreter, however, which treats the statement

```
IF c1 THEN IF c2 THEN s1 ELSE s2
```

as though it were

```
IF c1 THEN
   IF c2 THEN
      s1
ELSE
   s2
```

while the statement

```
IF c1 THEN s3: IF c2 THEN s1 ELSE s2
```

is treated as

```
IF c1 THEN
   s3: IF c2 THEN
      s1
   ELSE
      s2
```

We still haven't discussed what the "conditions" are which determine how an IF statement works, although their general form will be apparent from the above examples. There are actually two types of conditions – relational and logical.

A relational condition compares two items to establish their relation to each other using one of six relational operators shown in figure 10.1.

Thus we may write

```
IF a<b THEN ....
```

or

```
IF Name$ <> "Fred" THEN ....
```

The meaning of "less than" or "greater than" is quite clear for numbers, but we need to explain exactly what it means when applied to strings. What happens in this case is that the two strings are compared character by character until a difference is found. The ASCII codes (see figure 9.1) of these two characters are then compared and their relationship is taken as the relationship between the two strings. In particular this means that the digits 0–9 are in their correct order and less than any letters. The capital letters A–Z are in their alphabetic order and less than the lower case letters a–z, which are also in their correct order. In addition, a space is "less than" any other character. Thus

```
"ANNA"<"ANNE"
```
is true because A (65) is less than E (69)

```
"BILL"<"Bill"
```
is true because I (73) is less than i (105)

```
"Case1"<"CaseA"
```
is true because 1 (49) is less than A (65)

```
"William"<"Willie"
```
is true because a (97) is less than e (101)

If both strings match up to the end of one, but the other continues, then the shorter string is the lesser one. (This is equivalent to adding spaces to the shorter string – since these are less than any other character the shorter one will be the smaller.) Thus

```
"Pete"<"Peter"
```
is true because Peter is longer.

Incidentally, it is a good job that we don't use Roman numerals with computers because although "I" < "II" (1 < 2) and even "IV" < "V" (4 < 5), unfortunately "VIII" < "IX" (8 > 9)!

```
<    less than
=    equals
>    greater than
<=   less than or equal to
>=   greater than or equal to
<>   not equal to (i.e. less than or greater than)
```

Figure 10.1   Relational operators

Experiment 10.1

Write a program which reads two Roman numerals in the range I to C (1 to 100) and prints out a message to say which is the smaller.

Often a simple relational condition is not sufficient to determine which course of action is required, and we need to combine two or more simple conditions to produce a more complex one. We have already seen one example of this:

```
IF C%>135 AND C%<140 THEN ....
```

where the keyword AND is used to specify that both the first condition *and* the second must be true if the whole condition is to be true. This is an example of a *logical* operator, and another is OR, as in the statement

```
IF A$="Y" OR A$="y" THEN ....
```

which specifies that the whole condition is true if either the first condition *or* the second one is true.

We can build up more complicated tests by combining several simple relational conditions. For example

```
IF Age>21 AND Sex$="M" OR Salary>5000 THEN ....
```

In the case of a condition which contains both AND and OR operators it is important to realise that the AND operators have a higher priority than the OR operators (just as * and / have a higher priority than + or –). Thus the above condition is true either if Age is greater than 21 and Sex$ is male, or if Salary is greater than 5000. To avoid confusion we can use parentheses:

```
IF (Age>21 AND Sex$="M") OR Salary>5000 THEN ....
```

In general it is a good idea to use parentheses like this as it ensures that you and the computer are in agreement! It is very easy to write

```
IF Age>21 AND Sex$="M" OR Salary>5000 THEN ....
```

when what you mean is

```
IF Age>21 AND (Sex$="M" OR Salary>5000) THEN ...
```


10.2   THE UBIQUITOUS GOTO STATEMENT

As we have already stated, a complete IF...THEN...ELSE structure can only occupy a single program line. In many instances this is not sufficient for the statements required to carry out the necessary action, and we have to find a way of extending the scope of the statement. One way is by use of procedures:

```
IF condition THEN
    PROCone
ELSE
    PROCtwo
```

However, this is not appropriate in some situations and we must use a different approach with a special statement – GOTO. This can be very useful, but *must be used with great care* as it can easily lead to badly structured programs which are difficult to read and to correct. The GOTO statement takes the form

```
GOTO line_number
```

and causes the next statement to be obeyed to be the one at line line_number. We can thus write, for example,

```
100   IF Value>Av THEN
          ........: GOTO 150
110   REM Statements to be obeyed if Value<=Av
      •
      •
      •
150   REM Both cases back together again
      •
      •
```

Another, similar, situation occurs when a large number of alternative cases exist:

```
100 IF Case=1 THEN
        PROCone: GOTO 200
110 IF Case=2 THEN
        PROCtwo: GOTO 200
120 IF Case>2 AND Case<5 THEN
        PROCthree: GOTO 200
    •
    •
    •
190 IF Case=0 THEN
        PROCten
200 REM All cases back together again
```

Notice that in both situations the GOTO is used only to go to the end of what is otherwise a "multi-statement IF". You should only use GOTO for other purposes in very exceptional circumstances.

Experiment 10.2

A popular children's game is called Hangman. In this game one player chooses a word and indicates how many letters it contains. The other player then has to guess the word one letter at a time. If he/she guesses a letter correctly then that letter is written in each of the places in which it occurs in the word. If he/she is wrong then the first player adds one part to a drawing of a hanged man. The object is to guess the word before you are hanged! Figure 10.2 shows a game in progress; typically the drawing contains nine or ten parts as shown in figure 10.3.

You can write a program to play Hangman by storing a list of words in DATA statements and then using the RND function to READ up to a particular word. LEN can be used to find out how many letters it contains. Write a program to play the game.

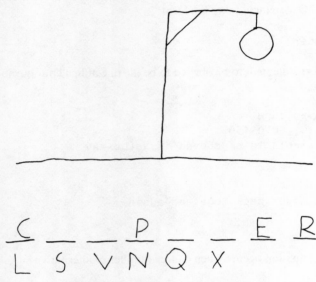

Figure 10.2   Hangman game in progress

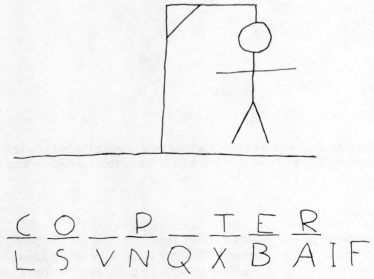

Figure 10.3   You lose! (and are hanged)

Note: This is a much more challenging experiment than any others so far, and it is important to tackle it in several stages. To begin with, write a program which simply chooses a name and prints out the appropriate number of dashes, and then prints out the word. Make sure that this works properly before proceeding to the next stage.

The second stage is to add the code to ask for a letter, check to see if it is in the word and take appropriate action. This is the heart of the program but is not too difficult if you think about it and remember the various facilities discussed in chapter 9 for character manipulation. Don't bother with any drawing at this stage – just print how many "lives" are left.

Once this is working you can add a section to draw the picture. This is quite easy apart from the head. If you can't work out how to do this there is a procedure to draw a circle in the Experimental Hints.

Finally, if you haven't already done so, you could add colour and some sound effects.

10.3   MORE FLEXIBLE LOOPS

In chapter 6 we introduced the concept of a FOR loop and we have used it in a number of examples since then. In fact it is a more powerful statement than it has appeared to be since, as well as the first and last values of the counter, we may specify the increment (or *step*) to be used. Thus if we write

```
70 FOR I=1 TO 10 STEP 3
```

the loop will be obeyed for I taking values 1, 4, 7 and 10. Similarly

```
90 FOR J=10 TO 0 STEP -2
```

will cause the loop to be obeyed for I taking values 10, 8, 6, 4, 2 and 0.

One question that arises with this extended form of FOR statement is "what happens if the counter never equals the final value?". For example

```
150 FOR I%=1 TO 10 STEP 2
```

would cause I% to take successive values of 1, 3, 5, 7, 9 and then 11. The answer is that the loop is always ended when the next value of the counter would be beyond the final value specified (i.e. greater when counting up, less when counting down). In this example, therefore, the loop would be obeyed five times with I% taking the values 1, 3, 5, 7 and 9.

Experiment 10.3

Write a program to produce a table showing Fahrenheit temperatures at ten degree intervals from 0 to 250 and their centigrade equivalents. Arrange for the temperatures to be listed in decreasing order, i.e. for 250°F to be at the top and 0°F at the bottom.

To make the results more interesting print the temperatures at or above the boiling point of water (100°C) in red, those at or below the freezing point of water (0°C) in blue, and all other temperatures in yellow.

For those who have forgotten (or never knew!), the centigrade equivalent of a

Fahrenheit temperature can be calculated by use of the formula

$$C = \frac{5}{9}(F-32)$$

The FOR loop is a very powerful feature of Basic but there are a great many occasions when we wish to create a loop (i.e. a sequence of statements which are to be repeated) but we either do not know how many times it is to be repeated, or the number of times it is repeated is not relevant. In these situations we may use an alternative form of loop which begins with the word REPEAT and ends with a statement of the form

```
UNTIL condition
```

We can use this to simulate a FOR loop by writing

```
100 I=First
110 REPEAT
120    REM Statements to be repeated
   .
   .
   .
170    I=I+Step
180    UNTIL I>Last
```

which is exactly equivalent to

```
100 FOR I=First TO Last STEP step
   .
   .
   .
180    NEXT
```

However, this is not a sensible use of a REPEAT loop, as the FOR loop is neater and more efficient. Consider the following however:

```
10  REPEAT
20     REM main part of proram
   .
   .
   .
250    INPUT "Another go?" A$
260    UNTIL A$<>"YES"
```

This will obey the main part of the program and then ask if "another go" is required. The program will repeat from line 20 as long as the answer is YES.

Note that a more flexible test would be

```
260    UNTIL LEFT$(A$,1)<>"Y" AND LEFT$(A$,1)<>"y"
```

which merely requires the reply to begin with either "Y" or "y" for the program to be repeated.

The condition does not, of course, need to be based on the reply to a question and will frequently be based on a value or values which are calculated during the loop. For example the main loop of Castle is to be repeated until the player finds his/her way into the tower where the princess is locked. This is deemed to be on a higher floor than the rest of the castle. Since the top floor of the castle is stored in F% (it varies depending on the skill of the player) and the current floor level is stored in Z%, the main loop can be expressed as

```
120 REPEAT
130    REM test for a key pressed and take appropriate action
   .
   .
180    UNTIL Z%>F%
```

This loop will therefore be repeated until the player finds his/her way into the tower (or until he/she is killed!).

Experiment 10.4

A musical tune can be stored in a DATA statement as a series of pairs of numbers – the first containing the pitch of the note, the second its duration. Write a program which will play a tune by READing the notes which have been stored in this way and using them in a SOUND statement. Since different tunes will have different lengths, make the program detect the end of the tune by, for example, having a negative value for the pitch.

Experiment 10.5

Make the program written in experiment 10.4 (or most of it) into a general procedure to play a tune. Then use this in a larger program which stores several tunes and plays one chosen from a list of tunes by the person using the program.

10.4   MULTIPLE SELECTION

The decision making and looping facilities described above will cater for all situations that you can possibly imagine (and many that you hadn't thought of!). In fact there are no requirements that cannot be met by an appropriate combination of FOR and/or REPEAT loops and IF statements (possibly including GOTOs). However, where a number of alternative courses of action are required which are dependent upon the value of a single number or character then a special statement can be used to simplify matters. This takes the form

```
ON value GOTO Line1,Line2, ...,LineN
```

and is really a "shorthand" way of writing

```
IF value=1 THEN
  GOTO Line1
ELSE
  IF value=2 THEN
    GOTO Line2
  ELSE
    .
    .
```

In practice, of course, we usually don't have a value which conveniently runs from 1 up to some value N which can be used to control the ON ... GOTO statement, and it may be easier to use IF statements (and will be much easier to read!). One way in which a suitable value can be created in certain situations, however, is by use of the INSTR function. This is written

```
INSTR(string1$,string2$)
```

and is used to determine if the second string appears in the first one, and if so where. If the second string *does* appear in the first one then the function returns the character position of the first character of the second string in the first one. Thus

```
INSTR("DRAIN","IN")
```

will return the value 4, since I is the fourth letter of DRAIN, while

```
INSTR("CRIBBAGE","RIB")
```

will return 2.
  If no match is made then the value 0 is returned, e.g.

```
INSTR("Cribbage","Rib")
```

will return zero because "Rib" does not appear in "Cribbage" (since "R" and "r" are quite different characters).
  This can be used in an ON statement like this:

```
795 ON INSTR("OGDI",CHR$(C%))+1 GOTO 860,800,810,820,830
```

which will first find the character represented by the number C% and then search for it in the string "OGDI", using the resulting value plus 1 in an ON statement. Thus if CHR$(C%) is "O" then the function will return 1 which (with one added) will cause the program to GOTO 800. The values corresponding to G, D and I will likewise cause the program to go to lines 810, 820 and 830. If C% represents none of these letters then a zero will be returned which (with one added) will cause the program to continue from line 860.

This is actually a (slightly) modified form of the first line (790) of PROCgetcom in Castle which was called, as we saw at the beginning of this chapter, if a key other than a cursor control key was pressed. The four letters O, G, D and I are the first letters of the four valid commands (OPEN, GET, DROP and INVENTORY) and are used to branch to statements which either call a procedure or print a list of items held. A similar technique is used at line 880 to identify the item to be collected or dropped (see figure 10.4).

Experiment 10.6

Modify the Castle program so that it will accept both capital and lower-case commands.

In the extracts from Castle it can be seen that INKEY (in line 130) and GET$ (in lines 880–900) are used instead of INPUT. This is because, as was discussed in chapter 7, they are acted upon immediately and do not need a RETURN to be pressed. They therefore provide a very powerful way of allowing the user of a program to obtain almost instantaneous response when only a limited range of possible answers are valid, as they can be used in IF or ON statements to choose an appropriate course of action without the program having to wait until RETURN has been pressed. (An early version of Castle had one or more crowns somewhere in the castle; these were changed to hats because CROWN and CROSS would have needed four letters to distinguish them while all other items could be identified by (at most) their first two letters.)

Experiment 10.7

Modify the program for experiment 10.5 so that RETURN does not need to be pressed

```
780 DEF PROCgetcom
790 VDU 4,28,0,31,19,26,31,3,0,17,3: C$=CHR$(C%):
    ON INSTR("OGDI",C$)+1 GOTO 860,800,810,820,830
800 PROCopn: ENDPROC
810 PROCget: ENDPROC
820 PROCdrop: ENDPROC
830 PRINT "Inventory": PRINT
    .
    .
    .
870 DEF FNitem: LOCAL n
880 PROCmtq: C$=GET$: n=INSTR("AREDBSCSHSNSLSFR",C$)-1:
    PRINT C$;
890 IF n=5 THEN
    S$=GET$: n=2*INSTR("WKAHP",S$)+3: IF n=3 THEN
      n=-3
    .
    .
    .
```

Figure 10.4   Lines 780–830, 870–890 of Castle

when choosing a tune. Furthermore arrange that if Q (for Quiet!) is pressed at any time during the playing of a tune then it will stop playing immediately and ask for another tune.

Experimental Hints

10.1 This experiment is to encourage you to think! If you try to find a way of directly comparing two character strings representing two Roman numerals then you will have an extremely difficult task. However a procedure to convert a Roman numeral into its integer value is much easier to write. You can then compare the two numbers very easily.

10.2 The following program will play the game as a simple text-based game with ten "lives":

```
 10 REM This program plays "Hangman" without any graphics
 20 REPEAT
 30   RESTORE
 40   R=RND(20)
 50   FOR I=1 TO R:
        READ R$: NEXT
 60   Rlen=LEN(R$): A$=LEFT$("----------",Rlen): G$=""
 70   REPEAT
 80     PRINT 'A$: INPUT "Next guess",X$
 90     Match=0
100     FOR I=1 TO Rlen
110       IF X$=MID$(R$,I,1) THEN
              A$=LEFT$(A$,I-1)+X$+RIGHT$(A$,Rlen-I): Match=1
120       NEXT
130     IF Match=0 THEN
            PROCwrong
140     UNTIL A$=R$ OR LEN(G$)=10
150   IF A$=R$ THEN
          PRINT '"Well done!"
        ELSE
          PRINT '"You have been hanged!"
160   PRINT "The word was ";R$
170   INPUT '"Another game",X$
180   UNTIL LEFT$(X$,1)<>"Y" AND LEFT$(X$,1)<>"y"
190 END
200 DEF PROCwrong
210 G$=G$+X$: PRINT '"Incorrect letters are: ";G$
220 ENDPROC
230 DATA  FOOTBALL,CRICKET,TENNIS,GOLF,ATHLETICS
240 DATA  BALLET,MUSIC,OPERA,CARPENTRY,METALWORK
250 DATA  SAUSAGES,KIPPERS,CASSEROLE,SPAGHETTI,HAGGIS
260 DATA  ARITHMETIC,SINGING,DRAWING,SCHOOL,UNIVERSITY
```

Conversion of this to use a drawing shouldn't be too difficult; the following procedure might be useful though:

```
1000 DEF PROCcircle(x,y,r)
1010 LOCAL theta
1020 MOVE x+r,y
```

```
1030 FOR theta=5 TO 360 STEP 5
1040   DRAW x+r*COS(RAD(theta)),y+r*SIN(RAD(theta))
1050   NEXT
1060 ENDPROC
```

10.4   The relevant part of the program should be along the following lines:

```
50 READ p
60 REPEAT
70   READ d: SOUND 1,-15,p,d: READ p
80   UNTIL p<0
```

10.6   Have you checked that it works?

10.7   Insert a statement such as

```
95 IF INKEY$(0)="Q" THEN ....
```

immediately before the UNTIL statement in the loop. If a "Q" has been pressed since the last time through the loop the program will obey the statements after THEN, which should stop the tune and set p to −1 so that a normal exit will then be made from the loop.

    You should *never* use a GOTO to jump out of a REPEAT loop (or a FOR loop) as this will upset the Beeb's counting since it thinks that it is still obeying the loop. In an extreme case it can cause the program to fail.

Improve your graphics

11.1 THE PLOT STATEMENT

In chapter 5 we saw how the MOVE and DRAW statements could be used to move the graphics cursor and to draw lines on the screen. We also met the PLOT statement, which takes the form

```
PLOT n,x,y
```

and saw how it could be used to move the cursor (n = 4), to draw a line (n = 5), and to fill a triangle with the foreground colour (n = 85). In fact these are only a few of a very wide range of options, as we shall now see.

The most important values of n are those from 0 to 7, since the effect of all other values relies on an understanding of these "base values". Figure 11.1 describes the meaning of these eight cases.

As we can see from figure 11.1 there are two groups (0–3 and 4–7) which differ only in the interpretation of x and y. If n is in the range 0–3 then x and y are *relative* values which are added to the co-ordinates of the current cursor position to find the new cursor position.

n	Meaning
0	**move** graphic cursor **relative** to last point
1	**draw** line **relative** in current graphics **foreground** colour
2	**draw** line **relative** in logical **inverse** colour
3	**draw** line **relative** in current graphics **background** colour
4	**move** graphic cursor to **absolute** position
5	**draw** line **absolute** in current graphics **foreground** colour
6	**draw** line **absolute** in logical **inverse** colour
7	**draw** line **absolute** in current graphics **background** colour

Figure 11.1   PLOT n,x,y for $0 \leqslant n \leqslant 7$

Thus if the cursor is at its initial position (0,0) the statement

```
PLOT 0,200,100
```

will move the cursor to the point (200,100), since 200 + 0 is 200 and 100 + 0 is 100. The statement

```
PLOT 1,100,150
```

will then draw a line in the current foreground colour from that point (200,100) to the point (300,250), since 100 + 200 is 300 and 150 + 100 is 250. The statements

```
PLOT 1,100,-150
PLOT 1,-200,0
```

will draw further lines from (300,250) to (400,100) and then to (200,100), thus drawing a triangle.

Experiment 11.1

Type in the following program and run it.

```
10 MODE 1
20 GCOL 0,129: CLG
30 GCOL 0,3
40 FOR a=0 TO 4*PI STEP PI/16
50    PLOT 4,100*a,500*(SIN(a)+1)
60    PROCtriangle
70    NEXT
80 END
90 DEF PROCtriangle
100 PLOT 1,10,20: PLOT 1,10,-20: PLOT 1,-20,0
110 ENDPROC
```

You will see a large number of triangles drawn in white on a red background following a "sine curve". The statement at line 50 (PLOT 4,. . .) is equivalent to MOVE and will position the cursor at a point on the curve. The procedure PROCtriangle then uses three PLOT 1,. . . statements to draw the triangle. Because PLOT 1,. . .. is a *relative* PLOT statement the triangle will be drawn with its bottom left-hand corner at the position moved to in line 50.

Experiment 11.2

Alter the statements in line 100 to PLOT 2,. . . instead of PLOT 1,. . . and run the program again.

This time the triangles will be in yellow.

Experiment 11.3

Alter the statements in line 100 to PLOT 3,. . . and run the program again.
    Nothing appears to happen. Now add an extra line

```
35 GCOL 0,128
```

and run it again. Does the result surprise you?

In these three experiments we have used the three different ways of drawing lines. In the first experiment PLOT 1,. . . specifies that a line is to be drawn in the current foreground colour (see figure 11.1). This is colour 3, which is white in mode 5, so the triangles were white.

In the next experiment PLOT 2,. . . specifies that a line is to be drawn in the logical inverse colour. You can calculate the *logical inverse* colour by subtracting the colour number from the maximum colour number for that mode. Thus in the two-colour modes 0 and 4 the logical inverse of 0 is 1, and the logical inverse of 1 is 0.

In the four-colour modes 1 and 5, the logical inverse of 0 is 3, of 1 is 2, of 2 is 1 and of 3 is 0. In mode 2, which has 16 colours, the logical inverse of 0 is 15, of 1 is 14, of 2 is 13, etc.

In this case, therefore, the triangles are drawn in the *logical inverse of the colour already on the screen* at the place where they are being drawn. Since the screen has been cleared to red (i.e. colour 1) the triangles will be drawn in the logical inverse of this, i.e. colour 2 or yellow (in mode 1).

Finally experiment 11.3 uses PLOT 3,. . . statements to draw the triangles. This draws lines in the current background colour (i.e. 129 or red), and they cannot be seen! When line 35 is added the background colour is changed to 128 and so the line is drawn in black. Notice that changing the background colour does not change the background on the screen – CLG will do that – but merely specifies the colour to be used when any plotting is to use the background colour.

Experiment 11.4

Alter line 50 to PLOT 5,. . .
    Before you run the program decide what you expect to see.
    Now run it. Were you right?
    Now alter line 50 to use PLOT 6,. . . and line 100 to use PLOT 0,. . .
    Once again, decide what you expect before you run the program. Were you right?
    If you are still not sure about what to expect with the various alternative forms of the PLOT statement try some more experiments with line 50, using PLOT n,. . . where n is in the range 4–7, and with line 100 using PLOT m,. . . where m is in the range 0–3.

11.2   DIFFERENT TYPES OF LINES AND POINTS

We can now move on to investigating what happens if we write PLOT n,x,y with n in the range 8–71. There are actually five separate cases here, as shown in figure 11.2, of which one (32–63) is not currently used.

n	Meaning
8–15	as for 0–7, but with last point omitted in inverse colour plots
16–23	as for 0–7, but with a dotted line
24–31	as for 0–7, but with a dotted line and the last point omitted in inverse colour plots
32–63	not currently used
64–71	as for 0–7, but only the final point is plotted

Figure 11.2   PLOT n,x,y for $8 \leqslant n \leqslant 71$

We shall begin this investigation with n in the range 16–23, when we expect to see a dotted line.

Experiment 11.5

Modify the program used in the earlier experiments so that the background is black, the curve is drawn as a dotted red line and the triangles are not visible.

Clearly this requires that line 20 contains the statement

GCOL 0,128

and line 30

GCOL 0,1

We know from our earlier experiments that to draw a continuous line in the foreground colour using absolute co-ordinates we should use PLOT 5,... and since dotted lines use 16–23 instead of 0–7 we therefore require a statement of the form

PLOT 21,...

at line 50.

The triangles are to be invisible and can either be drawn in the background colour (using PLOT 3,...) or the cursor can simply move without drawing by use of PLOT 0,... In either case line 35 can be deleted if required, since it now has no effect because line 10 also sets the background colour to black (128).

Modify this program so that dotted black triangles are drawn on a yellow background with no curve being visible.

The two groups 8–15 and 24–31 are the same as 0–7 and 16–23 except that the last point in the line is omitted in certain situations. We shall discuss these situations in section 11.4.

The group from 32–63 is reserved for a future Graphics Extension ROM, and values from 96–255 are not currently used. This leaves four groups of eight, of which three are concerned with filling areas with solid blocks of colour, while the fourth is more closely related to the line drawing groups discussed above.

If n lies in the range 64–71 then a single dot is drawn at the position (x,y), using the conventions of the group 0–7. Thus

PLOT 65,x,y

will draw a dot in the current foreground colour at a point whose co-ordinates are (x,y) relative to the current position of the graphics cursor. Similarly

```
PLOT 71,x,y
```

will draw a dot in the current background colour at the point whose absolute co-ordinates are (x,y).

Experiment 11.6

Modify the program used in earlier experiments (for the last time!) so that it draws only the vertices (or corners) of the triangles. Are all three vertices drawn? If not, why not? (See Experimental Hints if you can't get all three vertices.)

11.3   FILLING IN TRIANGLES AND OTHER SHAPES

In chapter 5 we saw how PLOT 85,x,y could be used to fill triangles with colour. We can now extend this to encompass the group 80–87.

We have already discovered that the statement

```
PLOT 85,x,y
```

fills a triangle defined by the last two points visited and the point (x,y), using the current foreground colour. The same pattern as was used with lines and points leads to the conclusion that, for example, the statement

```
PLOT 83,x,y
```

will fill a triangle defined by the last two points visited and the point (x,y) relative to the current cursor position (i.e. the last point visited), using the current background colour.

A triangle is the most useful basic shape from which to build up more complex shapes, and we saw in chapter 5 how The Final Test used this technique in CASTLE to draw dragons, skeletons and spirits, and also to produce the large letters used in the opening titles produced if the game is started from CASTLE.

In the early versions of the Beeb's operating system this was the only way of filling in solid areas of colour. In late 1982 however a new version of the operating system was introduced and computers produced from early 1983 have this as standard. This later operating system includes, amongst other things, two additional groups of PLOT statements.

If you don't know, you can find out which operating system you have by typing

```
*FX 0      (zero, not letter O!)
```

The computer will then display the version of the operating system which is installed. If this is the early version then the message will be

```
OS EPROM 0.10
```

(even if it is not on EPROM but is on ROM!) and the extra PLOT statements are not available to you. If it is some other message which gives the OS version as 1.0, 1.2 or some other value greater than 0.1 then you have the later version and the extra statements are available. The remainder of this section discusses these extra PLOT statements and can be omitted, therefore, if you only have the 0.1 version of the operating system. They will not be explicitly used in any subsequent examples or experiments, although there is no reason why those who have access to them should not use them in their experiments and other programs.

(If you do only have the 0.1 operating system you can replace it with the later version which provides a lot of extra facilities that you will value later. The replacement will be carried out by your local dealer for a charge of around £10, although if your version *really* is on EPROM then the new one should be free.)

The two extra groups of PLOT statement are groups 72–79 and 88–95; *they are not described in the User Guide.*

We shall start by examining the statement

```
PLOT 77,x,y
```

which will draw in the current foreground colour using absolute co-ordinates. The way that this works is not very easy to describe and it is important that you carry out the experiments so that you are fully aware of what will happen.

PLOT 77,... operates by starting at the point (x,y) and drawing a horizontal line to both the left and right until a point is met which is not in the current background colour, or until the edge of the screen is reached.

Experiment 11.7

Type the following commands:

```
MODE 5: GCOL 0,1
MOVE 200,0: DRAW 200,500
MOVE 800,0: DRAW 800,500
```

This will draw two vertical red lines in the bottom half of the screen. Now type

```
PLOT 77,400,400
```

You will see a horizontal red line drawn between the two vertical ones. Now type

```
PLOT 77,700,300
```

and another one will be drawn, slightly lower down.

In both these cases the point specified lay between the two vertical lines and so the horizontal line is drawn both left and right until it reaches one or other vertical line.

Now type

```
PLOT 77,900,350
PLOT 77,100,250
```

The first of these commands specifies a point to the right of the rightmost vertical line and so the horizontal line extends to the edge of the plotting area. In the second case the line extends to the left edge.

In the above experiment a single line was drawn, but clearly we can fill a complete shape by use of a loop. We know that there are 1024 addressable co-ordinates in the vertical direction (0–1023) and that the resolution in all modes is 256 lines in the vertical direction. It therefore follows that a loop which steps four units in the vertical direction each pass will move one "line" each pass. The following program uses this to draw a rectangle in the centre of the screen:

```
10 MODE 5: GCOL 0,1
20 MOVE 480,300: DRAW 480,724
30 MOVE 800,300: DRAW 800,724
40 FOR I=300 TO 724 STEP 4
50    PLOT 77,500,I
60    NEXT
```

Experiment 11.8

Modify the above program so as to produce a red rectangle on a yellow background. Do this in two different ways. (See Experimental Hints if necessary.)

In the above discussion we have used PLOT 77,. . . but the other variants work in the usual way (i.e. 72–75 with relative co-ordinates, 76–79 with absolute co-ordinates, etc.). The graphic cursor will normally be left at the right-hand end of the line which has been drawn; however if you intend to use this as the starting point for a line or triangle plot you should re-position it yourself with MOVE or an appropriate PLOT statement.

We are not, of course, restricted to using vertical lines for the boundaries with this type of PLOT statement – indeed the major advantage is that it becomes very easy to fill a complicated shape with colour. For example a procedure to draw a circle centred at (x,y) with radius r could be written as follows:

```
1000 DEF PROCcircle(x,y,r)
1010 LOCAL theta
1020 MOVE x+r,y
1030 FOR theta=5 TO 360 STEP 5
1040    DRAW x+r*COS(RAD(theta)),y+r*SIN(RAD(theta))
1050    NEXT
1060 ENDPROC
```

This can be modified to produce a solid disc by adding the line

```
1055 FOR yy=y+r TO y-r STEP -4: PLOT 77,x,yy: NEXT
```

and adding yy to line 1010

Experiment 11.9

Write a procedure which will draw a circle in the foreground colour, a solid disc in the foreground colour, or a solid disc in the inverse of the colour already present, depending upon the value of one of the procedure arguments.

Test this procedure and then use it in a program to produce an abstract pattern of random discs and circles.

(See Experimental Hints if necessary, but do run the program – you can get some quite dazzling effects!)

The other special variant of the PLOT statement uses group 88–95. This is similar in concept to the previous group and operates by starting at the point (x,y) and drawing a horizontal line to the right until a point is met which is in the current background colour, or until the edge of the screen is reached.

Notice the two differences between the two groups:

(i) Group 72–79 draws to both left and right; group 88–95 only draws to the right.
(ii) Group 72–79 draws until it finds a point which is *not* the background colour; group 88–95 draws until it finds a point which *is* in the background colour.

This last group of PLOT statements is generally less useful than the 72–79 group, but is nevertheless useful when it is required to fill in an area superimposed on top of other area(s) of colour. For example the program given in experiment 11.10 first uses a PLOT 93,... statement in a nested loop to draw vertical bands of all 16 colours in mode 2, and then uses a similar process to draw a series of horizontal bands which stop when they cross their own colour.

Experiment 11.10

RUN this program and ensure that you understand how it works:

```
10 MODE 2
20 FOR I%=1 TO 15
30    GCOL 0,I%: MOVE 80*I%,0
40    FOR J%=0 TO 1020 STEP 4
50      PLOT 93,80*I%,J%
60      NEXT:
   NEXT
70 FOR I%=15 TO 1 STEP -1
80    GCOL 0,I%: GCOL 0,128+I%
```

```
 90    K%=64*(15-I%): MOVE 0,K%
100       FOR J%=K% TO K%+60 STEP 4
110       PLOT 93,0,J%
120       NEXT:
       NEXT
```

11.4 MORE ABOUT COLOURS

In chapter 5 we said that the graphical foreground and background colours were specified by means of a statement of the form

```
GCOL n,lcol
```

where n was normally zero and lcol is the logical colour to be used. We can now investigate the effect of using different values for n.

The value of n determines the colour which will be put on the screen by reference to the (logical) colour specified in the GCOL statement and the colour already on the screen. Officially n must lie in the range 0 to 4 but, as we shall see, other values can also be used to provide a range of interesting effects.

Figure 11.3 shows the action taken for n in the range 0 to 4, and it can be seen that GCOL 0,col causes the colour specified to be plotted (unless over-ridden by a PLOT statement such as PLOT 6,...) while GCOL 4,col causes the inverse of the colour already there to be be plotted. Thus

```
GCOL 4,col: PLOT 5,x,y
```

is the same as

```
GCOL 0,col: PLOT 6,x,y
```

where in both cases the value of col is irrelevant.

The other three GCOL options, however, require some understanding of logical operations.

In chapter 10 we met the logical operators AND and OR and explained their use in terms of combining the results of relational expressions. However, these operators can also be used to combine any two numbers bit by bit as we shall see in the next chapter. Essentially the three GCOL options under discussion use the AND and OR operators, together with a third EOR operator, to combine the colour specified with the colour

n	Meaning
0	plot using the colour specified
1	plot using the logical OR of the colour specified and the colour already present
2	plot using the logical AND of the colour specified and the colour already present
3	plot using the logical Exclusive–OR of the colour specified and the colour already present
4	plot using the logical inverse of the colour already present

Figure 11.3   GCOL n,lcol for $0 \leqslant n \leqslant 4$

Colour present	GCOL 1 0	1	GCOL 2 0	1	GCOL 3 0	1
0	0	1	0	0	0	1
1	1	1	0	1	1	0

Figure 11.4   GCOL effects for modes 0 and 4

Colour present	GCOL 1 0	1	2	3	GCOL 2 0	1	2	3	GCOL 3 0	1	2	3
0	0	1	2	3	0	0	0	0	0	1	2	3
1	1	1	3	3	0	1	0	1	1	0	3	2
2	2	3	2	3	0	0	2	2	2	3	0	1
3	3	3	3	3	0	1	2	3	3	2	1	0

Figure 11.5   GCOL effects for modes 1 and 5

already present in order to create a third colour which is to be plotted. Chapter 12 will explain the details of how this works – for the present we shall simply use a table to show what will happen. Figure 11.4 shows the effect of the various GCOL options in the two-colour modes (0 and 4), while figure 11.5 shows their effect in the four-colour modes (1 and 5) and figures 11.6 to 11.8 show their effect in mode 2 with 16 colours.

(If you understand binary logic then you will realise that GCOL 1 carries out a *bitwise OR* of the two colours, GCOL 2 carries out a *bitwise AND* and GCOL 3 carries out a *bitwise Exclusive OR*. If this is gobbledegook to you then just use the tables!)

Colour present	0	1	2	3	4	5	6	GCOL 1 7	8	9	10	11	12	13	14	15
0	0	1	2	3	4	5	6	7	8	9	10	11	12	13	14	15
1	1	1	3	3	5	5	7	7	9	9	11	11	13	13	15	15
2	2	3	2	3	6	7	6	7	10	11	10	11	14	15	14	15
3	3	3	3	3	7	7	7	7	11	11	11	11	15	15	15	15
4	4	5	6	7	4	5	6	7	12	13	14	15	12	13	14	15
5	5	5	7	7	5	5	7	7	13	13	15	15	13	13	15	15
6	6	7	6	7	6	7	6	7	14	15	14	15	14	15	14	15
7	7	7	7	7	7	7	7	7	15	15	15	15	15	15	15	15
8	8	9	10	11	12	13	14	15	8	9	10	11	12	13	14	15
9	9	9	11	11	13	13	15	15	9	9	11	11	13	13	15	15
10	10	11	10	11	14	15	14	15	10	11	10	11	14	15	14	15
11	11	11	11	11	15	15	15	15	11	11	11	11	15	15	15	15
12	12	13	14	15	12	13	14	15	12	13	14	15	12	13	14	15
13	13	13	15	15	13	13	15	15	13	13	15	15	13	13	15	15
14	14	15	14	15	14	15	14	15	14	15	14	15	14	15	14	15
15	15	15	15	15	15	15	15	15	15	15	15	15	15	15	15	15

Figure 11.6   GCOL 1, effects for mode 2

Colour present	GGCOL 2															
	0	1	2	3	4	5	6	7	8	9	10	11	12	13	14	15
0	0	0	0	0	0	0	0	0	0	0	0	0	0	0	0	0
1	0	1	0	1	0	1	0	1	0	1	0	1	0	1	0	1
2	0	0	2	2	0	0	2	2	0	0	2	2	0	0	2	2
3	0	1	2	3	0	1	2	3	0	1	2	3	0	1	2	3
4	0	0	0	0	4	4	4	4	0	0	0	0	4	4	4	4
5	0	1	0	1	4	5	4	5	0	1	0	1	4	5	4	5
6	0	0	2	2	4	4	6	6	0	0	2	2	4	4	6	6
7	0	1	2	3	4	5	6	7	0	1	2	3	4	5	6	7
8	0	0	0	0	0	0	0	0	8	8	8	8	8	8	8	8
9	0	1	0	1	0	1	0	1	8	9	8	9	8	9	8	9
10	0	0	2	2	0	0	2	2	8	8	10	10	8	8	10	10
11	0	1	2	3	0	1	2	3	8	9	10	11	8	9	10	11
12	0	0	0	0	4	4	4	4	8	8	8	8	12	12	12	12
13	0	1	0	1	4	5	4	5	8	9	8	9	12	13	12	13
14	0	0	2	2	4	4	6	6	8	8	10	10	12	12	14	14
15	0	1	2	3	4	5	6	7	8	9	10	11	12	13	14	15

Figure 11.7   GCOL 2, effects for mode 2

Colour present	GCOL 3															
	0	1	2	3	4	5	6	7	8	9	10	11	12	13	14	15
0	0	1	2	3	4	5	6	7	8	9	10	11	12	13	14	15
1	1	0	3	2	5	4	7	6	9	8	11	10	13	12	15	14
2	2	3	0	1	6	7	4	5	10	11	8	9	14	15	12	13
3	3	2	1	0	7	6	5	4	11	10	9	8	15	14	13	12
4	4	5	6	7	0	1	2	3	12	13	14	15	8	9	10	11
5	5	4	7	6	1	0	3	2	13	12	15	14	9	8	11	10
6	6	7	4	5	2	3	0	1	14	15	12	13	10	11	8	9
7	7	6	5	4	3	2	1	0	15	14	13	12	11	10	9	8
8	8	9	10	11	12	13	14	15	0	1	2	3	4	5	6	7
9	9	8	11	10	13	12	15	14	1	0	3	2	5	4	7	6
10	10	11	8	9	14	15	12	13	2	3	0	1	6	7	4	5
11	11	10	9	8	15	14	13	12	3	2	1	0	7	6	5	4
12	12	13	14	15	8	9	10	11	4	5	6	7	0	1	2	3
13	13	12	15	14	9	8	11	10	5	4	7	6	1	0	3	2
14	14	15	12	13	10	11	8	9	6	7	4	5	2	3	0	1
15	15	14	13	12	11	10	9	8	7	6	5	4	3	2	1	0

Figure 11.8   GCOL 3, effects for mode 2

Experiment 11.11

Type in the following program and then RUN it:

```
10 MODE 2
20 MOVE 79,0: MOVE 79,1023
30 FOR I=1 TO 15
40 GCOL 0,I
50 PLOT 81,80,-1023: PLOT 81,0,1023
60 NEXT
```

This will produce a set of vertical bands in all 16 colours. Now type

```
GCOL 1,129: CLG
```

Do you understand what has happened? Refer to figure 11.6 if you don't.
   Now try

```
GCOL 2,134: CLG
```

Refer to figure 11.7 if you don't understand.
   Next type

```
GCOL 3,131: CLG
```

This is more interesting as you will see if you now type

```
CLG
```

and then again

```
CLG
```

Repeat this experiment with different variations of background colours – remember that
the background colour is specified as 128 plus the logical colour required.

When using GCOL 3,col as the means of defining the foreground colour, we can run into
difficulties when plotting a line. This is because, normally, *all* points on a line are drawn,
i.e. the statements

```
MOVE 100,400: DRAW 400,400
```

will draw a line which starts at the pixel containing the point (100,400) and finishes at the
pixel containing the point (400,400). If we now type

```
DRAW 400,600
```

then the new line will start at the pixel containing the point (400,400) and finish at the pixel
containing the point (400,600). The pixel containing the point (400,400) has therefore been
coloured *twice*.
   Normally this doesn't matter but, as we have just seen, when using GCOL 3,col this will
lead to that pixel reverting to its original colour – probably that of the background – which
is *not* what is required.
   The two groups of PLOT statements mentioned earlier (8–15 and 24–31) are provided
to deal with this problem and are the same as groups 0–7 and 16–23 except that the *last*
point in each line is not plotted, thus avoiding the double plotting of the end pixel.
   In experiment 11.11 you will have noticed that the CLG command caused the new
colours to be used everywhere including those areas which contain text. This can be used

148

to great effect in your programs, especially if the relationship of logical to actual colours is redefined. We shall investigate this further in the next chapter.

Experiment 11.12

Modify the program used in the last experiment so that after it has drawn the vertical bars it starts a new loop which draws horizontal bars using

```
GCOL n,I
```

where n is input from the keyboard.

This program can then be used to show the effect of plotting any colour on any other colour using different GCOL modes. Run it first with n in the range 0 to 4 and make sure that it works correctly. (See Experimental Hints if you have trouble.)

Finally try other, larger, values of n. The effects produced seem to vary depending upon which version of the operating system you have. You will find that only numbers in the range 0–255 need be tried and the results for values above 4 are difficult to predict. However you may well find some colour schemes that would be useful in particular situations – especially the pastel shades and/or striped patterns!

Experiment 11.13

In experiment 6.5 (chapter 6) we presented a short program to produce an almost hypnotic pattern of changing "boxes". Modify that program so that the way in which the foregound colour is plotted (see line 180) can be any of the five possibilities discussed in this section. Your modification should be such that pressing 0, 1, 2, 3 or 4 at any time during the running of the program will cause subsequent boxes to use that mode of colour drawing (i.e. GCOL 0, ..., GCOL 1, ..., etc.). Also arrange for pressing Q at any time to "quit" and end the program.

(Hint: Use INKEY to input the key value.)

11.5 THE VDU STATEMENT

The VDU statement is the key to most of the clever and/or sophisticated graphics and other effects that you can produce on the screen of your Beeb. It takes the form

```
VDU n1, n2,...
```

and essentially sends a string of characters to the special "chip" inside the Beeb (known as the VIA or Versatile Interface Adapter) which controls the screen. In fact

```
VDU n
```

is identical to

```
PRINT CHR$(n);
```

but is rather more concise, and

```
VDU a,b,c,
```

is the same as

```
PRINT CHR$(a);CHR$(b);CHR$(c);
```

In some situations, notably when producing mode 7 graphics (see chapter 13), it is convenient to use a VDU statement instead of a PRINT statement. Normally, however, a VDU statement is only used with values in the range 0–31, which correspond to control codes on the keyboard. Some of these special codes are followed by additional numbers to provide further information.

The *User Guide* gives a description of all of these special codes, but we shall consider some of them in more detail here.

VDU 12	is the same as CLS
VDU 16	is the same as CLG
VDU 14	is the same as CTRL+N i.e. turn on page mode
VDU 15	is the same as CTRL+O i.e. turn off page mode
VDU 17,c	is the same as COLOUR c
VDU 18,n,c	is the same as GCOL n,c
VDU 22,m	is the same as MODE m
VDU 25,n,x;y;	is the same as PLOT n,x,y

In this last case note the semi-colons after the values for x and y. This is necessary in several VDU commands because the numbers may be greater than 255. Normally each number in a VDU statement is sent to the VIA as a single byte, which must therefore lie in the range 0–255. If the number is followed by a semi-colon however it is sent as two bytes – first the low order byte and then the high order one. Thus

```
VDU 25,5,256;525;
```

is actually sent as though it had been written

```
VDU 25,5,0,1,13,2
```

where "0,1" means 0+256*1 and "13,2" means 13+256*2.

Obviously it is normally more convenient and readable to use PLOT, GCOL, CLG etc. than the corresponding VDU codes, but there are sometimes situations when it is useful to use the VDU codes as part of a larger string of such codes.

Some other useful VDU codes are

VDU 31,x,y	which is equivalent to PRINT TAB(x,y);
VDU 8	which moves the text cursor one space back
VDU 9	which moves it one space forward
VDU 10	which moves it down one line
VDU 11	which moves it up one line
VDU 13	which moves it to the start of the current line, and
VDU 30	which moves it to the top left-hand corner.

150

Thus

VDU 30

and

VDU 31,0,0

are exactly the same.

We have already met several of the other VDU statements but for completeness we shall repeat them here:

VDU 19,lcol,acol,0,0,0 ⎱	⎰ is used to redefine logical colour lcol
VDU 19,lcol,acol;0; ⎰	⎱ to represent the actual colour acol
VDU 20	restores the normal colour assignments for this mode
VDU 24,leftX;bottomY;rightX;topY;	defines a graphics window
VDU 28,leftX,bottomY,rightX,topY	defines a text window
VDU 26	restores the text and graphics windows to their default sizes – in which they occupy the whole screen
VDU 29,x;y;	sets the point (x,y) as the origin for future graphics operations. The values of x and y are always relative to the original (default) origin and not to any redefined origin.

Most of the remaining VDU statements are of little interest at this stage but will be listed for reference:

VDU 2	is used to cause output to be sent to the printer
VDU 3	is used to stop output being sent to the printer
VDU 1,x	causes the ASCII character x to be sent to the printer but not to the screen
VDU 21	stops all subsequent output to the screen
VDU 6	cancels the effect of VDU 21 and allows output to the screen to be displayed again
VDU 7	makes a short "beep"; the same effect can be obtained by pressing CTRL+G.
VDU 0 ⎱ VDU 27 ⎰	these do nothing
VDU 23	will be discussed in the next chapter

which leaves only VDU 4 and VDU 5:

VDU 4	causes text to be output at the text cursor position
VDU 5	causes text to be output at the graphics cursor position

There is, however, a lot more to these last two statements than is apparent from the above description of their effect, and the next part of this chapter will examine their use in more detail.

11.6 COMBINING GRAPHICS AND TEXT

The statement

VDU 5

causes the text cursor to disappear from the screen and any subsequent text to be printed at the graphics cursor position instead of at the text cursor position. However, because the text is now being printed as though it were a graphical drawing it uses the colours specified by GCOL instead of those specified by COLOUR.

Even more important is the way in which it is printed. As we have seen, when a PRINT statement is obeyed (in the normal way) the characters to be printed and their background are both placed on the screen at the specified position, thus totally obliterating whatever was there before (text or graphics). When a PRINT statement is obeyed after a VDU 5 statement has been obeyed, however, the characters to be printed are placed on the screen using the appropriate GCOL rule and the background is left as it was, thus permitting superimposed text, as can be seen in experiment 11.14.

Experiment 11.14

Type in the following program and RUN it:

```
10 MODE 1
20 GCOL 0,129: GCOL 4,2
30 CLG
40 MOVE 320,256: PLOT 0,640,0
50 PLOT 81,-640,512: PLOT 81,640,0
60 PRINT TAB(0,10) "This line is printed at the text cursor"
70 VDU 5
80 MOVE 0,320: PRINT "This line is at the graphics cursor"
90 VDU 4
```

You will see that lines 20–50 cause the screen to be cleared to the graphics background colour (red) and a solid rectangle to be drawn in the graphics foreground colour – which was defined (by GCOL 4,. . .) to be the inverse of whatever is there, i.e. yellow (colour 2) in this case.

Line 60 then prints a line of text across the screen in the normal text mode. The text is therefore white with a black background.

Line 70 causes text to be drawn at the graphics cursor. We must now MOVE and not TAB to the required position, and line 80 therefore prints a further line of text below the first one. However this is drawn in the graphics foreground colour, i.e. the inverse of what is there already, and so is yellow over the red background and red over the yellow rectangle. Because the text is being "printed" in graphics mode the letters appear over the existing drawing without any unpleasant extra background.

Experiment 11.15

Add the following extra lines to the program written in the last experiment:

```
65 PRINT TAB(0,10)SPC(5);"This"
85 MOVE 0,320: PRINT SPC(5);"This"
```

RUN this amended program. What do you observe? Do you understand why the two printed lines have been treated differently?

In the last two experiments we have seen how the use of VDU 5 can give us much greater flexibility with the positioning of text relative to graphics, but we have seen too that it can also cause problems. Because the previous character is not "blanked out" by a new one in the same place, any over-printing should be avoided in this mode. Where it is necessary to print in the same place it is necessary to return to text mode to ensure that the previous characters are deleted. For example in Castle the player's current score is printed at the end of every pass through the main loop.

The score is printed at the bottom of the screen and if it were printed in graphics mode (with VDU 5 in effect) the constantly changing score would quickly become unreadable. The relevant statement therefore reverts to text mode to print the score, and then returns to graphic mode ready for the next pass through the main loop:

```
170 H%=(C+S)*(M+W+M%): VDU 4:
    PRINT TAB(4,31) "Score: ";H%;" ";: VDU 5
```

Note that H% (the current score) is followed by a space. This is to deal with the situation in which the player's score is falling and is reduced from 3 digits to 2 (or from 4 to 3, or 2 to 1). If an extra space were not printed then the previous digit would be left on the screen.

Experiment 11.16

In chapter 5 we referred to the use of triangle filling in the drawing of the main title by CASTLE. At that stage we ignored the way in which the background (and foreground) colours are changed. Examine the relevant part of PROCtitle (lines 750–910) and make sure that you understand exactly how it works; you will need to make a small chart showing the logical colour at various points on the screen at each stage. Ignore lines 570–710 which define a special half-width character string and line 890 which prints it; these will be explained in the next chapter.

Once you are confident that you understand the effects of the various AND, OR, EOR and VDU statements, alter this procedure so that, instead of mainly altering the background while leaving the colour of the title unchanged, the foreground (title) colour is repeatedly altered in the early part of the sequence. If you created your own title in experiment 5.8 then use it in this experiment.

11.7 INVISIBLE PLOTTING AND SPECIAL EFFECTS

In experiment 7.10 (chapter 7) we wrote a program that used the VDU 19 statement to set logical colours 1–7 to 0 (black) before plotting a set of "coloured" bars, and then used

VDU 20 to suddenly make them all appear. This technique is a very useful one when you do not wish to see a picture being slowly built up, or merely wish to provide a dramatic effect.

For example in CASTLE the main title is initially plotted (quite slowly) in colour 15 which is assigned the actual colour 7 (see lines 760 and 770). If it were assigned actual colour 5 (which is the background colour – see line 750) then it would appear to be invisible and an extra VDU statement when it was fully drawn would reveal the whole title instantaneously.

Experiment 11.17

Carry out a similar modification to that discussed above on the title sequence you produced in the last experiment.

Experiment 11.18

At the end of CASTLE there is a "blinding flash" caused (as was mentioned in chapter 5) by a rapidly alternating sequence of VDU 19 commands which alternately set the background (colour 0) to red and white (see line 180). It would be possible to produce a quite different effect by having the background composed of bands of different colours, all of which were normally set to black. The "flashing" could then have a ripple effect as successive bands changed colour.

Modify the program to use at least four different logical colours for the background and to produce a more interesting effect for the flashing. *Note* that the dragons and spirits are drawn using GCOL 1,col (see lines 1030 and 1110) and so you will have to take this into account when choosing your colours.

The same techniques can, of course, be used to provide a form of animation in which successive copies of a shape are made visible as the object moves around the screen. In most cases, however, more subtle techniques than this are required for animation, and some of these are described in the next chapter.

Experimental Hints

11.4   PLOT 5,. . . draws the curve in the current foreground colour, which is white, while the triangles are drawn in the current background colour (i.e. black) as a result of the PLOT 3,. . . statement set up in experiment 11.3. Changing line 50 to use PLOT 6,. . . causes the curve to be drawn in the logical inverse of the colour already there. Since the colour there is colour 1 (red) the curve is drawn in colour 2, i.e. yellow. Changing line 100 to use PLOT 0,. . . means that only a move is made, and so no triangles are drawn.

11.6   If only two vertices are drawn it is probably because line 50 is drawing the curve in the background colour, thus making it invisible but also *overwriting one of the vertices*. If PLOT 4,. . . is used in line 50 to merely move along the curve then all three vertices should appear.

11.8   Mode 5 has four colours of which, by default, colour 1 is red and colour 2 is yellow. If a new line 15 is added to the program:

```
15 GCOL 0,130: CLG
```

then the screen will be cleared to yellow and the subsequent plotting will give a red rectangle.

If the DRAW statements in lines 20 and 30 are now changed to PLOT 6,... and the PLOT 77,... statement in line 50 is changed to PLOT 79,... then all plotting will be carried out in the logical inverse of the background colour – which is red in this case.

11.9   If you tried to use a variant of the procedure given you will have found that it didn't work properly for the discs! This is because PLOT 77,... or PLOT 79,... only fill a line until they reach a colour which is not the background colour. Once the screen has other circles or discs on it, therefore, there is a high probability that one of these will be met before the rim of the defining circle. The result may still look good, but it isn't what was wanted!

In this situation the discs should therefore be drawn by "triangle filling", and line 1040 in the procedure given should be replaced by

```
1040 PLOT mode, ....
```

where mode is 5 for a circle
                    85 for a disc in the foreground colour
                    87 for a disc in the logical inverse colour

11.12   Add the following lines to the program used in experiment 11.11:

```
  1 REPEAT
  5   INPUT "What mode for GCOL",mode
 70   MOVE 0,1023: MOVE 1279,1023
 80   FOR I=0 TO 15
 90     GCOL mode,I
100     PLOT 81,-1279,-64: PLOT 81,1279,0
110   NEXT
120   INPUT "Do you want to try another mode",A$
130   UNTIL LEFT$(A$,1)<>"Y"
```

12

Get animated

12.1 USER-DEFINED CHARACTERS

In the last chapter we discussed all the variants of the VDU statement except VDU 23. This is an extremely powerful statement which enables you to create your own characters which can then be printed in the usual way in either text or graphics mode. The Castle program uses this feature extensively to draw the player, the dragons, skeletons and spirits, the various objects found in the castle, and Morgan le Fey herself, and we shall refer to these to demonstrate how to use this special feature of your Beeb.

In operating system 0.10 only the 32 characters with ASCII values 224–255 may be redefined, but in later versions of the operating system all non-control characters may be redefined, i.e. any character whose ASCII value is in the range 32–255 may be redefined with Series 1 operating systems and beyond. We shall concentrate on the simple case, but will briefly mention how to redefine other characters in section 12.5

A character is given a user-defined form by the statement

```
VDU 23,char,b1,b2,b3,b4,b5,b6,b7,b8
```

where char is the number of the character to be defined and must normally lie in the range 224–255. The following eight numbers (b1 to b8) define the form that the character is to take, row by row. To understand how these eight numbers are created we must first examine how *any* character (in modes 0–6) is defined and drawn on the screen.

Figure 12.1 shows a greatly magnified drawing of the letter y in both its capital and

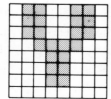

Figure 12.1   The characters Y and y (modes 0–6)

lower case forms. It will be seen that the letters are formed from small squares in an 8×8 grid and that, in this case, the extreme left and right columns are left blank to provide the spacing between letters. If we consider each row as a *binary number* we can uniquely identify each row by a single number in the range 0–255. If you don't understand binary numbers then we can allocate the value 128 to the first column, 64 to the second column, and so on, with the last column having the value 1. We can then add up the numbers in the appropriate columns.

Figure 12.2 shows how this works for a capital Y, and we see that the top three rows are represented by 102, the fourth row by 60, the next three rows by 24 and the bottom row (which is not used) by 0. The capital Y is thus defined by the eight numbers

102, 102, 102, 60, 24, 24, 24, 0

In a similar way the lower case y could be represented by the numbers

0, 0, 102, 102, 102, 62, 6, 60

Exactly the same technique is used with the VDU 23 statement, and, for example, the statement

VDU 23,229,56,124,84,108,124,68,56,56

is used in CASTLE2 to define character 229 as a skull (see figure 12.3).

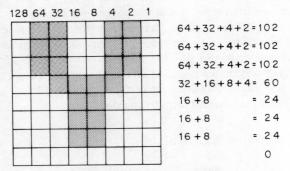

Figure 12.2   The character Y

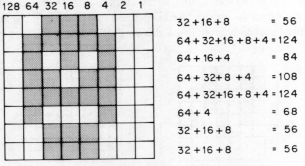

Figure 12.3   The skull in the Castle (character 229)

Experiment 12.1

In CASTLE2 lines 70–200 set up characters to represent the various items that can be found in the castle. These are as follows:

224   Axe
225   Ruby, Emerald, Diamond
226   Belt
227   Sword
228   Cross
229   Skull
230   Hat
231   Salt
232   Necklace
233   Shield
234   Lamp
235   Spear
236   Feathers
237   Ring

Design your own shapes to represent some or all of these items and produce a modified version of CASTLE2 containing them. RUN the game (from CASTLE) to check that they work properly.

12.2   AN EASY WAY OF DEFINING YOUR OWN CHARACTERS

Working out by hand how a character should be defined and hence what values to give in the VDU 23 statement is a time-consuming and error-prone activity. It is also difficult to accurately anticipate how a character will actually look on the screen, especially as its appearance in modes 1 and 4 will be quite different from modes 2 and 5. Appendix C contains four useful utility programs, of which the fourth is a program which helps you to create your own shapes in either mode 1 or mode 2 (or both) with great ease. The program works by drawing a large 8×8 grid and then using the cursor control keys to move the cursor around this grid. Any element may be filled in by pressing "X" or cleared by pressing the space bar. At the same time as this over-size character is being drawn a small (single character size) character is also drawn so that you can see what it looks like in the size that will be used when the character is printed.

When the program is run you are first asked whether you wish characters 224–255 to be initially blank, to be pre-set (with a set of characters described below), or whether you wish to load a set of definitions from tape (having saved them on a previous use of the program). You are then asked whether you wish to use mode 1 or 2.

The program then draws the large grid mentioned above and also prints all 32 characters from 224–255. You may then use the cursor control keys to move the cursor to the character you wish to define (or re-define) and press RETURN.

The character will then be copied into the large grid and also copied in its normal size. You can now use the cursor keys together with "X" and "space" as described above to create or modify your character. At any point you may also press "S" to save that definition or "Q" to quit. In the first case the character will be copied back to the table showing all user-defined characters; in the latter case it will not.

You then have the option of defining another character, of changing modes, or of leaving the program. In the latter case you may either list the VDU 23 statements which define the 32 user-defined characters, or you may save them on tape in a form suitable for inclusion in a program. If you choose to save the definitions on tape they will be saved as lines 32735 to 32766 and can be added to another program by use of *EXEC (see below).

The program itself uses a number of quite advanced techniques and actually alters itself every time you create a new character. *This is not a technique to be recommended* in general, and certainly not until you are experienced in both Basic programming and the use of the operating system. The program does, however, also use several useful facilities which are perfectly safe for you to use.

The first of these is the function POINT(x,y) which returns the logical colour of the screen at the point specified. This is used in PROCcursor (see figure 12.4) to control the colour in which the + is drawn in the large grid to represent a cursor.

If a cursor is to be drawn (IF on...) then the statement GCOL 0,1 is obeyed and the cross is plotted in colour 1. However, if the cursor is to be blanked out (prior to moving to an adjacent square) then the statement

```
GCOL 0,POINT(U%,V%)
```

is obeyed. This causes the cross to be plotted in the colour of the screen at the point (U%,V%), which is in the corner of the "current" square. Thus the cross will be plotted in the same colour as the square (either yellow if filled, or black if empty) and so will be blanked out.

The second useful technique is based on having two logical colours assigned the same actual colour. At the start of the program, just before the grid is drawn, the following colour assignments are made (see figure 12.5)

Logical colour 1 is actual colour 6 (cyan)
Logical colour 2 is actual colour 3 (yellow)
Logical colour 3 is actual colour 3 (yellow)

The grid is then drawn in colour 1 (cyan). When a square of the grid is to be filled, it is filled in such a way as to include the boundaries of the square using GCOL 1,2. This produces a logical OR of colour 2 with the colour already there. If that colour was 0 (black) or 2 (yellow) then the colour placed on the screen will be 2 (yellow); if it was 1 (cyan) then the colour used will be 3, which is also yellow. Thus the boundaries will disappear, giving a better look to the character.

```
1340 DEF PROCcursor(on)
1350 IF on THEN
        GCOL 0,1
     ELSE
        GCOL 0,POINT(U%,V%)
1360 IF M%=1 THEN
        MOVE U%+24,V%-24
     ELSE
        MOVE U%+8,V%-4
1370 PRINT "+": MOVE U%,V%
1380 ENDPROC
```

Figure 12.4   PROCcursor from SHAPES (lines 1340–1380)

700 VDU 19,1,6;0;19,3,3;0;23;8202;0;0;0;
.
.
.
850 VDU 19,1,6;0;19,2,3;0;23;8202;0;0;0;
.
.
.

Figure 12.5   Colour assignments in lines 700 and 850 of SHAPES

If the square is subsequently to be cleared then it is filled using GCOL 0,1 which produces a logical AND of colour 1 with the colour already there. Any areas containing colour 2 or 0 will therefore be filled with colour 0 (black) while any areas containing colour 3 will be filled with colour 1 (cyan), thus redrawing the cyan boundaries. Figure 12.6 illustrates these changes in tabular form.

The final point worth mentioning, although digressing slightly from the subject of this chapter, is the use of the cursor control keys. Normally these are only used in conjunction with the COPY key to edit a program. However the special instruction

*FX 4,1

instructs the operating system to allow these keys to be used as ordinary keys (with ASCII codes 136–139). They can then be read using GET or INKEY to allow the program to take appropriate action.

In the program, they operate differently at different stages. During the selection of a character, pressing one of the cursor control keys causes the cursor to move up, down, left or right to the next user-defined character. It is not possible to move to any other position.

During character definition however the (different) cursor is moved from the centre of one over-sized square to the centre of an adjacent one. Once again, it is not possible to move outside the grid.

The same technique is used in Castle to move the player around each floor of the castle. In that case moving into a wall or a closed door causes an error message to be produced, while walking through an open door leads to a fight with its guardian and/or travel along a passage to another floor.

The similar operating system instruction

*FX 4,0

restores these four keys to their normal mode of operation (see line 90 of SHAPES).

Initial logical colour	Logical colour after	
	GCOL 1,2	GCOL 2,1
0 black	2 yellow	0 black
1 cyan	3 yellow	1 cyan
2 yellow	2 yellow	0 black
3 yellow	3 yellow	1 cyan

Figure 12.6   Effect of GCOL 1,2 and 2,1 on colours 0–3 in SHAPES

Experiment 12.2

The four utility programs in Appendix C are available on a cassette if you don't wish to type them yourself. If you do not have the cassette and have not yet typed *and saved* the SHAPES program (C.4) then do so now.

Use the SHAPES program to experiment with creating various different shapes. *Note* in particular how the appearance of a character can change quite dramatically when you change from mode 1 to mode 2, or vice versa.

Experiment 12.3

Use the SHAPES program to create new (or at least different) representations of the various objects in the castle (as in experiment 12.1) and also the spirits, skeletons, dragons and Morgan le Fey. All of these should be defined in mode 2 and you should note that the spirits, etc. all occupy *two* characters, as specified below:

238 Spirit (top half)
239 Spirit (bottom half)
240 Morgan le Fey (top)
241 Morgan le Fey (bottom)
242 Skeleton (top)
243 Skeleton (bottom)
244 Left-facing dragon (left)
245 Left-facing dragon (right)
246 Right-facing dragon (left)
247 Right-facing dragon (right)

When you have created satisfactory shapes you should use the option in SHAPES to save these on tape.

Now load CASTLE2.

Next position the tape with the definitions in the correct place and then type

```
*EXEC "CharDefs"
```

The new definitions for characters 224–255 will now be added to CASTLE2 as lines 32735–32766; since these lines do not exist in CASTLE2 nothing is deleted. Now use the editing keys to renumber lines 32735–32758 as lines 70–300. This will cause your shape definitions to replace the original ones for characters 224–247; note that characters 248–255 should not be altered at this stage.

Finally delete lines 32735–32766

Before doing anything else save this program.

You can now run The Final Test and you should find that your own objects, spirits etc. have replaced those originally provided with the game.

Experiment 12.4

When SHAPES is run using initial option (c) – pre-set user-defined characters – the 26 characters 224–249 contain both upper- and lower-case alphabets only 4 units wide (instead of 8), 250–254 contains the digits 0–9 and 255 contains both full stop and comma. When displayed in mode 2 these give the same size characters as are found in modes 1, 4, 6 and 7. The copyright notice displayed in CASTLE by PROCtitle is produced by creating a sequence of characters based on the SHAPES pre-set ones (see lines 570–720) and then printing them in a short loop using a VDU statement (see line 890).

Write a program which enables you to use these characters to print simple messages in modes 2 or 5 with 40 characters to a line. (See Experimental Hints if you have difficulty with this.)

12.3 ANIMATION

We now have all the necessary skills and techniques to carry out animation on the screen. To understand how to do this we shall define a character in mode 1 which is not unlike the mode 2 spirits used in the Castle (see figure 12.7).

We can define this ghost character as follows:

```
VDU 23,224,0,60,90,126,66,126,90,0
```

and print it by typing either

```
PRINT CHR$224;
```

or

```
VDU 224
```

We could then move this character by overtyping with a space before typing it again in the next character position.

Experiment 12.5

Type in the following program:

```
10 MODE 1: COLOUR 2
20 VDU 23,224,0,60,90,126,66,126,90,0
30 *FX4,1
40 VDU 31,20,15,224,8
```

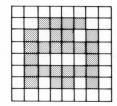

Figure 12.7   A ghost character

```
 50 REPEAT
 60    D=INKEY(0)
 70    IF D=136 THEN
          VDU 32,8,8,224,8: GOTO 110
 80    IF D=137 THEN
          VDU 32,224,8: GOTO 110
 90    IF D=138
          THEN VDU 32,8,10,224,8: GOTO 110
100    IF D=139
          THEN VDU 32,8,11,224,8
110    UNTIL D=81
120 *FX4,0
```

This program will first print the ghost in the centre of the screen and then use the four cursor keys to move it around. Pressing Q will end the program.

The program uses VDU statements to carry out all the printing and leaves the cursor at the current position (VDU 8 backspaces one character) so that the next movement can print a space (VDU 32) before moving the cursor to the next position of the ghost.

RUN this program, and remember that if you hold down a key it will automatically repeat several times a second.

Were you happy with this program and with the way in which the ghost moved?

(Keep this program – we shall use it again several times.)

There are two major problems with the program in experiment 12.5. The first is that the cursor remains, which detracts from the overall effect, and the second is that the movement is very jerky. We can switch the cursor off by the statement

VDU 23;8202;0;0;0;

(which actually defines a cursor of zero-size!) but switching it back on again is more difficult, although a MODE statement will cause it to return. If you have a Series 1 operating system then the cursor can be switched off by the statement

VDU 23,1,0;0;0;0;

and then switched back on again with

VDU 23,1,1;0;0;0;

However, this is not the real problem. The real problem is the jerky movement caused by the large steps (one full character) and the need to blank out the previous version before printing the new one.

An obvious improvement is to use graphic mode instead of character mode.

Experiment 12.6

Modify the program used in the last experiment by typing the following:

```
10 MODE 1: GCOL 0,2
40 VDU 5,25,4,600;500;224
70    IF D=136 THEN
          VDU 32,25,0,-36,0,224:GOTO 110
80    IF D=137 THEN
          VDU 32,25,0,-28,0,224:GOTO 110
90    IF D=138 THEN
          VDU 32,25,0,-32,-4,224:GOTO 110
100   IF D=139 THEN
          VDU 32,25,0,-32,4,224
130 VDU 4
```

In this case the text and graphics cursors are "joined" by the VDU 5 statement in line 40 and all subsequent cursor movement must be specified in graphics co-ordinates and carried out by PLOT, etc. VDU 25 is the equivalent of PLOT and VDU 25,4,. . . is therefore a move to an absolute position, while VDU 25,0,. . . is a move to a relative position.

The program thus moves around much as before except that each step is only 4 units (left, right, up or down) instead of 32 units (=1 character in mode 1). Are you happy with this program? If you are then RUN it.

Does the result surprise you? Can you see how to improve it?

The program written for the last experiment demonstrates once again the difference between the way in which characters are placed on the screen in graphic and text modes – and in particular the difference in the way that the background is handled. In text mode, printing a space blanks out any character already there with the background colour; in graphic mode, it leaves it exactly as it was – with disastrous consequences in this case. A solution is provided by the Exclusive OR or GCOL 3,col.

We saw in chapter 11, and especially in experiment 11.11, that GCOL 3,col had one very interesting property – namely that repeated plotting of the same (Exclusive OR) colour causes the display to alternate between two colours. We can explain this by examining in detail how it works.

Each colour from 0–15 can be expressed as a four-digit *binary number*, thus

0	= 0000	(0*8 + 0*4 + 0*2 + 0*1)
1	= 0001	(0*8 + 0*4 + 0*2 + 1*1)
2	= 0010	(0*8 + 0*4 + 1*2 + 0*1)
5	= 0101	(0*8 + 1*4 + 0*2 + 1*1)
7	= 0111	(0*8 + 1*4 + 1*2 + 1*1)
8	= 1000	(1*8 + 0*4 + 0*2 + 0*1)
13	= 1101	(1*8 + 1*4 + 0*2 + 1*1)

etc.

When an *Exclusive OR* is performed between two such numbers a third number is created which has a 1 where the original two numbers were different and a zero where they were the same. Thus

7 EOR 4

can be written as

```
      0111
EOR   0100
      0011
```

and this has the result 0011 (or 3). Notice, however, what happens if we repeat the operation:

3 EOR 4

leading to

```
      0011
EOR   0100
      0111
```

which is 7 once again. A few moments thought will show that this must always be the case and that

(a EOR b) EOR b = a

Notice, incidentally, that our other three GCOL options are also evaluated in a similar way. In the case of GCOL 1,. . . a logical OR is performed between the two numbers and the result has a 1 in every place in which *either* of the original numbers had a 1, thus

9 OR 5

can be written

```
     1001
OR   0101
     1101
```

and thus has the result 1101 (or 13). GCOL 2,. . . on the other hand uses a logical AND and sets a 1 in the result only if *both* the original numbers had a one there, thus

9 AND 5

can be written as

```
      1001
AND   0101
      0001
```

and thus has the result 1. Finally GCOL 4,... inverts the colour; which is the same as applying the logical NOT operator and changing all zeros to ones and vice-versa. Thus

NOT 9

can be written

NOT   1001
      ‾‾‾‾
      0110
      ‾‾‾‾

and has the value 6.

However it is GCOL 3,... (or EOR) which is of interest to us here, since we can clearly use it to create and then remove a character by suitable choice of colours.

Experiment 12.7

Alter the program used in experiment 12.6 so that the colour is specified by

GCOL 3,2

and the four VDU statements in lines 70–100 start

VDU 224,...

instead of

VDU 32,...

thus printing the ghost on top of itself. RUN this program.
    Now add an extra line to the program:

35 GCOL 0,131: VDU. 24,700;400;900;600;16,26

which will draw a white square to the right of the initial position of the ghost. (Do you understand how it does this? If not, see Experimental Hints.)
    RUN the program again. Does the result surprise you?
    Alter the program so that the ghost does not change colour as it passes in front of the "wall".
    When you have done that, alter the program so that the ghost appears to go behind the wall (i.e. it becomes invisible).
    See Experimental Hints if you have difficulty with these problems.

In Castle the spirits are moved about in exactly this manner, except that they are two characters high (using characters 238 and 239). The procedure PROCspirit plots a spirit at a defined place in the appropriate colour, while the procedure PROCmovespirit first plots it in its current position (to cause it to vanish) and then in its new position (see line 730).
    This method of animation produces reasonably smooth movement, and is good enough

for many purposes – especially when (as in Castle) it is flashing anyway. A still smoother method can be used in some circumstances, and this is described briefly in the next section. Before we look at that, however, there is one further aspect to consider.

Moving a shape such as a ghost (or a ball or an aeroplane) in the way described above is perfectly satisfactory, but it is not suitable for a man (or other animal) as can be readily seen by replacing line 20 of the program used in the last experiment by

```
VDU 23,224,28,28,8,124,28,28,22,50
```

which represents (rather crudely) a human figure.

RUN this modified program and you will see at once that it looks most unnatural because the legs (and arms) do not move. For this type of animation you should ideally use three different versions of the man in different positions (and another three facing in the opposite direction) and draw each one in turn. In practice you can often get away with two positions and the man walking around the Castle exists in four different forms – two facing right (248,249 and 254,255) and their mirror images facing left (250,251 and 252,253). In the program ("Castle") PROCmove first prints the man (using PROCman – line 460) and then alters the character and the position before printing him again (lines 510,520). To simplify matters A% contains the number of the first of the two current man characters and the change is made by altering A% to the value of 502–A% (unless a change of direction is required).

Experiment 12.8

Define a set of characters which represent a man walking and use them to simulate a man walking across the screen. (You can use the SHAPES program to help design your characters.)

Experiment 12.9

Write a program which draws a house and a tree and then make your man walk in front of one and behind the other.

Experiment 12.10

Using mode 2 write a program which draws a red house with a yellow roof, a green door and white windows, set against a black background. Then make a figure walk across the face of the house in such a way that when he passes the door he disappears inside the house.

12.4 SMOOTHER ANIMATION

It is possible to obtain even smoother animation, especially for static shapes, by eliminating the need to first delete the old character before printing the new one. To see how this works let us return to the ghost we used in experiments 12.5 to 12.7. Figure 12.8 shows two consecutive positions of the ghost and it can be seen that, because we left a blank row round each edge, the second character totally overlaps the non-blank areas of the first one.

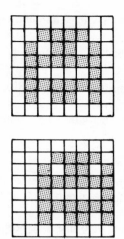

Figure 12.8   Two consecutive ghost positions

It should therefore be possible to define a character which when printed in the second position will directly change the original ghost character into one moved one space to the right.

In the last section we saw that

(a EOR b) EOR b = a

and so if

a EOR b = c

we find that

c EOR b = a

(and also that a EOR c = b). In other words, if a represents a row of the old character, b the special transformation row and c the corresponding row of the new character (so that a EOR b=c), we can find the value of b simply by evaluating a EOR c.

We can go further than this and write a program to calculate it for us since the new row, when moving right, is half the value of the old row. For example the top of the ghost's head has the value 60 (32+16+8+4), while in its new position it has the value 30 (16+8+4+2), relative to the old character position. We can use EOR, AND and OR as bitwise logical operators as well as for the purpose of evaluating logical expressions, and can therefore write the following program to calculate the transformation values:

```
10 REPEAT
20    INPUT "Old value",C%
30    PRINT "Transformation value is ";C% EOR (2*C%)
40    UNTIL C%<0
```

This program will give us the following character definition

```
VDU 23,225,0,68,238,130,198,130,238,0
```

which need only be printed one position to the right of the current position in order to produce an immediate shift to the right.

In a similar way we can create further characters to move left, up or down.

Experiment 12.11

Calculate the necessary transformation characters to move the ghost left, up and down, and modify the program written in experiment 12.7. RUN this program and ensure that it works correctly.

An improvement to this program is to use four procedures to move left, right, up and down, and to record the current character position. A check can then be made to avoid problems at the edges of the screen. Alter your program in this way.

One problem, of course, with this form of animation, is that it requires a lot of characters – five for the simple (one character) shape used above, and rather more for multi-character shapes. (*Note* that when moving a multi-character shape you must take particular care at the boundaries between characters as there will be a blank round the edge of the composite shape, but not round every edge of every character.)

In programs (such as The Final Test) which are designed to run with all versions of the Beeb operating system this can be an insurmountable problem, as only 32 user-defined characters are available. This restriction has been removed with later (Series 1) operating systems however, and so the method is more useful in those situations.

12.5   STILL MORE CHARACTERS TO DEFINE

With the original 0.10 operating system only characters 224–255 could be redefined by the user. With Series 1 operating systems, however, the 224 characters from 32 to 255 can be user-defined, although since 32–127 represent the standard character set a more realistic figure is the 128 characters from 128 to 255.

With all versions of the operating system the normal situation is for the 256 bytes of memory from &C00 (i.e. hexadecimal C00, or decimal 3072) to &CFF (decimal 3327) to be reserved for the definition of the 32 characters from 224 to 255. In fact, the characters from 128 to 233 are also "mapped" onto this area, and, for example, the statements

```
PRINT CHR$128
PRINT CHR$160
PRINT CHR$192
PRINT CHR$224
```

will all give the same character, and redefining character 224 will change all the other three. In this situation the character definitions are said to be *imploded* and it is not possible to redefine characters 32–127.

With the Series 1 operating system, however, it is possible to *explode* the character definitions and to redefine any character from 32 to 255. This is achieved by the command

`*FX 20,1`

However, this on its own is not enough, as space must be reserved in memory for the new character definitions. For this purpose characters are considered to be in seven blocks of 32 characters, and until any character in a block is redefined all characters in the block will be defined in the normal way (i.e. characters 32–127 will refer to the default characters in ROM and characters 128–255 will refer to the character definitions (if any) between &C00 and &CFF).

If it is required to redefine any characters other than 128–159 in this exploded mode then memory must be reserved as shown in figure 12.9, where OSHWM stands for the Operating System High Water Mark and is the first available byte of user memory – i.e. normally &E00 for cassette-based machines and &1900 for disc-based machines.

Thus on a disc-based computer the characters 160–191 (&A0–&BF) will occupy the area from &1900 to &19FF and any program that plans to define these characters must set PAGE to a higher than normal address by the statement

`PAGE = &1A00`

Note that in exploded mode, characters 224–255 are stored in what is normally part of the user program's data space, and so if exploded character definitions will be required you should start at 128 instead of 224 in order to minimise the amount of space which is lost to the program.

Experimental Hints

12.4 This experiment is not as easy as it may appear. The problem is that in order to take advantage of the half width characters they must either be printed one at a time at half-character intervals, or a single, composite, string must be created and printed together. Neither of these is possible with the character definitions provided in SHAPES!

It is not possible to print characters at half-character intervals except in graphic mode (after VDU 5) and then, as we have already seen, the character will not replace the unwanted half of the previous character but will be superimposed over it. Equally, it is clearly not possible to concatenate half-characters. The character definitions can, however, be used either to set up certain fixed messages (as is done

ASCII codes	Memory allocation in exploded mode
32–63 (&20–&3F)	OSHWM+&300 to OSHWM+&3FF
64–95 (&40–&5F)	OSHWM+&400 to OSHWM+&4FF
96–127 (&60–&7F)	OSHWM+&500 to OSHWM+&5FF
128–159 (&80–&9F)	&C00 to &CFF
160–191 (&A0–&BF)	OSHWM to OSHWM+&FF
192–223 (&C0–&DF)	OSHWM+&100 to OSHWM+&1FF
224–255 (&E0–&FF)	OSHWM+&200 to OSHWM+&2FF

Figure 12.9   Table of exploded character definition storage areas

by CASTLE for the copyright message – see lines 570–710) or the 32 characters 224–255 can be used just for capital letters, plus six other characters, and plotted at half-character intervals in graphic mode.

In the form defined in SHAPES the left-hand character (e.g. a capital letter) can be obtained by dividing the values given by 16, ignoring any remainder, and then multiplying by 16, while the right-hand character can be obtained (in the left-hand position) by dividing by 16, and using the remainder multiplied by 16. Thus the character 224 in SHAPES represents both "A" and "a":

```
VDU 23,224,064,160,174,226,174,170,174,000
```

A half-width capital A followed by a half-width space can therefore be defined as

```
VDU 23,224,64,160,160,224,160,160,160,0
```

while a half-width lower case a followed by a half-width space can be defined as

```
VDU 23,224,0,0,224,32,224,160,224,0
```

12.7   The VDU statement in line 35 can be broken down into three parts:

```
VDU 24,700;400;900;600;
VDU 16
VDU 26
```

These set up a graphics window (VDU 24,. . .), clear it to the background colour set up earlier in the same line (VDU 16), and then restore the normal (full-screen) window (VDU 26).

In addition, we could have used VDU 18 instead of GCOL and simply written

```
35 VDU 18,0,131,24,700;400;900;600;16,26
```

Because the ghost is being plotted using GCOL 3,2 it will be plotted in colour 1 (2 EOR 3) as it passes across the wall, i.e. red.

To make it appear to pass in front of the wall without any change of colour we must therefore make colour 1 the same as colour 2 (i.e. yellow in mode 1). This is achieved by the extra statement

```
25 VDU 19,1,3;0;
```

Note that the actual colour 3 is used (i.e. yellow) and not 2, which represents green.

To make the ghost go behind the wall we simply make colour 1 represent white:

```
25 VDU 19,1,7;0;
```

12.11   The necessary transformation characters are:

```
VDU 23,226,0,34,119,65,99,65,119,0
VDU 23,227,0,60,102,36,60,60,36,90
VDU 23,228,60,102,36,60,60,36,90,0
```

13

Another way of expressing yourself

13.1 THE TELETEXT CONCEPT

Up to this stage we have used modes 0–6 whenever we required any colour for either text or graphics, and have used modes 0, 1, 2, 4 and 5 for any graphics. Mode 7 has been the default mode and has only produced white text on a black background. However, we can do very much more than this in mode 7, as can be seen in the first program of The Final Test (FINALTEST) which only uses mode 7, and yet produces a wide range of colours and graphical effects, including some which are not available elsewhere. Mode 7 also has the advantage that it only requires 1000 bytes, while mode 6 (text only) uses 8192 bytes, modes 4 and 5 use 10240 bytes, mode 3 (text only) uses 16384 bytes, and modes 0, 1 and 2 use a massive 20480 bytes. How can this be?

The secret is a special coding/decoding "chip" inside the Beeb which uses the same system as is used by teletext services such as the BBC Ceefax service, the IBA Oracle service and the British Telecom Prestel service. The saving in space comes because in mode 7 each of the 40×25 characters requires just one byte to store it in, whereas in modes 0–6 each "dot" on the screen needs to be individually defined.

The teletext (mode 7) method of screen presentation is based on the inclusion of invisible control codes on the screen. These control codes can be used to define the foreground and/or background colour and a great many other things as well. To understand how these operate we shall examine a typical mode 7 line (or at least the first part of such a line).

Figure 13.1 shows how this will appear in the screen and also indicates the values of the invisible codes. This line could therefore be printed by typing

```
PRINT "White";CHR$129;"Red";CHR$131;"Yellow";CHR$132;"Blue"
```

The line, when printed, starts as usual using white letters but the control code 129 causes all subsequent text to be printed in red. The next control code (131) stipulates yellow text and the final one (132) specifies blue text.

Type this line on your Beeb and see that it really does work!

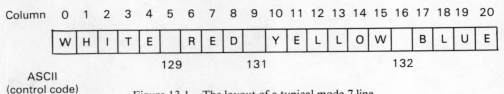

Figure 13.1   The layout of a typical mode 7 line

13.2   ALPHANUMERIC TEXT IN MODE 7

We have seen how some control codes can be used to change the colour of subsequent text, and figure 13.2 gives a full list of the colour codes available for this purpose.

Code 136 is used to cause the colour specified for the foreground to flash between that colour and the background colour. It is used, therefore, in conjunction with one of the other codes, for example

```
PRINT CHR$129;"Steady";CHR$136;"Flashing"
```

Like all the other teletext control codes the *flash code* continues in effect to the end of the line or until countermanded. In this case code 137 cancels the effect of a code 136 and restores steady colours:

```
PRINT CHR$129;"Steady";CHR$136;"Flashing";CHR$137;"Steady"
```

The control codes, of course, can only operate as long as they are present, and so altering an invisible control code can be used to quite dramatic effect.

Experiment 13.1

Type the following commands:

```
MODE 7
PRINT TAB(0,20)CHR$129;CHR$136;"Teletext is marvellous"
```

You will get the message flashing in red.

Code	Meaning
129	red alphanumeric
130	green alphanumeric
131	yellow alphanumeric
132	blue alphanumeric
133	magenta alphanumeric
134	cyan alphanumeric
135	white alphanumeric
136	flash foreground
137	steady foreground

Figure 13.2   Mode 7 (teletext) codes 129–137

Now type

```
PRINT TAB(0,20)CHR$130
```

Because of the TAB this will cause the control code 130 to replace 129, thus *instantly* changing all the text to green.
Now type

```
PRINT TAB(1,20)CHR$137
```

Did you expect the flashing to stop?
Now type

```
PRINT TAB(13,20)CHR$129
```

Character 13 was the space between the words "is" and "marvellous". Replacing it with code 129 therefore causes marvellous to be printed in red.
Finally, what effect do you expect the following to have?

```
VDU 31,0,20,133,136,9,9,9,9,9,9,9,9,137
```

Type it and see if you were right.

As well as flashing text for emphasis we can also cause it to be printed in *double height* characters. This is achieved by use of control code 141. However since a double height character must occupy two lines it is necessary to print the text twice, like this:

```
PRINT TAB(10,15)CHR$131;CHR$141;"Miles Ellis"
PRINT TAB(10,16)CHR$131;CHR$141;"Miles Ellis"
```

Type these two commands on your computer and notice that the first PRINT only prints the top half of each letter, while the second one prints the bottom half. A more convenient way of producing double height text is to use a loop, e.g.

```
100 DEF PROCdouble(text$,line,char)
110 REM This prints text$ in double height at the specified position
130 LOCAL lin
140 FOR lin=line TO line+1
150    PRINT TAB(char,lin) text$
160    NEXT
170 ENDPROC
```

Usually double height characters will be used for titles, etc. and will not be mixed with normal height characters. However if it is required to follow double height characters with further (normal height) characters then the code 140 will restore normal height.

Finally we come to *background colours*. Once again a special code is used – in this case 157, which defines the most recently specified colour *on this line* to be the background colour for the rest of this line.

Thus

```
PRINT CHR$131;CHR$157;CHR$132;"Blue on yellow"
```

will cause blue letters to be printed on a yellow background.

It is important to remember that control code 157 only sets the background for a single line. If we wish to set the background for the whole screen then we must put the appropriate control codes at the start of every line. For example the command

```
FOR I%=0 TO 24: PRINT TAB(0,I%)CHR$129;CHR$157;: NEXT
```

will cause the whole screen to have a red background.

Notice that the PRINT statement in the above command could have been replaced by

```
VDU 31,0,I%,129,157
```

When using mode 7 colour and (especially) graphics the VDU statement often gives a more compact and easily read form than does a PRINT statement.

Experiment 13.2

Type in the following short program

```
10 MODE 7
20 FOR I%=0 TO 24
30    VDU 31,0,I%,134,157
40    NEXT
50 FOR I%=0 TO 24
60    C%=129+(I% MOD 5)
70    PRINT TAB(10,I%)CHR$(C%);"This is line ";I%
80    NEXT
```

What do you expect to see?

Now RUN the program. Were you right? Can you correct the error in it?

Now modify the program so that instead of printing 25 lines saying "This is line n" it prints 50 such lines (*all on a cyan background*).

The FINALTEST program uses two procedures to create most of the special effects – PROCback and PROCclear.

PROCback (lines 1410–1450) uses a loop to put a new background colour at the start of all lines between two limits which are supplied as arguments. There is a very small delay after each pass through the loop which slows down the process to approximately the same speed as CLG.

175

PROCclear (lines 1460–1490) first clears the screen and then uses a similar loop to PROCback, but without any delays, thus providing an almost instantaneous colour change.

Because PROCback does not clear the screen but only alters the background colour, it can easily be used to provide the interesting effects of the opening title in which the new background colour appears to "wipe" down *behind* the title which remains unaltered. This is carried out by the loop on line 260, and also by lines 280–310 (see figure 13.3). The similar effect of "wiping" a new colour down the title without affecting the background is achieved by the loop at line 270, which alters the foreground colour codes in column 3 which were placed there initially by the loop at line 70 (see figure 13.4).

You may have noticed in figure 13.2 that there is no code for black. It is therefore impossible in mode 7 to produce black text on a coloured background. However, it is necessary to be able to specify a *black background* (this, after all, is the normal situation) and this is achieved by use of code 156.

Thus the statement

```
PRINT CHR$129;CHR$157;CHR$131;"First";CHR$156;"Second"
```

will print the word "First" in yellow on a red background followed by a space (occupied by CHR$156) and then the word "Second" also in yellow, but on a black background.

The use of mode 7 colour can very easily brighten up the results produced by a program and can also be used to distinguish between various items on the screen. For example the four utility programs in Appendix C all start in a uniform manner.

First the title of the program is displayed in double-height green characters with a red copyright notice beneath it. Then a set of questions and answers establish how the program is to be used. The questions are displayed in green and the answers in yellow by statements

```
260 FOR J%=145 TO 149:
       PROCback(0,24,J%): PROCwait(0.1): NEXT
270 FOR I%=2 TO 20:
       VDU 31,3,I%,148: PROCwait(0.03): NEXT:
    PROCwait(1)
280 PROCback(0,7,145): PROCwait(0.5)
290 PROCback(8,14,150): PROCwait(0.5)
300 PROCback(15,24,146): PROCwait(0.5)
310 PROCback(22,24,147): PROCwait(0.5)
```

Figure 13.3   Lines 260–310 of FINALTEST

```
70 FOR I%=2 TO 20:
      VDU 31,3,I%,151: NEXT:
       .
       .
       .
270 FOR I%=2 TO 20:
       VDU 31,3,I%,148: PROCwait(0.03): NEXT:
    PROCwait(1)
```

Figure 13.4   Lines 70 and 270 of FINALTEST

176

such as

```
310 PRINT TAB(3,15)CHR$130;"What line width do you want?";CHR$131;
320 INPUT ""Width%
```

Note that in this case it is necessary to use separate PRINT and INPUT statements as it would be awkward to include the colour codes in the INPUT prompt message.

Experiment 13.3

Can you find a way of replacing the separate PRINT and INPUT statements in the above example by a single INPUT statement which produces the identical effect?

In some cases the program will refuse to accept the reply to a question (e.g. line width must be between 20 and 120 characters) and an error message is printed in red to highlight it before the user is invited to try again (by having his previous answer replaced by spaces).

   This colour coding is trivially easy once you have mastered the use of the teletext codes, but creates an impact out of all proportion to the effort required.

13.3   GRAPHICS IN MODE 7

Mode 7 also provides a quite powerful graphics system which can be used with great effect when space is at a premium. In the FINALTEST program, for example, the main title "THE FINAL TEST" is drawn using these graphics but, more obviously, so are the various scenes in the forest and outside the castle.

   Mode 7 graphics are produced by a special set of *graphic characters*, each of which occupies the full height of one line and the full width of one character (i.e. including the gaps left between lines and between characters in normal text mode). Each of these special characters consists of a 2×3 arrangement of small blocks as shown in figure 13.5.

   In order to use these graphic characters you must specify their colour using codes which are 16 greater than those used for text colours (see figure 13.6).

   The characters used for graphics are those numbered from 160 to 191 and from 244–255 and can be calculated by use of the diagram below

in which each of the six "cells" is allocated a number. The sum of the numbers of the cells which are to be numbered is added to 160 to give the ASCII code of the graphic character.

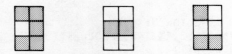

Figure 13.5   Enlarged view of mode 7 graphic characters

Code	Meaning
145	red graphics
146	green graphics
147	yellow graphics
148	blue graphics
149	magenta graphics
150	cyan graphics
151	white graphics

Figure 13.6   Mode 7 graphic colour codes

Thus the character

will be produced by ASCII code 185 ($=1+8+16+160$).

(Notice, incidentally, that in the above drawing the white squares are the coloured ones, while the black squares represent the background.)

Experiment 13.4

Write a program which prints a small castle, e.g.

in red such that it is on the skyline separating a green field from a pale blue sky. (This is similar to part of the opening picture in FINALTEST, but greatly simplified.) The castle should be very small and should occupy only a single line.

When you have done this, modify the program to produce a castle two lines high.

The above experiment will have demonstrated that the VDU statement is considerably easier to use for this purpose than a PRINT statement. Remember that

VDU a,b,c

and

PRINT CHR$(a);CHR$(b);CHR$(c);

are identical in their effect, and also that

VDU 31,x,y

and

PRINT TAB(x,y);

are identical. Furthermore, the VDU codes 8, 9, 10 and 11 can be used to move the cursor left, right, down and up. Thus the statements

```
PRINT TAB(30,10)CHR$145;CHR$255;CHR$240;CHR$255;CHR$240;CHR$255;
PRINT TAB(30,11)CHR$145;CHR$255;CHR$255;CHR$163;CHR$255;CHR$255;
```

can be replaced by

```
VDU 31,30,10,145,255,240,255,240,255,31,30,11,145,255,255,163,255,255
```

which is both shorter and, in this context, easier to read.

The work involved in planning a mode 7 picture is quite considerable as the last experiment will have shown you. If you intend to produce large or complex scenes (such as those in FINALTEST) you will find it best to draw your picture on graph paper in such a way that one square represents one "dot" in a graphics character. The various different characters can then be relatively easily read off (with a bit of practice). Figure 13.7 shows all 64 graphic characters with their ASCII codes so that it is not necessary to work them out by hand.

One potential problem with this method of drawing pictures is that the control characters in a line will appear as spaces, in other words as solid characters in the background colour. You will have noticed this in the last experiment as the castle door will have been pale blue (the colour of the sky) and there is no obvious way of changing this. One special feature that can come to our aid in this situation is known as *hold graphics* and is initiated by code 158.

After a hold graphics code, all subsequent control characters in a line (including the hold graphics code itself) will be displayed as the last graphics character instead of a space. For example let us consider the following command:

```
VDU 31,15,12,147,172,172,172,172,172,172,172,172
```

which will draw a horizontal yellow line in the centre of the screen. (If you aren't sure about this, look at figure 13.7 and then try it on your computer.)

If we wished to change colour half-way along the line we could write

```
VDU 31,15,12,147,172,172,172,172,145,172,172,172
```

but this will leave a gap in the middle of the line. Try it and see for yourself.

However, if we type

```
VDU 31,15,12,147,172,172,158,145,172,172,172,172
```

then the two control characters (158 and 145) will both be replaced by the previous character (i.e. a yellow line) before the colour change takes effect and causes the rest of the line to use red as the foreground colour.

Experiment 13.5

The very small castle that we drew in experiment 13.4 only occupied one line and so the

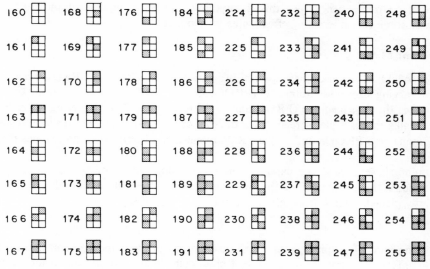

Figure 13.7   Mode 7 graphic codes

same colour background must, inevitably, appear behind both the crenellations at the top and the gateway at the bottom. The larger one, however, used two lines and so we can do something about the door. Modify the program you wrote earlier so that the door is yellow. The castle should be two lines high and five characters wide.

This problem requires quite a lot of careful thought. If you *really* can't work out how to do it then see Experimental Hints but do try to work it out yourself (and try it on the computer) before you get help.

If necessary you can cancel the hold graphics option by the code 159 which returns to the normal default state in which control codes appear as spaces.

In the forest scenes in FINALTEST you will have noticed that the tops of the trees are not solid blocks but are broken up to give a better effect. This is achieved by use of control code 154 which gives *separated graphics*. In this mode the six "cells" which make up each graphic character are reduced slightly in size so as to leave a grid (or border) between them in the background colour. Thus in the normal (or *contiguous graphics*) mode the character 255 appears as

while it appears as six separate cells in separated graphics mode;

As usual there is another code (153) to return to (normal) contiguous graphics. It is important to remember to use this if anything else is to appear on the same line as otherwise some very interesting effects may be produced!

Experiment 13.6

The FINALTEST program uses a set of procedures (PROCtree1,. . .,PROCtree4) to draw trees of varying sizes and another set (PROCcastle1,. . .,PROCcastle5) to draw the castles. It also uses three procedures (PROCman1,. . .,PROCman3) for animating the man figure as he walks across the screen towards the castle. (In fact the walking uses only PROCman1 and PROCman2, while PROCman3 is used only when he reaches the castle gate.)

Examine these procedures carefully until you think you understand how they work. Then modify the main part of the program (lines 470–900) so that the trees etc. are differently placed. (Don't forget about the control characters!)

Developing mode 7 graphic pictures can be a lengthy process and you can find some very peculiar effects occurring due to control characters being omitted or accidentally over-written, especially if the picture is animated. We had some hilarious (as well as frustrating) experiences when developing the graphics in FINALTEST, so don't give up!

Experiment 13.7

In chapter 5, experiment 5.8 required you to create a new (mode 2) title sequence for use in CASTLE. Modify FINALTEST to use the same title in mode 7.

Figure 13.8 shows the effects of the various special graphic control codes that have been discussed above together with one extra code (152) that has not yet been mentioned. Quite simply the *conceal display* code does just that – for the rest of the line, or until another control code is encountered. The concealed display can then be revealed by replacing code 152 with some other appropriate value (e.g. a colour code).

Conceal display operates with both graphics and text and can therefore be used in some forms of animation, or to reveal hidden answers to questions. It is of limited use in general but can be used sometimes to provide apparently instantaneous drawing of complex shapes. For example if line 70 in FINALTEST were replaced by

```
70 FOR I%=2 TO 20: VDU 31,3,I%,152: NEXT
```

then the main title would be drawn invisibly! An extra statement

```
245 FOR I%=2 TO 20: VDU 31,3,I%,151: NEXT
```

Code	Meaning
152	conceal display
153	contiguous graphics
154	separated graphics
158	hold graphics
159	release graphics

Figure 13.8   Special graphic codes

would reveal the full title in a fraction of a second in a very similar way to that achieved by use of VDU 19 in experiment 11.17.

In general, however, the conceal facility is of only limited use – its primary purpose being for use in broadcast teletext services such as the BBC Ceefax and the IBA Oracle systems.

Experiment 13.8

Write a program which will use only mode 7 to produce a moving picture of two figures playing tennis. The picture should include a green court, a blue sky, two players, a net and a ball and any other items that you care to add!

Experimental Hints

13.2   The program provided moves the cursor to the next line after printing (see line 70). When it does this on line 24 then the screen will scroll up, including the control characters, thus producing a black line at the bottom of the screen. Changing line 70 to

```
70    PRINT TAB(10,I%)CHR$(C%);"This is line ";I%;
```

will not move the cursor down, thus solving the problem.

For 50 lines, however, it will be necessary for lines 25–49 to start with the control characters since the screen will have to be scrolled. The following changes will suffice:

```
50 FOR I%=0 TO 49
70    PRINT TAB(0,I%)CHR$134;CHR$157;SPC(8);CHR$(C%);
      "This is line ";I%;
```

13.3   The trick here is to get the control character itself into your prompt text. The way to do this is by use of the COPY key.

First clear the screen, and then type (for example)

```
PRINT TAB(0,20)CHR$130;"What line width do you want?";CHR$131;
```

This will display the question (in green) near the bottom of the screen. Now type

```
310 INPUT "
```

and then use the cursor control keys to move the editing cursor to the beginning of the line just printed (in green). The cursor should be positioned at the extreme left-hand side of the screen, immediately before the letter "W" which starts the (visible) text. The cursor is therefore positioned at the (invisible) control code. Now COPY up to and including the (invisible) control code after the question mark at the end of the (visible) text.

Finally, complete line 310 by typing

```
" Width%
```

You will see that line 310 starts (as usual) in white, then turns green for the prompt text, and ends up yellow!

When used in a program, the message will be printed in green, and the answer will be in yellow as required.

13.4   A suitable program for the first case is

```
10 CLS
20 FOR I%=0 TO 9
30    VDU 31,0,I%,150,157
40    NEXT
50 FOR I%=10 TO 24
60    VDU 31,0,I%,146,157
70    NEXT
80 VDU 31,19,9,145,253,237,181
90 VDU 31,38,24
```

13.5   The two lines to draw the castle (on lines 8 and 9) should be:

```
80 VDU 31,18,8,145,255,240,255,240,255
85 VDU 31,17,9,158,145,157,147,252,160,150,157
```

If you still don't understand, then draw yourself a plan so that you can compare the layout of the various characters with the screen display.

Dealing with sets of data

14.1 THE CONCEPT OF AN ARRAY

In all the programs and examples that we have discussed so far we have assumed that each variable name refers to a single memory location (or variable). However, we frequently need to refer to *sets* of data and to access individual items within those sets. For example experiments 7.3 to 7.5 were concerned with the collection of simple health statistics, but because the same variables were used to store details of every person in the survey it was not possible to analyse the full set of data other than by calculating various averages. The input in these exercises was carried out by a statement of the form

```
INPUT name$,age,ht,wt
```

and therefore each time the statement is obeyed (in a loop) the previous values are lost.

If we knew that there were (say) five out-patients in the survey we could write

```
INPUT name1$,age1,ht1,wt1
INPUT name2$,age2,ht2,wt2
INPUT name3$,age3,ht3,wt3
INPUT name4$,age4,ht4,wt4
INPUT name5$,age5,ht5,wt5
```

but this is extremely poor programming style and, far more important, will only work for five patients.

The solution to this problem is to use what is called an *array*.

An array is a set of consecutive memory locations which are all referred to by the same name plus an index, or subscript, to identify the individual *elements* of the array. The identifying number is called a subscript because the array concept is derived from the mathematical vector or matrix in which members of the set are written as a_1, a_2, a_3, etc. In Basic, of course, we cannot actually write this identifying number as a subscript and so it is enclosed in parentheses immediately after the name:

```
age(1)  age(2)  age(3)  etc.
```

The identifying subscript can be a constant, as above, but it is more usually a variable:

```
age(I)  name$(J%)  etc.
```

Life is never that easy though, and there is still one slight problem!

Normally the Basic Interpreter allocates memory space for each variable as it comes to it during the execution of the program. However, an array will require a substantial amount of space to be allocated, since all the elements of the array must be stored consecutively in the memory. Unfortunately there is no way that the Interpreter can know when it first comes to a reference to an array what the largest value of the subscript is going to be, and so it cannot know how much space to allocate. It is as though we were booking seats for the theatre and said to the booking clerk

"I'll be having some friends along later and we all want to sit together please."

The clerk cannot sell us the right number of tickets unless we tell him how many friends will be coming!

Figure 14.1 "... and some tickets for my friends please"

In Basic, we deal with this problem by means of a special statement

```
DIM name(size)
```

where name is the name of the array and size is the maximum value of the subscript.

Experiment 14.1

Type in the following program

```
10 INPUT "How many exams",N
20 DIM mark(N)
29 REM Input marks
30 FOR I=1 TO N
40    INPUT "Next mark: " mark(I)
50    NEXT
60 total=0
69 REM Calculate average mark
70 FOR I=1 TO N
80    total=total+mark(I)
90    NEXT
100 average=total/N
110 PRINT: PRINT "Average mark was ";average
119 REM List above average marks
120 PRINT '"Above average results were"
130 FOR I=1 TO N
140    IF mark(I)>average THEN
         PRINT mark(I);" in exam ";I
150    NEXT
160 PRINT
```

This program first asks for the number of exams for which marks are available, and uses this to DIMension the array mark. It then uses a loop to input the marks into this array. A second loop then adds up these marks so that an average mark can be calculated. (This could also have been done during the input loop if required.) Finally a third loop uses the array again to print the marks which were above average, and the exams in which they were obtained.

RUN this program and make sure that you understand how it works.

Experiment 14.2

Modify the program presented in the last experiment to print the average mark when the best and the worst marks are ignored.

Important note: When you are testing your programs it is not enough to ensure that they produce an answer — it must be the right answer! Before running your revised program did you work out by hand what answer you expected? If you did not, then how do you know it worked correctly? This leads to another important point — start your testing with small, carefully chosen, sets of data.

Experiment 14.3

The program developed above analyses the exam results for one pupil. We could modify it to deal with more than one by adding the extra lines

```
500 INPUT "Another pupil",A$
510 IF A$="Y" THEN
        GOTO 10
```

Add these to your program and test them. Does the result surprise you? What should we have done?

Normally an array will have constant dimensions and it is good practice to place the DIM statement at or near the beginning of the program (or at the start of a procedure in the case of a local array). As we have seen, however, it is also possible to use a variable to define the size of the array, but in this situation it is important to ensure that the DIM can only be obeyed once.

One important point to note about array dimensions is that the first subscript is 0 and not 1 — because that's the way computers count! Thus if we dimension an array as

```
DIM Xa(20)
```

it actually contains 21 elements, with subscripts running from 0 to 20. We don't need to refer to the first element (with a zero subscript) if we don't want to, but it is always there and as you get used to using arrays you will find it quite natural to start counting at zero.

A second point is that if, as is often the case, we have several arrays to dimension then we can list them all, separated by commas, in the same DIM statement. Thus the four statements

```
10 DIM A(10)
20 DIM B(5)
30 DIM N$(15)
40 DIM X%(25)
```

could be more succinctly written as

```
10 DIM A(10),B(5),N$(15),X%(25)
```

14.2   INITIALISING AN ARRAY

The above experiments have illustrated the power of an array when used in conjunction with a loop, and, indeed, arrays are normally to be found in loops of various kinds. However, just as with variables, it is frequently necessary to initialise the elements of an array before the start of processing so that they have a known and defined value. If all the elements are to have the same value, for example zero, then a simple loop is sufficient:

```
10 DIM Xa(20)
20 FOR I%=0 TO 20
30    Xa(I%)=0
40    NEXT
```

However, if different elements are to have different values then READ and DATA provide an elegant way of carrying out the initialisation:

```
10 DIM Xa(20)
20 FOR I=0 TO 20
30    READ Xa(I)
40    NEXT
50 DATA 1,4,0,7,0, ...
```

In this case the DATA statement at line 50 has a list of 21 values which are to be the initial values of the 21 elements of the array Xa. On each pass through the loop in lines 20–40 the next value is READ into the Ith element of the array. When the loop is completed, therefore, the whole array will have been initialised with the values supplied in the DATA statement.

An example of this technique occurs in the CASTLE2 program which sets up the main aspects of the game for Castle. Line 60 reads

```
60 RESTORE 1900: FOR I=0 TO 15:
    READ Item$(I): NEXT:
   *FX15,1
```

Ignoring the *FX15,1 (which clears the input buffer), this is in exactly the same form as the earlier example, with a RESTORE statement to ensure that the correct data is read. Examination of line 1900 shows that it is a list of items to be found in the castle:

```
1900 DATA Axe,Ruby,Emerald,Diamond,Belt,Sword,Cross,Skull,Hat,Salt,
     Necklace,Shield,Lamp,Spear,Feathers,Ring
```

The array Item$ is thus set up with a list of the items to be found in the castle – a list whose order is the same as the user-defined characters used to display the various items, and also the same as the array Item% which will contain details of their location, magic power, etc.

One very important point to note concerns the use of character arrays whose contents (unlike Item$ above) can be altered during the program's execution. In chapter 9 we emphasised that to avoid wasted space you should always initialise a character variable to a string which is at least as long as any that will subsequently be assigned to it. *This is doubly important in the case of a character array.*

For example if the array name$ is to be used to store names input from the terminal with a maximum length of (say) 20 characters, you can initialise the array as follows:

```
10 DIM name$(50)
20 FOR I=0 TO 50
30    name$=STRING$(20," "): name$=""
40    NEXT
```

This will first assign a 20 character string (of spaces) to each element, followed by a null (or empty) string to clear it ready for use.

Experiment 14.4

Write a short program to input a list of ten names of no more than 12 characters each. Then for each consecutive pair print a random message created by inserting a (random) verb between the names, e.g.

Paul likes Mary
Mary hits Susan
Susan hates Nathaniel
etc.

Arrange for your program to detect a name of more than 12 characters without wasting any array space.

14.3   GETTING SOME ORDER INTO THINGS

When a program is using arrays to store information it frequently needs to print (or display) some or all of the information. When we do this by hand we usually arrange it in an appropriate order – for example alphabetic order or in increasing (or decreasing) numeric order. We can add considerably to the usefulness of our programs if we arrange for them to sort their results in a similar way.

Sorting is quite a tricky task and over the years a considerable amount of research has gone into developing highly efficient methods (or algorithms). The increased speed of these sophisticated methods, however, does not normally concern us unless we have several hundred or thousand items to sort. For the types of problems we are likely to face on the Beeb (certainly to begin with) one of the simple methods will be more than adequate.

The simplest method of all is known as the "Bubble Sort" and operates on the principle of repeatedly examining successive pairs and exchanging them if they are in the wrong order. If we assume that there are N numbers stored in an array called num then the following structure plan shows the steps needed to sort them into increasing order:

Repeat for J from 1 to N−1
  Repeat for I from 1 to N−j
    If num(I)>num(I+1) then
      Exchange num(I) and num(I+1)

Figure 14.2 shows how this works with a simple sequence of 5 numbers. The two numbers exchanged in each pass (if any) are circled, and it can readily be seen why it is called a bubble sort, since each number in turn "bubbles" along to its correct position. (If you draw the array in a vertical direction this is even more apparent!)

Experiment 14.5

Write a program which inputs a set of names and then lists them in alphabetic order.

One problem with the bubble sort is that, although it is delightfully easy to understand and to program, it is very inefficient. Its very name gives us a clue as to the reason for this, and an examination of figure 14.2 will show that a relatively large number of exchanges take place (8) for such a small number of items.

Examination of the method shows that on the first pass through the *outer* loop (J=1) the largest value gradually "bubbles" up to its correct place. On the second pass (J=2) the next largest value (4) bubbles into its correct place, and so on. A considerable improvement in efficiency can therefore be made by simply identifying the largest number not yet sorted and exchanging it with the number currently occupying its correct place.

Figure 14.3 shows the way in which this works.

This type of sort, which is called a "Straight Selection" sort is also easy to program, as can be seen from the following structure plan:

Repeat for J from N to 2 in steps of −1
  max=J
  Repeat for I from 1 to J−1
    If num(I)>num(max) then max=I
  If max<>J then exchange num(max) and num(J)

J	I	num(1)	num(2)	num(3)	num(4)	num(5)
Initially		3	5	4	2	1
1	1	3	5	4	2	1
	2	3	④	⑤	2	1
	3	3	4	②	⑤	1
	4	3	4	2	①	⑤
2	1	3	4	2	1	5
	2	3	②	④	1	5
	3	3	2	①	④	5
3	1	②	③	1	4	5
	2	2	①	③	4	5
4	1	①	②	3	4	5

Figure 14.2   The Bubble Sort in action

	J	num(1)	num(2)	num(3)	num(4)	num(5)
Initially		3	5	4	2	1
	5	3	①	4	2	⑤
	4	3	1	②	④	5
	3	②	1	③	4	5
	2	①	②	3	4	5

Figure 14.3   A Straight-selection sort

In this algorithm the value of J indicates the position in the sorted list which is next to be filled; it thus counts down from N to 2. (Obviously once positions 2 to N are filled correctly then the first position must also be correctly filled!) The variable max is set to the value of J and the inner loop then searches for a number greater than the one in the maxth position; if it finds one then max is set to the position of that number and the process is continued. At the end of this inner loop max therefore identifies the position of the largest number remaining to be sorted and this is then exchanged with the number currently in its new (correct) position (J), unless it is already there (i.e. max=J).

Experiment 14.6

Modify the program written in experiment 14.5 to use a straight selection sort.

Experiment 14.7

We have stated that the straight selection sort is more efficient than the bubble sort. Write a program to prove (or disprove!) this assertion.

Use numbers set up at random and use the value of TIME as a means of timing your program. (TIME is a pseudo-variable which was introduced in chapter 7.) Use the same sequence of numbers with each method and use successively larger sets. (See Experimental Hints if you are not sure what to do.)

What conclusions do you draw from this?

Sometimes we wish to sort several arrays at the same time into an order determined by just one of them. For example in the health survey mentioned at the start of this chapter we might wish to list all the patients and their relevant details in alphabetic order, or in order of their ages (or their heights or weights!). Manipulating all these arrays would be both time consuming and inelegant and the approach normally used is to create a pointer array and then to sort that.

Each element of the pointer array contains a number which is used as a subscript to the other arrays. The key array which is being used to define the order is used in the search for the next item to be placed, but the exchanges are carried out only on the pointer array. The following structure plan shows how this works with the array key being the basis for the

```
 10 DIM name$(50),age(50),ht(50),wt(50),seq(50)
 20 FOR I=1 TO 50:
       seq(I)=I: NEXT
 30 REM Input data, etc.
        .
        .
        .
100 REM Sort into alphabetical order
110 FOR J=50 TO 2 STEP -1
120    Jlast=J: last=seq(J)
130    FOR I=1 TO J-1
140       IF name$(seq(I))>name$(last) THEN
              last=seq(I): Jlast=I
150       NEXT
160    IF Jlast<>J THEN
          temp=seq(Jlast): seq(Jlast)=seq(J): seq(J)=temp
170    NEXT
180 REM Now print data in alphabetical order of names
190 FOR I=1 TO 50
200    J=seq(I): PRINT name(J),age(J),ht(J),wt(J)
210    NEXT
```

Figure 14.4   An example of a pointer sort

sorting and the array ptr being the pointer array:

Initialise ptr(1)–ptr(N) to the values 1–N
Repeat for J from N down to 2
  Jmax=J
  max=ptr(J)
  Repeat for I from 1 to J–1
    If key(ptr(I))>key(max) then max=ptr(I): Jmax=I
  If Jmax<>J then exchange ptr(Jmax) and ptr(J)

Figure 14.4 shows how this technique could be used to sort the health statistics, referred to above, into alphabetic order before printing.

14.4   ADDING ANOTHER DIMENSION

In all the above examples the arrays have had a single subscript and can, therefore, be visualised as a row of consecutive elements, as in figure 14.5.

However, in many situations it would be more natural to use two subscripts. For example it might be necessary to count the number of people of different ages in various salary bands. An array called NumPeople could be set up in which the first subscript represented the age less 15 and the second the weekly wage (in, say, tens of pounds). Thus

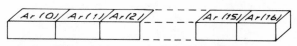

Figure 14.5   A one-dimensional array

NumPeople(0,5) would contain the number of people aged 15 earning £50–£59.99 while NumPeople(20,25) would contain the number of people aged 35 earning £250–£259.99 per week.

A two-dimensional array such as this is written with two subscripts, separated by a commma, and must be DIMensioned in the same way:

```
10 DIM NumPeople(50,100)
```

Figure 14.6 shows a visual representation of such an array.

The example given above of NumPeople also serves as an example of one major potential problem when using two-dimensional arrays. As defined in the DIM statement the first subscript can run from 0 to 50, corresponding to ages from 15 to 65, while the second subscript can run from 0–100, corresponding to weekly wages from £0.00 to £1009.99. However, this utilises a total of 51×101 elements, i.e. 5151 elements or just over 25K bytes! Even in mode 7 this is virtually all the available memory (and more than the available memory on a disc-based model), and there will be no room for the program!

When using two-dimensional arrays it is therefore very important to be aware of the implications on memory usage. In the above example the array NumPeople uses real numbers and each element occupies five bytes. In fact it could equally well have been declared as an integer array:

```
10 DIM NumPeople%(50,100)
```

In this case only four bytes are used for each element with a consequent saving of about 5K bytes! The array is still too long but the example does show that significant savings can be made by using integer arrays when only whole numbers are to be stored in them. (The use of integers also leads to faster arithmetic and no loss of accuracy, but the space requirement is the main reason in this case.)

The Castle program uses an array Door% to store information about the layout of the castle. It is dimensioned as

```
DIM Door%(7,9)
```

and the first subscript defines the floor (from 0–7) while the second defines which of the ten doors on each floor (from 0–9) is being referred to. Each element uses special data compression techniques to store the following information:

a) The location at the other end of the tunnel (floor and door).
b) The existence (if any) of a trapdoor down to the dungeon.
c) The type of creature (if any) guarding the tunnel.
d) The physical and magical strengths of the guardian.

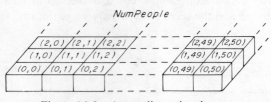

Figure 14.6   A two-dimensional array

The method used to store all this in a single element is too difficult to explain until you have read and understood all of this book, especially chapter 17. If you are interested at that point then you will find the details in Appendix B.

Whenever a door is opened, this array is used to determine what character (if any) is to be revealed, and when an attempt is made to enter a guarded door it is used to determine the fighting strength of the guardian (skeleton, dragon or Morgan le Fey). If the guardian is defeated (or if the doorway is unguarded) the array is again used to determine the direction of travel (up, down or level), whether the player falls into the dungeon, and which floor and doorway he finally appears at.

The array is set up in the program CASTLE2 by the procedure PROCdoors and transferred to Castle together with other initial data by a method described in chapter 17.

Two-dimensional arrays are not the end of the story however, as there is no limit to the number of dimensions an array may have — other than memory space. Thus we may define an array multdim as follows:

```
20 DIM multdim(5,3,7,4,3)
```

Notice, though, that this seemingly innocuous array has 6*4*8*5*4 elements and occupies almost 19K bytes!

Experiment 14.8

Write a program to play "Noughts and Crosses" (or "Tic-Tac-Toe" as our American cousins call it).

For anyone who has never played this game, a grid is drawn as shown in figure 14.7 and then each player fills one square alternately — one using a 0 (zero or *nought*) and the other an X (or *cross*). The object is to get a straight line of three of your mark, as shown in figure 14.7.

Your program should draw a playing grid and then ask each player in turn to make a move. The move (at this stage) can be defined by two numbers "row, column". The program should check the validity of the move and then draw the appropriate mark. It

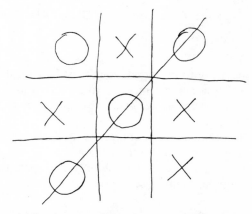

Figure 14.7   A game of Noughts and Crosses (conclusion)

should also check to see if it completes a winning line. If there are any vacant squares it should then invite the second player to move.

Use colour and sound to make it interesting.

Experiment 14.9

Modify the program written for the last experiment so that the computer plays against a single player.

This will require some careful thought to work out a strategy for choosing the best move. Remember that four lines go through the centre square, three through each corner, and only two through the other four squares.

14.5 ARRAYS IN PROCEDURES

A limitation on the use of arrays is that they cannot be used as parameters to procedures. If we wish a procedure to use information stored in an array then the array must be a global array. It is, of course, possible to declare a local array within a procedure, but since this cannot be accessed in any way from outside the procedure (unless the procedure copies it into a global array) local arrays are not very widely used.

It is, however, possible to write a procedure which expects to be passed information in an array by using a special global name and copying the actual array into it. Suppose, for example, that we wished to write a procedure to sort a collection of names into alphabetic order, using a straight-selection sort. We could write this as follows:

```
500 DEF PROCalphasort(num%)
510 LOCAL I%,J%,max%,temp$
520 REM This procedure sorts num% strings in the array STR_$ into
    alphabetic order
530 FOR J%=num% TO 2 STEP -1
540   max%=J%
550   FOR I%=1 TO J%-1
560     IF STR_$(I%)>STR_$(max%) THEN max%=I%
570   NEXT
580   IF max%<>J% THEN
        temp$=STR_$(max%): STR_$(max%)=STR_$(J%): STR_$(J%)=temp$
590   NEXT
600 ENDPROC
```

In the calling program the array to be sorted would first be copied into STR_$ and then PROCalphasort called with the number of items to be sorted as its only parameter. On return from the procedure the sorted names could be copied back to their original array or to another array, as required.

The special array STR_$ should not, of course, be used for any other purpose and has been deliberately given an unusual name for this reason.

A possible improvement to this procedure would be also to pass the maximum length of name as a parameter and use this to initialise temp$.

Experiment 14.10

A computer game which goes back to long before the days of microcomputers used to be known as "Cows and Bulls". Indeed it may even be the original computer game! More recently this was revived as a board game called "Mastermind" and even more recently as an electronic version of the board game – thus completing the circle!

In its original form the computer generates a random four-digit number and you, the player, have to guess what it is. For every correct digit in the correct place you are awarded a "bull", while for every correct digit in the wrong place you are awarded a "cow"! By a combination of logic and guesswork you can then attempt to find the number, as shown in figure 14.8.

The board game uses coloured pegs instead of numbers and awards black and white pegs instead of bulls and cows, respectively.

Write a program to play Cows and Bulls (using numbers).

This is quite a difficult task and falls into four main stages. The first stage is concerned with general initialisation and the generation of a random number (or rather of four random digits which together form the number). The remaining stages are repeated in a loop until the number is guessed and consist of obtaining and analysing the player's guess, checking for "bulls", and checking for "cows". Work out a plan before you start and remember not to count bulls (digits in the right place) as cows (digits in the wrong place) as well. If you have difficulty you will find a suitable structure plan in Experimental Hints.

Experiment 14.11

Modify the program you have just written to use coloured dots instead of numbers, as in the Mastermind board game.

```
Your guess: 1234      2 cows

Your guess: 5678      2 cows

Your guess: 9090      1 cow

Your guess: 2350

Your guess: 4150      1 bull    1 cow

Your guess: 4510      2 bulls

Your guess: 6970      2 cows

Your guess: 4619      3 bulls

Your guess: 4719      4 bulls

Another go?
```

Figure 14.8   A game of Cows and Bulls

Experimental Hints

14.3   The new line 510 causes the DIM statement at line 10 to be obeyed again, and this is forbidden. An array may only be dimensioned *once* in a program.

The only exception to this rule is that the statement

```
CLEAR
```

will erase all variables and arrays apart from the resident integer variables. In general this is not very useful, but in certain situations it can be valuable to be able to clear the memory (apart, possibly, from a few key integer values) and start again. In this particular experiment, for example, we could write

```
510 IF A$="Y" THEN
       CLEAR: GOTO 10
```

which would be perfectly acceptable.

14.4   To avoid wasting array space the following input sequence could be used:

```
10 DIM Name$(9)
20 FOR I%=0 TO 9: Name$=STRING$(" ",12): NEXT
30 String$=STRING$(" ",20)
40 PRINT "Please give names with a maximum of 12 letters"
50 FOR I%=0 TO 9
60    INPUT "Next name: " String$
70    IF LEN(String$)>12 THEN
          PRINT CHR$129;"Only 12 letters!": GOTO 60
80    Name$(I%)=String$
90    NEXT
   .
   .
   .
```

14.7   It is important, when carrying out comparative tests such as this, to ensure that you are comparing like with like. In this case we can ensure that the same set of random numbers is sorted with each method by first calling RND with a negative number to initialise the random number generator to a repeatable sequence (see chapter 8, section 8.3).

One method, therefore, would be to write two procedures (PROCbubble and PROCstraight) which use the appropriate method to sort N% numbers in an array called (say) Number%. The main program could then be along the following lines:

```
10 DIM Number%(1000)
20 REPEAT
30    INPUT "How many numbers",N%
40    IF N%>1000 THEN
          N%=1000
50    PROCsetup
```

```
 60    TIME=0: PROCbubble: B%=TIME
 70    PROCsetup
 80    TIME=0: PROCstraight: S%=TIME
 90    PRINT "Bubble sort took ";B%/100;" seconds for ";N%;" numbers"
100    PRINT "Straight selection sort took ";S%/100;" seconds"
110    PRINT: INPUT "Another test",A$
120    UNTIL LEFT$(A$,1)<>"Y"
130 END
140 DEF PROCsetup
150 X%=RND(-N%)
160 FOR I%=0 TO N%
170    Number%(I%)=RND
180    NEXT
190 ENDPROC
200 DEF PROCbubble
       .
       .
       .
```

14.10   A suitable structure plan is

> Repeat until a non-zero digit is generated
>> Generate first (random) digit
>
> Generate remaining digits
> Repeat until number is guessed
>> Input player's guess
>> Split guess into its four digits
>> Initialise count of "bulls" to zero
>> Repeat for I from 1 to 4
>>> If Ith digits are equal then
>>>> Add one to count of "bulls"
>>>> Modify both digits
>>
>> If number not yet guessed then
>>> Initialise count of "cows" to zero
>>> Repeat for I from 1 to 4
>>>> Repeat for J from 1 to 4
>>>>> If Ith guessed digit equals Jth computed digit then
>>>>>> Add one to count of "cows"
>>>>>> Modify both digits
>>> Print number of "cows" and "bulls"
>>> Reset computed digits
>> otherwise
>>> Print congratulations

Notice how the indented layout of this structure plan emphasises the structure of the program design.

One point that may need some comment concerns the statements in both "checking" loops which say "Modify both digits". It is important that when a digit has been accepted as a "bull" or a "cow" that it should not be counted again! The best way to do this is to alter both digits to values which could not possibly match; for example, the guessed digit could have ten added to it (thus making it lie in the range 10–19), while the computed digit could have twenty added. If the number is not guessed then the computed digits must be reset, either by means of a previously saved copy or by reversing the earlier transformation.

15

Saving your results

15.1 PROGRAM FILES AND DATA FILES

By now the concept of saving a program on a cassette tape (or on a disc) is a familiar one. When we type

```
SAVE "filename"
```

in direct mode, the Beeb's operating system sets in motion a train of events which will cause the current program to be recorded on tape (or disc) as a number of 256 byte blocks. If the program is being saved on tape then the filename will be displayed together with the number of the current block in hexadecimal; when the final block is written this will show the size of the program. If the program is being saved on disc then normally there will be no messages as the whole process only takes a second or two.

The information saved in this way constitutes a *file* which consists of one or more *blocks*, and this chapter will discuss other ways in which files may be written and read. Such files may contain either programs or data (or results) or both. However, we must first make a clear distinction between loadable program files and other files.

A *loadable program file* (or simply a program file) is a file that has been produced by the SAVE command (or the *SAVE command) and contains a Basic program in its internal form. In this form all Basic keywords are represented in a coded form as single bytes and various other aspects of the program such as line numbers are also stored in coded form. Such a file can be loaded into the computer by the LOAD or RUN command. (A loadable program file may also contain a machine code program, but that is another story!)

All other files can be loosely grouped together and defined as *data files*.

Data files will normally be stored on tape (or disc) in internal format (i.e. as stored in the computer's memory), but they can also be stored as blocks of ASCII coded characters which can, if required, be used to simulate keyboard input by using the *EXEC command which was discussed briefly in chapter 12; this latter use of files is discussed in more detail in section 15.4. The main use of data files, however, is to preserve information (e.g. stock lists, accounts, etc.) from one run of a program to the next. We shall discuss this important use of files in section 15.3 but first we must examine the various forms of storage media and their implications for data (and program) files.

15.2 TAPES, DISCS AND OTHER FILE STORAGE MEDIA

The purpose of a file storage medium is to preserve the information in a file for as long as the user wishes to keep it. It provides the *backing store* for the computer system. Unlike the (semi-conductor) memory which forms the main (run-time) storage medium of the computer, the backing store must, therefore, require no electrical power, or other outside energy source, to maintain its information. In practice, today, this implies some form of magnetic storage.

The simplest and cheapest form is the humble cassette tape. Unfortunately, since this was originally designed for domestic audio use it is also slow and relatively prone to errors.

A far more sophisticated and more expensive method is the use of magnetic discs (or *floppy discs*). These provide fast information transfer and a very low error rate and are in every way better than cassettes. Unfortunately the cost of the cheapest disc drive together with the modifications necessary to your computer to provide the Disc Filing System firmware (on a ROM "chip") almost doubles the price of the computer.

A compromise is to use a "floppy tape" system which uses a special type of micro-cassette recorder to provide many of the advantages of discs at a much lower price.

As well as their higher speed, automatic operation and increased reliability, discs (and floppy tapes) provide facilities for *random access* to files as well as the normal form of *sequential access* (i.e. starting at the beginning and going on to the end). However, such use of files is beyond the scope of this book and we shall therefore concentrate on cassette tape systems for the rest of this chapter. If you have some other system then what follows will apply equally to it, although the extra facilities available will have to be ascertained from the file system's own documentation.

15.3 CREATING AND USING DATA FILES IN YOUR PROGRAMS

The basic commands used to write and read files are variants of the PRINT and INPUT commands which are used to communicate with the keyboard and display screen. However, before we can use them we must tell the computer that we wish to do so, in order that it may carry out certain initialisation, set the tape running, etc. We do this with the OPENOUT function in a statement of the form

```
100 File=OPENOUT("filename")
```

or simply

```
100 File=OPENOUT "filename"
```

This instructs the Beeb's operating system to prepare to create a file called filename, and the computer will respond by switching on the cassette recorder's motor and displaying the familiar message

```
RECORD then RETURN
```

You should now position the cassette tape, set the recorder in recording mode and press

RETURN, just as when you are saving a program. As soon as you press RETURN the cassette motor will be switched off.

The OPENOUT function will return a *channel* or *file number* which will be used to identify the file in all subsequent statements. When using a cassette tape this number is somewhat irrelevant as it is not practicable to deal with two files at once. With discs or floppy tapes, however, several files may be in use at the same time on the same disc or tape and so the channel number is vital. The channel number is also used for cassette tapes so that the same statements can be used for all file systems.

In the earlier example the channel number was stored in the variable File, and information will then be written to the file by statements of the form

```
150 PRINT #File, list of items....
```

where the list of items to be "printed" takes the same form as in an ordinary PRINT statement, except that TABs are obviously redundant.

It is important to realise that the file will still be written in 256 byte blocks and that a single PRINT# statement will not necessarily cause anything to be recorded on the tape. The items to be output will actually be copied to a special 256 byte *buffer* area in the computer's memory and only when this is full will it be written to tape. During the running of the program the recorder will stop and start at intervals as the buffer gets filled.

When there is no more information to be written to the file it is *vital* that the operating system is informed so that it may output any characters remaining in the buffer and record a special mark on the tape to indicate the end of the file. This is achieved by the CLOSE# statement, which takes the form

```
999 CLOSE #File
```

Note that, because a data file is normally being produced by a program while it is doing something else, it would be confusing for the usual messages to be produced when the file was being recorded. Apart from the initial request to press Record, therefore, there will normally be no messages produced concerning the progress of the recording. In particular there will be no indication that the file has been closed. If it is important to know this then you should include a print statement to inform you of this fact, e.g.

```
770 CLOSE #File
780 PRINT "Data file closed - Press STOP"
```

The subsequent input of such a file is carried out by a very similar procedure.

First the file is opened using the OPENIN function:

```
150 File=OPENIN("filename")
```

or simply

```
150 File=OPENIN "filename"
```

This will switch on the cassette recorder but will *not* normally display the usual

"Searching" message. Once the start of the file has been found the first block will be read into a buffer and the motor switched off.

The file is read, as might be expected, by a statement of the form

```
210 INPUT #File, list of names
```

where the list of names follows the same form as for a normal INPUT statement. The data will be read from the buffer and the cassette motor switched on as and when necessary to read a further block from the tape. Once again, no messages will normally be displayed.

During input it is possible to detect whether the end of the file has been reached by use of a special function EOF# which returns the value TRUE if it has and FALSE otherwise. It can be used, therefore, in a sequence such as shown below:

```
10 File=OPENIN "Mydata"
20 REPEAT
30    INPUT #File,A$,B,C,D
40    PRINT A$,B,C,D
50    UNTIL EOF #File
60 CLOSE #File
```

Note that the file should still be closed by using CLOSE# as this enables the operating system to clear its tables. It is good programming practice to close input files when they are finished with, and may be essential if your program is likely to use any further files.

Experiment 15.1

Write a short program which inputs a number of sets of three co-ordinates (X,Y,Z). Decide for yourself how to determine the end of this data. Your program should write all this data to a file.

Write a second program to read the file and print the data on the screen in three columns like this:

X	Y	Z
1.5	2.7	0.3
2.25	1.9	-4.1
.	.	.
.	.	.
.	.	.

Think carefully about this problem before you start.

As you will be aware, the motor of your cassette recorder is normally switched on and off by the computer via the REMote socket on the recorder. There are, however, occasions when it would be useful to be able to switch the motor on and off without issuing any form of input/output statement. An example of this would be when it is necessary to position the tape before one of several identically named files before reading.

It is, of course, possible to position the tape once the program has initiated the reading, or to remove the REMote control jack plug and position it earlier. If the user has, as is usual, simply left the recorder in PLAY mode once it stops under remote control then in some circumstances it might start to read the wrong data before the user realises that it has started to do so. It is possible, therefore, to directly control the motor *without any input or output taking place* by use of the *MOTOR command.

The command

```
*MOTOR 1
```

switches the cassette motor on and the appropriate light on the keyboard will be illuminated. The command

```
*MOTOR 0
```

will switch it off again.

Note that these two commands are operating system commands (as are all commands that start with *) and must not be followed by any other characters on the same line, as everything following the asterisk will be passed to the operating system instead of being processed by the Basic Interpreter.

An example of the use of these commands might be as follows:

```
150 PRINT "Position tape and then RETURN"
160 *MOTOR 1
170 REPEAT UNTIL GET=&D
180 *MOTOR 0
```

Obviously the use of *MOTOR in this way implies that the user has some way of knowing where to find the required data file, i.e. by having noted the tape counter reading.

Experiment 15.2

In a golf tournament each player normally plays four rounds of 18 holes. The winner is the player with the lowest total number of strokes after all 72 holes. Each round takes one day and it is therefore necessary to keep a record of the daily and cumulative totals.

Write a program to keep the scores at a golf tournament in which a maximum of 30 golfers are taking part.

During the first round the program should accept player's names and scores and build up a table of scores. When all the scores are in, it should print an ordered list (i.e. the leading player first, etc.) and store the details in a file.

During the remaining rounds the details of this file will be updated to show the score in each round and the total to date. After each round the list should be printed in the current order.

Run this program with your own data.

(*Hint:* Think about this carefully and remember the advantages of modular, step-by-step, design.)

Experiment 15.3

A slight improvement to the above golfing program would be to ensure that players with the same score were grouped together in alphabetic order, e.g.

```
279   Ballesteros     (71, 69, 68, 71)

280   Jacklin         (70, 68, 72, 70)

      Lyle            (73, 69, 69, 69)

      Watson          (68, 70, 73, 69)

282   Faldo           (73, 69, 70, 70)

      Langer          (71, 70, 70, 71)
         .

         .

         .
```

(If you have already done this – well done!)

15.4   USING FILES TO SIMULATE THE KEYBOARD

As we have already mentioned, PRINT# creates a file in internal format. It is, however, also possible to create files of ASCII-coded characters which can, if required, be used to simulate keyboard input. The most common use of this facility is to incorporate part of one program in another without the necessity of retyping it. The easiest way of creating such a file is by use of the *SPOOL command, which is used as described below.

The command

```
*SPOOL "textfile"
```

instructs the Beeb's operating system that henceforth everything that is output to the screen is to be also sent to a file called *textfile*. Thus, for example, the statements

```
*SPOOL "SortFile"
LIST 500,670
```

will cause lines 500–670 of the current program to be sent to the file SortFile.

The command

```
*SPOOL
```

without any file name will close the file and return the computer to its normal mode of operation.

This file can then be used to simulate keyboard input by the command

```
*EXEC "SortFile"
```

which will read the contents of SortFile exactly as though they had been typed at the keyboard. If, as in the above example, the file contains numbered lines of Basic then these lines will therefore be added to any program currently resident in the computer, replacing any similarly numbered lines.

Experiment 15.4

Write a short program which uses a procedure to sort the contents of an array into alphabetic order. Test this program to ensure that it works.

Now use *SPOOL to save the procedure in a file called, for example, AlphaSort.

Finally delete the original program and write a program which reads a set of names and telephone numbers, sorts them into alphabetic order using the sort procedure stored in the file AlphaSort, and prints a well laid-out list of names and numbers.

(*Hint:* Think about line numbers before you *SPOOL the procedure.)

Although the primary use of *SPOOL and *EXEC is to merge programs in the way discussed above, they can also be used for other purposes and, indeed, can even be used in a program. For example the following program will display the numbers from 0 to 100 while simultaneously creating a file containing these numbers:

```
10 *SPOOL "Numbers"
20 FOR I=0 TO 100
30    PRINT I
40    NEXT
50 *SPOOL
```

This file could then be input by the following:

```
10 DIM Num(100)
20 *EXEC "Numbers"
30 FOR I=0 TO 100
40    INPUT Num(I)
50    NEXT
60 FOR I=0 TO 100
70    PRINT Num(I)
80    NEXT
```

When this program is run, the first loop (30–50) will input its data from the file identified in the *EXEC command on line 20. It will therefore read the numbers sent to the file by the first program. *Note* that because it is simulating the keyboard these numbers will also be displayed as they are input.

Experiment 15.5

Type and run the two programs listed above to create and then input a file of numbers.
   Now alter line 30 to read

```
30 FOR I=0 TO 50
```

and line 60 similarly. What do you expect to happen when you run this?
   Run the modified program and see if you were right.

15.5   ANOTHER WAY OF WRITING AND READING FILES

As well as using *SPOOL to create an ASCII-coded file it is possible to do so by use of the BPUT# statement, which takes the form

```
BPUT #channel,byte
```

where byte is a number in the range 0–255. (If byte is greater than 255 then the value of byte MOD 256 will be used.)
   The file must already have been opened by OPENOUT and the statement will then cause the single ASCII code stored in byte to be written to the file – or rather to be sent to the output buffer for subsequent writing.
   A file written using BPUT# is in a form suitable for subsequent input using *EXEC, or it may be input one byte at a time by use of BGET#, which is a function used in statements such as

```
50 next=BGET#(channel)
```

or simply

```
50 next=BGET #channel
```

The use of BGET# and BPUT# is only necessary in specialised situations and so will not be discussed further in this book. An example of their use is in the utility program SHAPES (see chapter 12 and Appendix C.4) which uses BPUT# to create a file containing lines 32735 to 32766 of itself. These lines contain the 32 VDU statements used to specify the user-defined characters 224–255. The file so produced can be incorporated into another program by use of *EXEC or it can be loaded by the SHAPES program using BGET# to replace part of itself. PROCsave (lines 1640–1850) writes the file and PROCsaved (lines 340–490) reads it back. Notice that PROCsave starts by sending the two characters &A followed by &D to the file, and terminates each line in the same way. These are the codes for LF CR (line feed, carriage return) and are necessary to cause *EXEC to perform correctly.

Important Note: SHAPES modifies its own code both by reading from a file (in PROCsaved) and during character definition. This is very dangerous and should normally *never* be attempted!

Experiment 15.6

The main part of Castle may take a considerable time to play (especially at the higher skill levels). Modify the program so that you can save the current stage of the game in a file and then re-activate it later.

Castle has got very little spare space and so it will be necessary to deal with the re-activation largely in one of the earlier programs. The variable information that must be saved is shown in figure 15.1, and in addition the array Item$ contains the names of the items to be found. It will be necessary to ensure that the user-defined characters are all set up.

If you find that you are short of space during this experiment use the program compacter described in Appendix C.2 to reduce the program's size.

Experimental Hints

15.1   A common mistake is to write the file with a statement such as

```
PRINT #File,X,Y,Z
```

This will write the numbers to the file in the normal output format, i.e. with a number of spaces between them. When the file is being read by a statement of the form

```
INPUT #File,X,Y,Z
```

however, there are no separators between the numbers (spaces don't count!) and the

Name	Type	Purpose
Door%	Array (7,9)	Plan of the castle and tunnel guardians
Item%	Array (29)	Details of items in the castle
Item$	Array (15)	Names of items in the castle (permanent)
C	Variable	Player's courage
S	Variable	Player's strength
M	Variable	Player's magic
W	Variable	Player's weapon strength
A%-H% ⎫ ⎬ M%-Z% ⎭	Resident Integer Variables	See figure 8.3

Figure 15.1   List of variables and arrays to be saved in Castle

file will not be read correctly. The solution is to either write each number to a separate "line", or to include separators in the file. Thus both of the following statements would produce a readable file:

```
PRINT #File,X'Y'Z

PRINT #File,X;",";Y;",";Z
```

15.2   A suitable structure plan is as follows:

> Input number of round
> If this is the first round then
>   Initialise player and score arrays
> otherwise
>   Read players and scores from file
> Repeat until there are no more players
>   Input player's name and score for this round
>   If this is the first round then
>   Insert player's name and score in appropriate arrays
>   otherwise
>   Find this player's name
>   Store this score with his previous scores
>   Calculate and store player's total score to date
> Sort arrays into order of total score to date
> If this is not the last round then
>   Write the arrays to file
> Print ordered list of scores to date

Do not try to write the whole program at once. One approach would be to develop it in stages, as described below:

1. Write program to input data and list it.
2. Add a sorting procedure to sort data before printing.
3. Add a section to write data to a file.
4. Add a section to read data from a file.
5. Complete the whole program.

15.4   Since you will be including your sorting procedure in a second program, it is important to use large line numbers when writing the procedure in order to avoid any possible clashes when loading it with *EXEC. You can always RENUMBER the program once it is all together.

15.5   The altered program only inputs 51 numbers; however, the *EXEC command causes the *whole* file to be treated as keyboard input. When the program has finished, therefore, the remaining items (i.e. the numbers 51 to 100) will be waiting in the input buffer, and will be input as though they had been typed at the keyboard. In this case this will have the effect of deleting any lines with these line numbers! List the program and you will find that lines 60 to 80 are no longer there!

16

More advanced sound

16.1 THE SOUND STATEMENT REVISITED

In chapter 3 we defined the SOUND statement as taking the form

SOUND c,a,p,d

where the four numbers after the keyword SOUND define the sound channel, the amplitude of the sound (or the envelope to be used), the pitch of the note (or the type of sound effect) and the duration of the note. Thus

SOUND 1,-15,100,40

will sound a high C (one octave above middle C) on channel 1 at maximum volume for two seconds (i.e. 40 twentieths of a second). Similarly

SOUND 0,-10,4,10

will produce a half-second burst of high frequency "white noise" at medium volume (on channel 0).

We can now extend this definition to provide a number of other useful effects.

The fourth parameter (d) defines the duration of the note in units of one-twentieth of a second and must lie in the range -1 to 255. There are, however, two special cases.

If d=-1 (or d=255) then the duration of the note is considered to be infinite and it will continue until stopped by some form of interruption such as the pressing of ESCape or a special form of SOUND statement described below.

If d=0 then the duration of the note is not zero but is actually 0.005 seconds in duration (one two-hundredth of a second). This is so short that it is difficult to hear, but the following experiment will convince you that it really is there!

Experiment 16.1

Type in the following program and run it:

```
 10 PROCnext: SOUND 1,-15,100,0
 20 PROCnext: SOUND 1,-15,100,0: SOUND 1,-15,100,0
 30 PROCnext: SOUND 1,-15,100,0: SOUND 1,-15,100,0
 40 SOUND 1,-15,100,0: SOUND 1,-15,100,0
 50 PROCnext
 60 FOR I=1 TO 100
 70   SOUND 1,-15,100,0: NEXT
 80 END
 90 DEF PROCnext
100 PRINT "Press RETURN for next sound"
110 A%=GET
120 ENDPROC
```

This will sound successive notes of duration 0 (i.e. 0.005 seconds), 2*0 (i.e. 0.01 seconds) and 4*0 (i.e. 0.02 seconds), followed by a loop producing 100 "zero duration" notes.

The third parameter (p) specifies either the pitch of the note (in the range 0–255) or the type of sound (in the range 0–7) produced on channel 0. The definition given in chapter 3 is complete for this parameter. However, it should be emphasised that there are a number of peculiarities in the behaviour of the Beeb's sound producing circuits. For example the note produced for a pitch of 92 is lower than that produced for 91, and the note for 96 is lower than 95! At the top end of the range extremely peculiar things happen and, for example, the pitch values for 239, 242 and 243 all give the same note, while 238, 240 and 241 all give a lower note (the same one)! As long as the values given in figure 3.1 are used there will be no real problems, but intermediate values will not necessarily give the correct intermediate notes! These errors are described in considerable detail in the article by B. M. Landsberg referred to in chapter 3 ("Extending the BBC's Sound Command – What the Manual Doesn't Tell You", *Electronics & Computing*, February 1983).

Experiment 16.2

Write a program to investigate the notes produced for pitches in the range 84–104 and the range 200–255.

Experiment 16.3

Write a program to play the chromatic scale over an interval of several octaves (i.e. each note is one semitone higher than the preceding one – or has a pitch value 4 more). This will play notes whose pitches have the values 4*N over some range of N, e.g. 52, 56, 60, 64, . . .

Now try it for pitches 4*N+1 (e.g. 53, 57, 61, 65, . . .) which corresponds to the values given in the User Guide, 4*N+2 (e.g. 54, 58, 62, 66, . . .) and 4*N+3 (e.g. 55, 59, 63, 67, . . .).

Now do you see why 4*N is best?

The second parameter (a) either specifies the sound envelope to be used (in the range 1–4) or the amplitude (volume) of the note (in the range −15 to 0). In the latter case an amplitude of −15 represents the maximum volume and −1 the minimum, while 0 indicates total silence. This too is exactly as defined in chapter 3.

Finally we come to the first parameter (c). Up to now we have considered this to represent the channel number in the range 0-3; however, it is actually far more complex than this. The first parameter should really be thought of as a hexadecimal number

&hsfc

where each of the four "digits" h, s, f and c controls some aspect of the sound generation.

The last, and least significant, "digit" (c) defines the channel number (in the range 0–3), and thus if the other "digits" are all zero has the same effect as before,

i.e.   SOUND &0002,−10,96,20

is the same as

SOUND 2,−10,96,20

since the hexadecimal number &0002 clearly has the value 2 (0*4096 + 0*256 + 0*16 + 2).

The third "digit" (f) is a *flush control indicator* and may take the value 0 or 1. Normally, as we have seen, a SOUND command causes a note to be placed in a queue for the specified channel and only to be sounded when it reaches the head of the queue. However, if the flush control indicator is set to 1 then the appropriate queue is flushed (i.e. emptied) and any note being played on that queue stopped; the new note is therefore played at once.

Experiment 16.4

Type in the following program which will play a two-octave chromatic scale (i.e. rising in semitone intervals):

```
10 FOR I=52 TO 148 STEP 4
20    SOUND 1,-15,I,4
30    NEXT
```

Run the program.

Now alter line 20 to read

```
20 SOUND 17,-15,I,4
```

Note that 17 is the same as &11 (=0*4096 + 0*256 + 1*16 + 1)

Run this program.

As you can hear, this new program gives a very rapid "glissando" through the two octaves with each successive note cutting off its predecessor almost immediately it has started. However, the last note continues for its full half second.

We can shorten this last note by adding an extra line:

```
40 SOUND 17,0,0,0
```

which will send a silent note of "zero" duration to channel 1, *flushing the queue at the same time*, thus stopping the last (audible) note.

Now alter line 10 to read

```
10 FOR I=0 TO 255 STEP 4
```

and run the program again to produce a glissando from the bottom of the tonal range to the top. As you can hear, some parts are much better than others!

The second hexadecimal "digit" (s) is a *synchronisation control indicator* and may take a value in the range 0–3. It is used to synchronise notes on different channels so that accurate chords, or other effects, may be obtained. The value of s indicates the number of other notes which are to be synchronised with this one.

If s is zero then no notice is taken of the other channels, and the note is sounded as soon as it reaches the head of its queue (or is "flushed" to the head of the queue). This is the normal situation which we have been using in our programs up to now.

If s is 1, 2 or 3 however, the note is not played when it reaches the head of its queue until s similarly synchronised notes reach the heads of their queues. Thus a value of 1 causes two channels to be synchronised, a value of 2 causes three channels to be synchronised and a value of 3 causes all four channels to be synchronised.

Experiment 16.5

Type the following statements

```
SOUND 1,-15,52,40
SOUND 2,-10,68,40
SOUND 3,-15,80,40
```

Unless you are an extremely fast typist the three notes (C, E, G) will sound one after the other.

Now type

```
SOUND &201,-15,52,40
SOUND &202,-15,68,40
SOUND &203,-15,80,40
```

This time nothing will happen when the first and second SOUND commands are typed.

When the third one is typed, however, the synchronisation requirements are satisfied and all three notes are sounded *together*.

Now type

```
SOUND &301,-15,52,40
SOUND &302,-15,68,40
SOUND &303,-15,80,40
SOUND &201,-15,60,40
SOUND &202,-15,76,40
SOUND &203,-15,88,40
```

This time nothing happens because the first three lines (for channels 1, 2 and 3) require four-channel synchronisation. The next three lines put a second note into each queue – these will be played together as a chord when they all reach the head of their queues.

Finally type

```
SOUND &300,0,0,0
```

This will produce a silent "noise" of 0.005 seconds duration! However, it will also satisfy the synchronisation requirements and act as a "trigger" for the first of the two synchronised chords. The second synchronised chord will then be sounded as soon as the first one is completed.

The first hexadecimal "digit" (h) is a *continuation control indicator* and is only of relevance in connection with envelopes; it will be discussed in the next section. One point that should, however, be mentioned here is that if the continuation control indicator is non-zero then the amplitude pitch and parameters are ignored; such a note is therefore a *dummy note* which produces no sound.

16.2 THE ENVELOPE STATEMENT

In chapter 3 we indicated that the ENVELOPE statement could be used to produce a dramatic range of different effects from a single SOUND command. We can now begin to investigate how we can control these effects, but before we do that we need to establish what we mean by a sound envelope.

In fact, there are two, quite distinct, types of sound envelope – amplitude and frequency – and we shall consider each of them separately before examining how the ENVELOPE statement allows us to define both types.

An *amplitude envelope* is a measure of the way in which the amplitude, or *loudness*, of a sound varies with time. For example figure 16.1 shows a (simplified) graph of the loudness of the sound of an express train as it approaches a station, passes through, and disappears on its way.

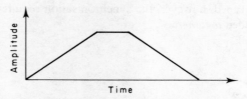

Figure 16.1   Amplitude envelope for a train

This is an extreme example, and of more relevance to us is, perhaps, the amplitude envelope of a musical instrument. Here we find a marked difference between, for example, a percussive instrument such as a piano or guitar and a wind instrument such as an oboe or an organ (see figures 16.2 and 16.3).

A common method for simplifying and idealising such envelopes is known as the ADSR envelope. In this the sound is considered to have four phases – Attack, Decay, Sustain and Release – as shown in figure 16.4.

The Attack phase is the period during which the sound (normally) builds up to its maximum loudness. In a percussive instrument this is a very rapid growth period, in a wind instrument it is much more gradual.

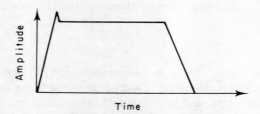

Figure 16.2   Amplitude envelope for a piano

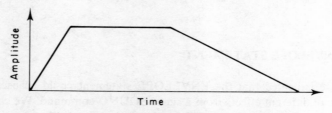

Figure 16.3   Amplitude envelope for an organ

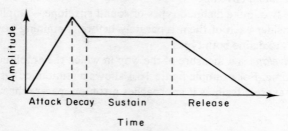

Figure 16.4   A typical ADSR envelope

This is followed by the Decay phase during which the volume drops (slightly) to its required loudness.

The third phase is the Sustain phase, during which the loudness usually remains constant.

Finally there is the Release phase when the player has stopped playing the note and the loudness fades to zero.

The ENVELOPE statement allows you to define your own ADSR amplitude envelope, and thus to dramatically alter the type of sound produced.

A *frequency envelope* on the other hand, is not concerned with the loudness of a sound but with its *pitch* or frequency. Thus figure 16.5 shows the frequency envelope for the same train whose amplitude envelope was illustrated in figure 16.1, and shows the well-known Doppler effect which causes a drop in frequency as the train passes.

Another example of a frequency envelope is a police siren, as illustrated in figure 16.6.

The ENVELOPE statement allows us to define both of these types of frequency (or pitch) envelopes, and a wide range of others as well.

The statement itself takes the following form

```
ENVELOPE n,t,pi1,pi2,pi3,pn1,pn2,pn3,aa,ad,as,ar,ala,ald
```

and is clearly the most complicated statement that we have met so far (or, indeed, will meet at any time). It actually consists of three main parts.

The first two parameters (n and t) define the envelope number and the overall timing to be used. The next six parameters define the pitch envelope, and the last six define the amplitude envelope. We shall examine each group in turn.

The envelope number (n) lies in the range 1–4 and is used to ensure that the correct envelope is used with a SOUND statement which has its second parameter (a) set to a value in the range 1–4.

The second parameter (t) in the ENVELOPE statement specifies the length of each step in hundredths of a second. We shall return to the full meaning of this step length when we

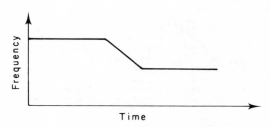

Figure 16.5   Frequency envelope for a train showing the Doppler effect

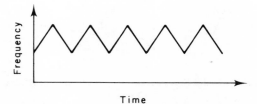

Figure 16.6   Frequency envelope for a police siren

discuss the pitch and amplitude envelopes. It will usually be 1, but can be any value in the range 0–127. Values in the range 128–255 are also permitted but are considered to be the same as 0–127 except that the pitch envelope will not auto-repeat; we shall discuss this feature later in this section.

We now come to the six parameters which define the *pitch envelope*. These define an envelope which consists of three sections, each of which is defined by two parameters (pi1 and pn1, etc.), as shown in figure 16.7.

The pitch envelope starts at the *base pitch* specified in the SOUND statement, and alters in steps of pi1 for pn1 steps, where each step lasts for a time specified by the parameter t. It then alters in steps of pi2 for pn2 steps, and in steps of pi3 for pn3 steps. The values of the three increments (pi1, pi2, pi3) may take any value in the range −128 to +127, while the three parameters giving the number of steps per section (pn1, pn2, pn3) may take values in the range 0–255.

This completes one cycle of the pitch envelope and normally the process will then be repeated (with an abrupt jump back to the base pitch if necessary). This auto-repeat of the pitch envelope will continue as long as the note is sounding (see figure 16.8).

However, if the value of t is greater than 127 then the auto-repeat does not take place and the pitch will remain at the value it had at the end of the cycle (which is not necessarily the base frequency, see figure 16.9). In this case the length of each step is t−128.

In general it is difficult to work out exactly how a pitch envelope will sound, especially as the irregular behaviour of the sound generator can significantly effect the end result. The final section of this chapter describes a utility program which will greatly simplify the design of envelopes.

The *amplitude envelope* is easier to visualise and to use as it corresponds exactly to the ADSR envelope described earlier.

The amplitude starts at zero and rises at the rate of aa per step (t) until it reaches the level ala. It then decays at the rate of ad per step until it reaches a level of ada. Both aa

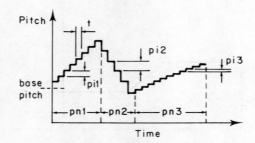

Figure 16.7   The pitch envelope

Figure 16.8   An auto-repeating pitch envelope

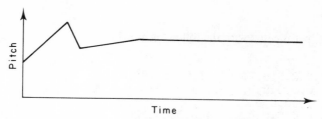

Figure 16.9 A non-repeating pitch envelope

and ad may lie in the range −127 to +127 (although a negative value for aa is not particularly useful!), while the two levels (ala, ada) must lie in the range 0 to 126.

Note that the (current) sound generator only has 16 sound levels (i.e. 0 to −15 in the SOUND statement). The greater range of values in the ENVELOPE definition does not, therefore, give a greater range of sound levels but simply operates by using (sound) level 0 for (envelope) levels 0 to 7, (sound) level −1 for (envelope) levels 8 to 15, etc. The reason why the ENVELOPE statement uses this wider range of amplitude values is to allow for a (possible) future sound chip with greater control over the amplitude of the sounds produced.

The envelope then enters the sustain phase which lasts until the duration of the sound (d) specified in the SOUND statement has elapsed. During the sustain phase the amplitude changes at the rate as per time step.

If there is another note waiting to be played on the same channel then the current note will be terminated at the end of the sustain phase; however, if there is no note waiting then the release phase of the envelope is entered. During this phase the amplitude will decay at the rate ar per step until a zero amplitude is reached or until a new note on the same channel is ready to be played.

Both as and ar may take values in the range −127 to 0, and you should notice, in particular, that a value of zero for ar will cause the note to continue indefinitely (in the absence of any further notes).

Figure 16.10 shows the structure of the amplitude envelope.

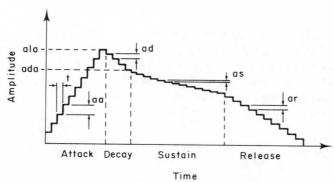

Figure 16.10 The amplitude envelope

Experiment 16.6

In chapter 3 we experimented with the following envelopes:

```
ENVELOPE 1,10,0,0,0,0,0,0,3,-1,0,-3,126,76
ENVELOPE 2,25,0,0,0,0,0,0,10,-4,-1,-10,126,90
ENVELOPE 3,3,0,0,0,0,0,0,1,-30,0,-5,126,66
ENVELOPE 4,10,0,0,0,0,0,0,1,4,0,0,50,126
```

```
ENVELOPE 1,25,4,-4,4,12,24,12,126,0,0,0,126,126
ENVELOPE 2,1,1,-1,1,1,2,1,126,0,0,0,126,126
ENVELOPE 3,50,4,-8,4,1,1,1,14,-50,0,-4,126,76
ENVELOPE 4,1,3,-6,3,1,1,1,1,0,0,-1,126,126
```

Try to draw a sketch of both amplitude and (for the last four) pitch envelopes. Then try them out with SOUND statements of the form

```
SOUND 1,1,100,250
```

Do the effects match your drawings?
   What would you expect the following statements to produce?

```
ENVELOPE 1,5,10,-15,10,5,5,10,1,-1,-1,0,126,110
SOUND 1,1,100,255
```

Type them in and see if you were right.
   Now, *without doing anything else first*, type the following

```
SOUND 0,-15,3,-1
```

Does the result surprise you? Do you understand what has happened? (See Experimental Hints if you don't understand.)

We have seen that, in general, the release phase of a sound envelope is terminated by the presence in the queue for the same channel of a note ready to be played. However, in some circumstances we may wish the release phase to be completed before the next note is played, instead of the first note being abruptly cut off. We can arrange for this to happen by use of a dummy note with its *continuation control indicator* set.
   In the last section we said that a SOUND statement of the form

```
SOUND &1sfc,a,p,d
```

is treated as a special *dummy note*, and that the values of a and p are ignored. However, such a note does not terminate the release phase of the currently playing note (if any). The values of s, f and c are interpreted as usual, although there is little point in having non-zero values for s or f.

Experiment 16.7

Type the following commands

```
ENVELOPE 1,10,0,0,0,0,0,0,126,0,0,-1,126,126
SOUND 1,1,52,50
SOUND 1,1,100,50
```

The envelope defined will only die away very slowly, but the second SOUND statement will truncate the release phase abruptly.
  Now type

```
SOUND 1,1,52,50
SOUND &1001,0,0,250
SOUND 1,1,100,50
```

Notice that, once defined, the envelope will remain defined and so an ENVELOPE command is not required this time. However, because of the extra (dummy) statement the release phase of the first SOUND command is allowed to continue to completion before the second note is played.

16.3 NOISE ENVELOPES

The above discussion of envelopes has implied that they are for use only with the music channels (1–3); however they can also be used with the noise channel 0.
  There are two distinct cases here, depending upon whether the SOUND command for channel 0 refers directly to an envelope, or whether it refers to a note on channel 1 which is using an envelope. We shall consider the direct use of envelopes first:

```
SOUND 0,n,p,d
```

The amplitude envelope operates in exactly the same way for channel 0 as for channels 1–3 and so, for example, the statements

```
ENVELOPE 1,4,0,0,0,0,0,0,1,0,0,-1,126,126
SOUND 0,1,5,100
```

will cause a medium frequency "white noise" to gradually grow in volume over a period of about 5 seconds and then die away over another 5 seconds.

A pitch envelope is, however, of less use since there is no regular progression as the value of p changes. Thus an envelope such as

```
ENVELOPE 1,25,2,-1,3,3,6,3,126,0,0,-126,126,126
```

when used with, for example,

```
SOUND 0,1,0,240
```

will produce sounds as follows

$\frac{1}{4}$ second low frequency "buzzing" (p=2)
$\frac{1}{4}$ second high frequency white noise (p=4)
$\frac{1}{4}$ second low frequency white noise (p=6)
$\frac{1}{4}$ second medium frequency white noise (p=5)
$\frac{1}{4}$ second high frequency white noise (p=4)
$\frac{1}{4}$ second buzzing related to channel 1 pitch (p=3) – or "clicking"
$\frac{1}{4}$ second low frequency buzzing (p=2)
$\frac{1}{4}$ second medium frequency buzzing (p=1)
$\frac{1}{4}$ second high frequency buzzing (p=0)
$\frac{1}{4}$ second white noise related to channel 1 pitch (p=3) – or "clicking"
$\frac{1}{4}$ second low frequency white noise (p=6)
$\frac{1}{4}$ second medium frequency buzzing (p=9 i.e. p=1)

which will sound most peculiar! (If you don't believe us, try it and see!) The whole sequence lasts for three seconds and will, therefore, be repeated four times.

Note that when the next step in the pitch envelope would take the value greater than 7 or less than 0 then it simply "loops round", i.e. 8 is the same as 0 and −1 is the same as 7.

One way of varying the pitch (or frequency) of the noise channel in a predictable way is to use a value for p of 3 (or 7), which relates the pitch of the noise channel to the pitch of the note on channel 1. In experiment 16.7 we did this after the amplitude on channel 1 had decayed to zero, although the pitch envelope was still auto-repeating, and thus affecting the pitch of the "buzzing" produced by the subsequent SOUND statement on channel 0.

We shall investigate this further in the next section.

16.4   AN EASY WAY OF DEFINING ENVELOPES

The extraordinarily wide range of effects that can be obtained with the SOUND and ENVELOPE statements can only be fully appreciated by experiment. To enable such experiments to be carried out easily and usefully in a controlled manner a special utility program is provided in Appendix C.3.

This program allows you to quickly alter the various parameters and to display a graph of both the pitch and amplitude envelopes. It displays an ENVELOPE statement for envelope 1 and SOUND statements for both channels 1 and 0.

When you run the program it will first ask what time period you wish to be displayed – any period between 1 and 20 seconds may be chosen. After giving you some instructions (which are repeated here) it draws axes for time (horizontal) and pitch/amplitude (vertical).

An initial envelope which simulates a piano is set up – this appears to best effect on the (default) time-scale of 2 seconds. You may then alter any of the parameters, redraw the envelopes, or sound the notes on channel 1, channel 0, or on both together.

Pressing "E" allows you to alter the envelope parameters, and pressing the cursor control keys (← or →) will move the cursor to the next parameter. An attempt to type an out-of-range value will result in a "raspberry" from the computer and the value will be set to zero.

Pressing "S" allows you to alter the sound channel (1) in a similar way, while "N" selects the noise channel (0) for alteration. Only one of these statements is allowed to refer to the envelope.

Pressing "D" draws both pitch and amplitude envelopes. If the sound channel refers to the envelope then both envelopes are drawn. Normally the pitch envelope will only be drawn for as long as the amplitude envelope has a non-zero value. However, if the noise channel has a non-zero amplitude then the pitch envelope will be drawn for the full duration of that (noise) sound (cf. experiment 16.6).

If the noise channel refers to the envelope then the pitch envelope is not drawn, for the reasons explained in the previous section.

Pressing the space bar will sound both channels. If, for example, only channel 1 is required then the amplitude of the SOUND statement for channel 0 should be set to zero (and vice-versa).

Pressing "Q" will stop any sounds that are currently being made. This is particularly important when a long or infinite sound has been produced.

Pressing "X" will terminate the program.

Pressing ESCape or BREAK will simply start the program again.

Experiment 16.8

If you have not obtained the ENVELOPE program on a tape, type it in and SAVE it.

Use the ENVELOPE program to experiment with various types of envelopes. Here are some interesting ones to try out – see what you can develop for yourself:

```
ENVELOPE 1,1,1,-10,8,200,20,32,3,0,0,-1,126,126
SOUND 1,1,150,250

ENVELOPE 1,50,8,-8,8,6,12,6,126,0,0,-1,126,126
SOUND 1,1,100,200

ENVELOPE 1,1,8,-8,8,6,12,6,126,0,0,-1,126,126
SOUND 1,1,100,200

ENVELOPE 1,1,0,0,0,0,0,0,126,-10,0,-2,126,50
SOUND 0,1,4,2

ENVELOPE 1,1,-5,0,0,50,1,1,126,0,0,-126,126,0
SOUND 1,1,255,10
SOUND 0,-15,7,10

ENVELOPE 1,30,8,4,8,80,90,80,1,-1,-1,-1,126,125
SOUND 0,1,2,-1
```

Experiment 16.9

The opening music of FINALTEST uses an envelope (see line 980) to produce a flute-like sound. Experiment with the ENVELOPE program to produce envelopes so that PROCtune can sound like other instruments, e.g. piano, organ, accordion, xylophone, etc.

Experimental Hints

16.6 The last SOUND statement for channel 1 has a duration of 255, which means "for ever". The associated envelope decays the amplitude to zero, but the (silent) pitch envelope is still auto-repeating. The statement

```
SOUND 0,-15,3,-1
```

also creates an infinitely long sound, but one whose pitch is related to the pitch on channel 1. Even though the earlier sound appears to have ended, therefore, it controls the frequency of the buzzing produced on channel 0.

ESCape will be necessary to end the sounds (or further notes on both channels 0 and 1).

Some other useful features of BBC Basic

17.1 MORE CONTROL OF TEXT LAYOUT

We have seen how the use of TAB and various separators (such as ; , and ') can enable you to have considerable control over the layout of your results. However, there are still two more aspects of the layout that we can alter if we wish.

The first of these relates to the length of each line. By default, there is no maximum line length and when PRINTing or LISTing reaches the physical end of a line (i.e. the right-hand edge of the screen or the printer paper) the output will simply continue on the next line. However, it is possible to define the required line length by the statement

```
WIDTH n
```

which specifies that the *maximum* line length is n characters. After n characters have been output on a line the Beeb automatically outputs a new line (i.e. Line Feed, Carriage Return) before it continues outputting.

This is not a particularly useful command when the results are only being sent to the display, but it can be very useful when listing to a printer which might otherwise produce wider listings than are required.

The statement

```
WIDTH 0
```

cancels the insertion of new line characters and returns to the "infinite line length" which is the normal default.

Note that a WIDTH statements affects *all* subsequent text output to the screen or printer; this includes PRINTed output, program LISTings and even mode 7 (teletext) graphics.

The other aspect of printing over which we have, so far, had no control is the printing of numbers, which have always been printed in a "sensible" way, but one which we have been unable to influence.

The format in which numbers are printed is controlled by a special resident integer variable — @%. Like all integer variables, @% occupies four bytes of memory, and each individual byte of @% has a particular significance. We can write a four byte integer as &ddddddd, where each pair of "digits" represents a hexadecimal number in the range &00–&FF (i.e. 0-256 in decimal notation).

The special variable @% can be defined as the hexadecimal number

&ssffddww

where the four pairs of "digits" have the following effect.

The first pair (ss) is used by the function STR$. If ss has the value 01 then STR$ will use the format defined by the rest of @% when converting numbers to strings. If ss is zero then STR$ will ignore the rest of @% and use format G9 (see below).

The second (ff) and third (dd) pairs select the format in which numbers are to be printed. The basic format is determined by ff and can be a General format (ff=00), an Exponent format (ff=01), or a Fixed format (ff=02). The way in which each of these formats works is dependent also upon the number of digits to be printed (dd).

In *General format* (G) the value of dd must lie in the range 1–9 and specifies the maximum number of digits that can be printed in this format. In G format any integers or whole numbers are printed as integers, while any numbers in the range 0.1 to 0.999999999 are printed as 0.1, etc. Thus in G8 format (i.e. 8 digits) the statement

PRINT 100'100.1'0.1'.25'.888888888'.999999999

will cause the following to be printed

```
       100
     100.1
       0.1
      0.25
0.88888889
         1
```

Notice, in particular, the last two lines. The value 0.888888888 would require *ten* digits including the initial zero, and so the final digit is rounded (up) to a nine. A similar situation occurs with 0.999999999, except that in this case rounding up leads to the value 1.00000000, which is printed as an integer.

If a number is less than 0.1 then it is printed in *exponent format* as a number (greater than or equal to 1 and less than 10), followed by the letter E and the number of times by which the first number must be divided by 10 to give the required result; this last number is expressed as a negative number. Thus

PRINT 0.01'0.0125'.0000123456

will lead to the following result:

```
      1E-2
   1.25E-2
1.23456E-5
```

(The number before the letter E is called the *mantissa* and the number after it is called the *exponent*.)

If a number is too large to be printed in normal G format then it too will be printed in exponent format, except that in this case the exponent is positive and indicates the number of times the mantissa is to be *multiplied* by 10. Thus, for example, in G4 format the statement

```
PRINT 1234'12345'123456789
```

will lead to

```
    1234
1.235E4
1.235E8
```

Note that the total number of digits *before* the E is the same as the value given by the dd "digits" in @%. The last two numbers have thus been rounded so as to have mantissas of 1.235.

If ff has the value 01 then *Exponent format* (E) is used for all numbers. This is essentially the same as used by the G format for large and small numbers except that the mantissa will always be expressed as a real number (greater than or equal to 1 and less than 10). The value of dd specifies the number of digits in the mantissa and, as with G formats, must lie in the range 1–9. Thus in E4 format the statement

```
PRINT 10000'12345'123.456789'.123456789
```

will lead to

```
1.000E4
1.235E4
1.235E2
1.235E-1
```

The third format type is *Fixed format* (F), which is used to print numbers with a fixed number of decimal places, as specified by the value of dd – which must lie in the range 0–9. In this format all the decimal points will be aligned vertically, which can be very useful for accounting programs and also for tables and other regularly laid out columns of results. In F2 format, therefore, the statement

```
PRINT 10000'12345'123.456789'.123456789
```

will lead to the following result:

```
10000.00
12345.00
  123.46
    0.12
```

As usual, the number is rounded (if necessary) to fit the available space. If it would require more than 10 digits, including any trailing zeros after the decimal point, then G format is used instead. Thus if the field width is ten characters (the default value) and the format is F7 then the statement

```
PRINT 1.23456789'1234.56789'123456.789'12345678900
```

will be printed as

```
   1.23457          (rounded in F format)
1234.56789
123456.789          (G format)
1.23456789E10       (rounded in exponent G format)
```

In all three format modes the value of dd is taken as 9 if it is set to a value which is too large or too small.

The final part of @% defines the field width to be used when a comma is used to separate items in a PRINT statement. It may have any value in the range 0–255 (i.e. &00 to &FF in hexadecimal).

The initial value of @% when your computer is switched on is &AOA which specifies that G9 format is to be used (ff=00; dd=0A, i.e. 10 – which is too large, so 9 is used!), that the field width is to be ten characters (&0A) and that STR$ is not to take note of @%.

Experiment 17.1

Write a program to print a table of trigonometrical functions for angles from 0° to 90° in steps of 5°. Each line of the table should contain the following details:

V	the angle (as an integer in the range 0–90)
SIN(V)	the sine of V
COS(V)	the cosine of V
TAN(X)	the tangent of X

The three function results should be printed with five decimal places.

17.2 A BIT MORE LOGIC

In chapter 10 we introduced the concept of *logical operations*, and met the six relational operators ($<, =, >, <=, >=$ and $<>$) and the two logical operators (AND and OR).

In chapter 12 the concept of bitwise logical operations was explained in the context of the GCOL statement, and in particular, its use for animation. The two operators AND and OR can also be used for *bitwise operations*, as can a third EOR operator. All three operators work by carrying out the appropriate logical operation on corresponding *bits* of their operands. Thus

```
&14273AD6 AND &46235462
```

can be written as

```
     0001 0100 0010 0111 0011 1010 1101 0110
AND  0100 0110 0010 0011 0101 0100 0110 0010
     0000 0100 0010 0011 0001 0000 0100 0010
```

which leads to the result

&04231042

Similarly

&14273AD6 OR &46235462

will lead to

&56277EF6

while

&14273AD6 EOR &46235462

will give

&52046EB4

There is also a fourth (monadic) operator – NOT, which inverts every bit, changing 0s to
1s and vice versa. Thus

NOT &14273AD6

is equal to

&EBD8C529

Since the Beeb sets the value TRUE to be −1 (i.e. &FFFFFFFF) and FALSE to zero, the
NOT operator applied to a TRUE condition returns FALSE, and vice versa.

In addition, it is possible to use two special functions TRUE and FALSE to set variables
to the appropriate value. The following program illustrates this very simply

```
10 True=TRUE: False=FALSE
20 IF True THEN
     PRINT "True =";True;" which is TRUE"
30 IF NOT False THEN
     PRINT "False =";False;" which is FALSE"
40 And=True AND False
50 Or=True OR False
60 Eor=True EOR False
```

```
 70 PRINT "True AND False is ";FNtrue(And)
 80 PRINT "True OR False is ";FNtrue(Or)
 90 PRINT "True EOR False is ";FNtrue(Eor)
100 END
110 DEF FNtrue(true)
120 IF true THEN ="TRUE" ELSE ="FALSE"
```

Experiment 17.2

Type in the above program and run it.

Do you understand what it is doing, and how it works?

Now replace "False" in lines 40–90 by "True" and run it again. Is the result what you expected?

Finally replace "True" in lines 40–90 by "False" and run it again. Did this do what you anticipated?

17.3   MANIPULATING YOUR MEMORY

Up to this point we have not concerned ourselves in any detail with the actual allocation of the Beeb's memory. A model B has a total of 64K bytes of memory, while a model A normally has only 48K bytes; 32K bytes of this total are used for the operating system ROM (read only memory) and the Basic interpreter ROM, leaving either 32K or 16K of user-accessible RAM (random access memory). This part of the memory is shared between the operating system and the user program and constitutes what is usually called the *memory*.

Figure 17.1 shows how the memory is used for five major purposes, with the three main boundaries being defined by the three variables PAGE, LOMEM and HIMEM.

PAGE defines the start of the user area, once sufficient space has been allowed for various operating system and Basic Interpreter variables and input/output buffers. It is the address at which Basic programs will always start.

When the computer is switched on, or re-initialised by BREAK being pressed, PAGE is set to an appropriate value for the particular computer system, for example 3584 (&E00) for a standard cassette-based model or 6400 (&1900) for one which contains the Acorn Disc Filing System. However, it can be altered by an ordinary assignment statement

```
PAGE=&1200
```

One important point to note here is that *PAGE is always rounded down to a multiple of 256*. This means that a statement such as

```
PAGE=6600
```

will, in fact, set PAGE to 6400. If PAGE is always set to a hexadecimal value ending in two zeros then there will be no difficulty:

```
PAGE=&1A00
```

If PAGE is altered then any Basic program in memory will become inaccessible, since it

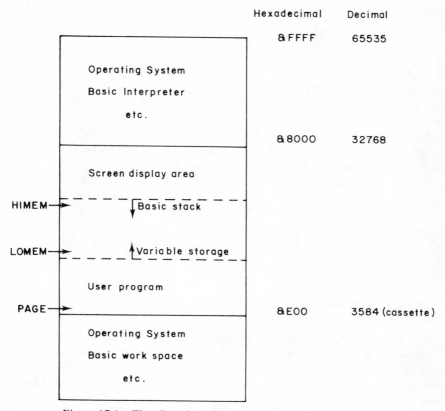

Figure 17.1   The allocation of memory (cassette based system)

will not begin at the new value of PAGE. However, since all variable storage uses space *above* the top of the program it follows that increasing the value of PAGE creates an area of memory which is totally inaccessible (and thus protected). If PAGE is increased to a value higher than the top of the current program it is therefore possible to load another program at the new PAGE and run it without in any way damaging or corrupting the original program. Resetting PAGE will then restore the original program.

The two utility programs SLIST and COMPACTER described in Appendix C use this principle to allow them to be loaded and run without destroying the program already in memory, which is to be listed or compacted.

The other two variables (LOMEM and HIMEM) define the first and last bytes of the general memory area which can be used for variable and other data storage. The value of LOMEM is automatically set to the address of the first byte after the end of the current program. Any alteration to that program therefore causes LOMEM to be altered, thus making all variables and arrays inaccessible. HIMEM is set to the address of the first byte below the area set aside for the screen display; it is reset whenever a MODE change is carried out.

This general memory area is used for two types of variable storage – program variables, which start at LOMEM and work upwards, and the Basic Interpreter's working "stack", which starts at HIMEM and works downwards. If these two meet then the dreaded message

"No room"

will appear!

Both LOMEM and HIMEM can be altered, but should only be changed by experienced programmers who know the full implications of what they are doing, otherwise the results can be catastrophic.

In addition to these three special variables there is a function, TOP, which returns the address of the first free byte above the top of the current program. This is usually the same as LOMEM, unless the latter has been altered by the programmer or his program.

When working with large programs it is often useful to find out the size of the program, and there are occasional reasons for altering PAGE. As a general rule, however, these memory control variables should not be altered (or even used) except in machine-code programs or when using direct addressing. Machine-code is outside the scope of this book, but direct addressing is the subject of the next, and final, section of this book.

17.4 DIRECT ADDRESSING

BBC Basic has three rather unusual operators, in addition to the arithmetic and logical ones already described elsewhere, which enable you (or your program) to directly address locations in the computer's memory. This is not normally a useful thing to do and is, potentially, *very dangerous*; in some situations, however, it provides a very powerful (or even essential) extra facility.

The three operators are known as *indirection operators*, and enable you to refer directly to any byte in the computer's memory, any group of four bytes, or any sequence of bytes which represents a character string. The three operators are written using the three characters ? (pronounced "query" – for byte addressing), ! (pronounced "pling" – for four-byte addressing) and $ (pronounced "dollar" – for string addressing). They are all, primarily, monadic operators, and are written before the variable or constant on which they are to operate.

The expression

?N

refers to the contents of the byte whose *address* is N. It can be used anywhere that a variable name could have been used, such as

```
100 ?N=&3A
150 Byte=?N
170 IF ?N=&FF THEN...
etc.
```

In an assignment to a variable the byte will be at the least significant end, with the rest of the value being zeros. Line 150 above will therefore store the five byte "real" value &00000000bb in Byte, where &bb is the byte stored at the address stored in the variable N.

The operator ! is very similar except that

```
!N
```

refers to the contents of the *four* successive bytes starting at *address* N. Since an integer variable occupies four bytes we may write

```
200 Int%=!N
250 !N=123
280 IF !N=Test% THEN...
```

In both cases, of course, N may be a decimal integer or a hexadecimal integer in addition to being a variable. Thus, for example, we may write

```
300 ?&1F00=&FF
350 Type%=!1756
```

In practice, because memory addressing is normally carried out in hexadecimal, statements such as that in line 300 are more usual than those using decimal, as in line 350.

Experiment 17.3

One very valuable use of ! is to copy an area of memory, or even a complete program, to some other part of the memory. For example, the following line will copy the current program to an area starting at &6000:

```
D%=&6000-PAGE: FOR I%=PAGE TO TOP: !(D%+I%)=!I%: NEXT
```

As long as the program only uses mode 7 (and is not too demanding of memory) it can be run in its new location by typing

```
PAGE=&6000
RUN
```

Load the Compacter program (Appendix C.2) and then copy it as described above. Run the copy to produce a compacted version of itself.

Note that you cannot run the version at the lower address without running the potential risk of overwriting the other copy unless HIMEM is altered. It is normally preferable to run the higher version and protect the lower one by ensuring that it is below the address of PAGE.

Both of these operators may also be used as diadic operators, in which case the expression

```
N?M
```

means the contents of the byte whose *address* is N+M, while

```
N!M
```

means the contents of the *four* consecutive bytes starting at *address* N+M. In this form of usage, however, the first operand (N) must be a variable and not a constant.

In the Castle program this form of expression is used extensively to access individual bytes of the arrays Door% and Item%. Both these arrays combine a large number of pieces of information into a single (integer) element, and, for example, the other end of a corridor (i.e. the floor and door number) is contained in two bytes of the relevant element of Door%. The statement

```
!XX=Door%(Z%,d)
```

copies the relevant element to a special four-byte area whose address is stored in the variable XX, and then the statements

```
f=XX?1:  d=?XX
```

extract the relevant values and store them in the variables f and d.

In a similar way the strength of the "guardian" of the door is extracted by the statement

```
p=XX?2
```

while the colour of the guardian (and hence its type) is obtained by

```
c=XX?3 MOD 16
```

Note that since dragons are drawn facing either left or right it is important that the correct version is plotted. This is achieved by using colours 17 and 18 for left-facing dragons and colours 1 and 2 for right-facing ones. The full detail of any element of Door% is shown in figure 17.2, while details of all the storage arrangements are given in Appendix B.

One very important aspect of the above examples concerns the four bytes addressed by

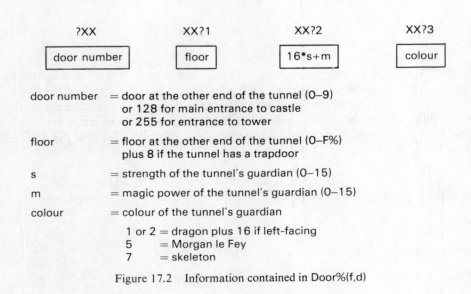

?XX	XX?1	XX?2	XX?3
door number	floor	16*s+m	colour

door number	= door at the other end of the tunnel (0–9) or 128 for main entrance to castle or 255 for entrance to tower
floor	= floor at the other end of the tunnel (0–F%) plus 8 if the tunnel has a trapdoor
s	= strength of the tunnel's guardian (0–15)
m	= magic power of the tunnel's guardian (0–15)
colour	= colour of the tunnel's guardian

1 or 2	= dragon plus 16 if left-facing
5	= Morgan le Fey
7	= skeleton

Figure 17.2   Information contained in Door%(f,d)

the variable XX. The statement

```
!XX=Door%(Z%,d)
```

clearly stores the four bytes which constitute the array element Door%(Z%,d) in an area which starts at the address stored in the variable XX. But where is this?

When manipulating memory contents directly (or when using assembly code) it is frequently necessary to reserve an area of memory at a known address, in such a way that the Basic variables or stack do not overwrite it. A special form of the DIM statement is used for this purpose, and takes the form

```
DIM name n
```

where name is a variable name and n is an integer number. *Note* that the space between name and n is *essential* and enables the Basic Interpreter to distinguish between them. The statement causes the Basic Interpreter to reserve n+1 bytes of memory and to store the address of the first byte in the variable name. Thus

```
DIM Table 20
```

will reserve 21 bytes (0 to 20) and will store the address of the first one in Table.

Line 50 of Castle contains a number of DIMensions for arrays and one special reservation:

```
50 DIM Door%(7,9),Item%(29),Item$(15),Sx%(3),Sy%(3),XX 3
```

The variable XX thus refers to a four byte area and the statement

```
!XX=Door%(Z%,d)
```

transfers the contents of the array element to this area. Subsequent references to ?XX, etc. will select the appropriate byte of the array element.

The third operator ($) can only be used as a monadic operator and refers to a character string at the specified address. Thus

```
$&1234
```

refers to a *character string* starting at byte &1234. Every valid character string is terminated by a CR character (&0D) and the string specified by the above expression therefore occupies one byte more than the length of the string.

Experiment 17.4

The Final Test uses the ! and $ operators to store various information in fixed locations so that it can be passed from one program to another. The locations used are areas in the Operating System's work space which are not otherwise used. *This is not normally recommended* unless you are very sure of what you are doing; it is, however, the only easy method (in the absence of discs) of passing data from one program to another.

For example, FINALTEST stores the player's name in the area used for the resident integer variables. The variable @% is stored in &400–&403, A% in &404–&407, B% in &408–&40B etc., and the statement

```
2150 A%=LEN(Name$): $&408=Name$
```

therefore stores the length of the name in A% and the name itself in the area reserved for B% to E% (since a maximum of 15 characters is allowed).

CASTLE examines these locations at line 40 in order to decide whether FINALTEST has already been run. If A% is the length of a string starting at &408 then the name is extracted; if it is not then a full (mode 2) title sequence is started and the name explicitly requested and stored as before.

CASTLE2 sets up the castle tunnels, etc., the placement of items, and the names of those items in the three arrays Door%, Item% and Item$. The statements at lines 420 and 430 copy the first two arrays into a 440 byte area starting at &900. This is an area used mainly for file buffers and is not used in CASTLE2 or Castle. The array Item$ and the player's name (Name$) are stored by the statements on line 440 in a 114 byte area starting at &D00; this area is not used in cassette based systems and is available for the programmer's own use.

Finally Castle extracts this information and puts it back into arrays in lines 60–80. As long as these areas are not corrupted (and they shouldn't be) Castle can re-create the starting conditions for that particular scenario at will.

Run "The Final Test". Once you have reached the final program (Castle) interrupt the game by pressing ESCape or BREAK and use indirection operators to modify such items as the strength or type of the tunnel guardians, the physical and magical power of various items or their location, and the existence of trapdoors in tunnels. Appendix B gives full details of the format of these items. Then press the f0 key to restart the program.

Did your changes work?

The details discussed in this section are only for quite advanced programmers – normally you will never need to use them, and you should avoid their use unless absolutely essential as they are potentially very dangerous. Finally we should say that if you have read (and understood) this far, then you won't need much more help from us! So enjoy your Beeb, and good luck!

Experiment 17.5

As you will be aware, the two programs CASTLE and CASTLE2 carry out various initialisations between them. See if you can combine them into a single program which has a proper opening title and some instructions and/or advice. Since FINALTEST is not necessary, you will then only need your XCASTLE and Castle to play the game.

Experiment 17.6

Castle contains one "bug" that you may have noticed, which means that sometimes you will be told that you can't go through an unguarded open door, although a second attempt will work. For your "graduation test", see if you can find the error, and correct it! (Don't write and tell us – we already know!)

Experimental Hints

17.1　You will need to alter the value of @% in different parts of your program. For example, the value &20509 will cause all numbers to be printed with five decimal places; this is what is required for the function values, but the angle should be printed as a whole number and not to five places of decimals!

Appendix A

The Final Test

The four programs listed in this appendix are available in cassette tape form from your local bookshop, computer store or the publisher.

A.1 THE PROGRAMS AND HOW TO TYPE THEM

The four programs which constitute The Final Test are listed in the remainder of this Appendix. They are listed in the "structured" form produced by the utility program SLIST which is listed in Appendix C.1. Both The Final Test and the utilities given in Appendix C are essential parts of this book and are available on cassette tapes; you are strongly recommended to purchase these tapes. However, if you do not wish to purchase the tapes then the programs may be typed by you and saved. In this case you should save the COMPACTER program given in Appendix C.2 before attempting to type and save any of The Final Test.

The four programs FINALTEST, CASTLE, CASTLE2 and Castle are all close to the maximum size possible, and care must be taken to avoid redundant spaces etc. or you may find that there is "No Room" when you come to run them. The procedure you should adopt, therefore, is as follows:

1) Type in a program (e.g. CASTLE), omitting all REMarks.
2) Save it on a tape (see section 1.5 with regard to checking your recording).
3) Load the COMPACTER program at a high address (see Appendix C.2 for details of how to do this).
4) Run the COMPACTER program. This will produce a "compacted" version of the program you typed at step 1 (e.g. CASTLE), in which all redundant spaces are removed. See Appendix C.2 for more information.
5) Save the compacted program

At steps 2 and 5 you should check your saved program using the technique described in chapter 1 (section 1.5).

If you have typed the programs without any unnecessary spaces then the first three programs should run without being compacted if the REMarks are removed, but the above procedure will make sure. The last program (Castle) will almost certainly need to be compacted.

A.2 FINALTEST

```
  1 REM IMPORTANT!
  2 REM Only those lines whose line numbers end in 0
  3 REM (10, 20, 30, etc.) should be typed.
  4 REM All other lines (1, 2, 3, etc.) are for
  5 REM information only, and will make the program
  6 REM too big if they are typed.
  7 REM You can therefore use AUTO and ignore lines
  8 REM which are not multiples of 10.
  9 REM
 10 *KEY10OLD|M
 20 ON ERROR GOTO 2290
 27 REM
 28 REM Author:  Miles Ellis, 1983
 29 REM
 30 REM Copyright 1984, John Wiley & Sons, Limited
 40 MODE 7: Birds=FALSE
 50 VDU 15,23;8202;0;0;0
 57 REM
 58 REM Set up screen and play 1st half of Greensleeves
 59 REM
 60 PROCback(0,24,133): PROCtune
 70 FOR I%=2 TO 20:
      VDU 31,3,I%,151: NEXT
 77 REM
 78 REM Draw title one word at a time
 79 REM
 80 VDU 31,9,2,252,252,252,252,252,160,160,232,180,160,160,232,180,
    160,160,252,252,252,252,252
 90 VDU 31,11,3,255,31,16,3,234,181,160,160,234,181,160,160,255
100 VDU 31,11,4,255,31,16,4,234,253,252,252,254,181,160,160,255,
    252,252,180
110 VDU 31,11,5,255,31,16,5,234,183,163,163,235,181,160,160,255,
    163,163,161
120 VDU 31,11,6,255,31,16,6,234,181,160,160,234,181,160,160,255,
    240,240,240,240
130 VDU 31,11,7,163,31,16,7,162,161,160,160,162,161,160,160,163,
    163,163,163,163: PROCwait(1)
140 VDU 31,4,9,255,175,175,175,175,160,160,170,239,191,165,160,160,
    255,245,160,160,255,160,160,160,224,254,253,176,160,160,160,
    255
150 VDU 31,4,10,255,31,12,10,234,181,160,160,160,255,239,180,160,
    255,160,160,232,191,161,162,239,180,160,160,255
160 VDU 31,4,11,255,255,255,181,31,12,11,234,181,160,160,160,255,
    162,255,176,255,160,160,234,255,255,255,255,181,160,160,255
170 VDU 31,4,12,255,31,12,12,234,181,160,160,160,255,160,170,253,
    255,160,160,234,181,160,160,234,181,160,160,255
180 VDU 31,4,13,255,31,11,13,232,254,253,180,160,160,255,160,160,
    235,255,160,160,234,181,160,160,234,181,160,160,255,252,252,
    252,252: PROCwait(1)
190 VDU 31,6,15,240,240,240,240,240,160,160,224,240,240,240,240,
    176,160,160,160,224,240,240,31,29,15,240,240,240,240,240
200 VDU 31,6,16,163,163,255,163,163,160,160,234,183,163,163,163,
    161,160,160,250,191,163,171,255,164,160,160,163,163,255,163,
    163
```

```
210 VDU 31,8,17,255,31,13,17,234,245,240,240,31,21,17,239,244,240,
    240,31,31,17,255
220 VDU 31,8,18,255,31,13,18,234,191,175,175,31,22,18,163,163,171,
    253,176,160,160,160,255
230 VDU 31,8,19,255,31,13,19,234,181,31,21,19,248,244,160,224,254,
    165,160,160,160,255
240 VDU 31,8,20,175,31,13,20,170,175,175,175,175,165,160,160,162,
    171,175,175,163,31,31,20,175
247 REM
248 REM Title is complete - play 2nd half of Greensleeves
249 REM
250 VDU 31,5,23: PROCwait(1): PROCtune
257 REM
258 REM Cycle through background colours
259 REM
260 FOR J%=145 TO 149:
      PROCback(0,24,J%): PROCwait(0.1): NEXT
267 REM
268 REM Change title colour to blue
269 REM
270 FOR I%=2 TO 20:
      VDU 31,3,I%,148: PROCwait(0.03): NEXT:
    PROCwait(1)
277 REM
278 REM Change background to stripes
279 REM
280 PROCback(0,7,145): PROCwait(0.5)
290 PROCback(8,14,150): PROCwait(0.5)
300 PROCback(15,24,146): PROCwait(0.5)
310 PROCback(22,24,147): PROCwait(0.5)
317 REM
318 REM Print flashing copyright notice
319 REM
320 PRINT TAB(2,23);CHR$(136);CHR$(132);
    "(c) 1984, John Wiley & Sons, Ltd."
327 REM
328 REM Play Greensleeves and freeze copyright notice
329 REM
330 RESTORE 2310: PROCtune: PRINT TAB(2,23);" ": PROCtune
337 REM
338 REM Clear screen and start story
339 REM
340 PROCback(0,24,148)
350 PROCclear(132): PROCwait(1)
360 PROCtell
370 FOR I%=6 TO 7:
      PRINT TAB(14,I%);CHR$(141);CHR$(131);"CAMELOT": NEXT:
    PROCwait(5)
380 PROCtell: *FX15,1
390 PRINT TAB(6,24);CHR$(136);CHR$(134);
    "Press any key to continue";: X=GET
397 REM
398 REM Clear screen for next page of story
399 REM
400 PROCclear(129)
410 PROCtell: *FX15,1
```

```
417 REM
418 REM Get player's name
419 REM
420 PRINT TAB(3,17);CHR$(136);CHR$(131);"<<<<<<";:
    INPUT TAB(5,17)""""Name$: A%=LEN(Name$)
430 IF A%>15 THEN
       PRINT TAB(3,17);CHR$(135);
       "Please limit name to 15 characters";: PROCwait(3):
       PRINT TAB(3,17);SPC(35);: GOTO 420
440 IF A%<6 THEN
       PRINT TAB(5+A%,17);SPC(5);
450 PRINT TAB(3,17);CHR$(137);
460 Name$=FNconvert(Name$): PROCwait(3)
467 REM
468 REM Clear screen for opening picture
469 REM
470 PROCclear(134)
480 Birds=TRUE: PROCtell
490 PROCback(10,24,130)
500 PROCtree1(6,9): PROCtree1(22,9): PROCtree1(13,10):
    PROCtree1(28,11)
510 PROCtree2(17,13): PROCtree2(7,16)
520 PROCtree3(27,20): PROCwait(5)
530 PROCtell
537 REM
538 REM Walk man through trees
539 REM
540 FOR I%=6 TO 14 STEP 2
550    PROCman1(I%,23): PROCwait(0.3): PROCclearman(I%,23):
       PROCwait(0.01): PROCman2(I%+1,23): PROCwait(0.3):
       PROCclearman(I%+1,23): PROCwait(0.01): NEXT
560 PROCman3(16,23): PROCwait(1)
570 PROCtell
577 REM
578 REM Draw castle
579 REM
580 PROCcastle1(33,11): PROCwait(5)
587 REM
588 REM Clear screen for second picture
589 REM
590 PROCclear(134)
600 PROCtell
610 PROCback(11,24,130)
620 PROCtree3(6,11): PROCtree3(18,14)
630 PROCcastle2(28,14): PROCwait(1)
637 REM
638 REM Walk man towards castle
639 REM
640 FOR I%=0 TO 4
650    X%=6+2*I%: Y%=24-I%
660    PROCman1(X%,Y%): PROCwait(0.3): PROCclearman(X%,Y%):
       PROCwait(0.01): PROCman2(X%+1,Y%): PROCwait(0.3):
       PROCclearman(X%+1,Y%): PROCwait(0.01): NEXT
670 PROCman3(16,19): PROCwait(1)
680 PROCtell
```

```
690 PROCcry(1): PROCwait(2)
700 PROCtell
707 REM
708 REM Clear screen for third picture
709 REM
710 PROCclear(134): PROCback(12,24,130)
720 PROCtree4(6,17): PROCcastle3(22,17)
727 REM
728 REM Walk man towards castle
729 REM
730 FOR I%=0 TO 3
740   X%=11+2*I%: Y%=24-I%
750   PROCman1(X%,Y%): PROCwait(0.3): PROCclearman(X%,Y%):
      PROCwait(0.01): PROCman2(X%+1,Y%): PROCwait(0.3)
760   IF I%<3 THEN
         PROCclearman(X%+1,Y%): PROCwait(0.01)
770   NEXT:
    Birds=TRUE: PROCwait(1)
777 REM
778 REM Clear screen for fourth picture
779 REM
780 PROCclear(134): PROCback(14,24,130)
790 PROCcastle4(17,21)
797 REM
798 REM Walk man up to castle
799 REM
800 FOR I%=0 TO 3
810   X%=6+2*I%: Y%=24-I%
820   PROCman1(X%,Y%): PROCwait(0.3): PROCclearman(X%,Y%):
      PROCwait(0.01): PROCman2(X%+1,Y%): PROCwait(0.3)
830   IF I%<3 THEN
         PROCclearman(X%+1,Y%): PROCwait(0.01)
840   NEXT:
    Birds=TRUE: PROCwait(1)
847 REM
848 REM Clear screen for last picture
849 REM
850 PROCclear(134): PROCback(15,24,130)
860 PROCcastle5(12,24)
867 REM
868 REM Walk man up to castle door
869 REM
870 FOR I%=0 TO 3
880   X%=18+2*I%
890   PROCman1(X%,24): PROCwait(0.3): PROCclearman(X%,24):
      PROCwait(0.01): PROCman2(X%+1,24): PROCwait(0.3):
      PROCclearman(X%+1,24): PROCwait(0.01): NEXT
900 PROCman3(X%+2,24): PROCwait(1)
910 PROCtell
920 PROCcry(2): PROCwait(3)
926 REM
927 REM Ask whether player will enter castle
928 REM and take appropriate action
929 REM
930 PROCtell: Y$=GET$: Birds=FALSE
```

```
 940 IF Y$="Y" OR Y$="y" THEN
        PRINT "Yes": PROCwait(1): PROCbrave
     ELSE
        IF Y$="N" OR Y$="n" THEN
           PRINT "No": PROCwait(1): PROCcoward
        ELSE
           PRINT Y$;: INPUT ""Y$: PROCwait(1): PROCfool
 950 END
 957 REM
 958 REM Procedure to play a tune from DATA
 959 REM
 960 DEF PROCtune
 970 LOCAL a,p,d
 980 ENVELOPE 1,1,0,0,0,0,0,0,20,5,0,-2,100,126
 990 READ p: REPEAT
        READ d: IF d=0 THEN
          a=0
        ELSE
          a=1
1000    SOUND 1,a,p,d: READ p: UNTIL p<0:
     PROCwait(2)
1010 ENDPROC
1017 REM
1018 REM Procedure to wait for t seconds
1019 REM
1020 DEF PROCwait(t)
1030 LOCAL a
1040 t=TIME+100*t
1050 REPEAT
        IF Birds THEN
           PROCcheep(4)
1060    UNTIL TIME>t
1070 ENDPROC
1077 REM
1078 REM Procedure to "cry out"!
1079 REM
1080 DEF PROCcry(n)
1090 ENVELOPE 1,15,3,-1,0,1,1,255,126,-1,-n,-n^2,16*n^2,16*n^2
1100 SOUND 1,1,224,20: SOUND 3,1,210,20
1110 ENDPROC
1117 REM
1118 REM Procedure to sound a random "cheep"
1119 REM
1120 DEF PROCcheep(d)
1130 LOCAL c,a
1140 IF d=1 THEN
        c=18
     ELSE
        c=2
1150 a=8*(RND(10)-1): ENVELOPE 2,4,20,10,0,1,1,1,126,0,0,-126,a,a:
     SOUND c,0,0,d*RND(5): SOUND 2,2,210,5
1160 ENDPROC
1166 REM
1167 REM Function to convert a character string to
1168 REM correct use of upper and lower case
```

```
1169 REM
1170 DEF FNconvert(n$)
1180 LOCAL i,n,c$
1190 n=LEN(n$)
1200 n$=FNupcase(n$,1,1)+FNlocase(n$,2,n)
1210 FOR i=2 TO n
1220   c$=MID$(n$,i,1)
1230   IF c$=" " OR c$="-" OR c$="'" THEN
          n$=MID$(n$,1,i)+FNupcase(n$,i+1,1)+MID$(n$,i+2)
1240   NEXT
1250 =n$
1257 REM
1258 REM Function to convert a string to upper case
1259 REM
1260 DEF FNupcase(n$,n1,n2)=FNcase(n$,n1,n2,-32)
1267 REM
1268 REM Function to convert a string to lower case
1269 REM
1270 DEF FNlocase(n$,n1,n2)=FNcase(n$,n1,n2,32)
1277 REM
1278 REM Function to convert a string to upper or lower case
1279 REM
1280 DEF FNcase(n$,n1,n2,d)
1290 LOCAL min,max,i,c,c$,a$
1300 a$=STRING$(16," "): a$="": IF d<0 THEN
        min=97: max=122
     ELSE
        min=65: max=90
1310 FOR i=n1 TO n2:
        c$=MID$(n$,i,1): c=ASC(c$)
1320   IF c>=min AND c<=max THEN
          a$=a$+CHR$(c+d)
       ELSE
          a$=a$+c$
1330   NEXT
1340 =a$
1347 REM
1348 REM Procedure to print text from DATA
1349 REM
1350 DEF PROCtell
1360 LOCAL lin,col,line$
1370 READ lin: REPEAT
        READ col,line$: PRINT TAB(3,lin);CHR$(col);line$;
1380   READ lin: IF lin<0 THEN
          PROCwait(-lin): READ lin
1390   UNTIL lin>24
1400 ENDPROC
1407 REM
1408 REM Procedure to change background colour
1409 REM
1410 DEF PROCback(lin1,lin2,col)
1420 LOCAL i,t
1430 t=TIME+10: REPEAT
        UNTIL TIME>t
1440 FOR i=lin1 TO lin2:
```

```
      VDU 31,0,i,col,157: t=TIME+3: REPEAT
        UNTIL TIME>t:
      NEXT
1450 ENDPROC
1457 REM
1458 REM Procedure to clear screen to colour col
1459 REM
1460 DEF PROCclear(col)
1470 LOCAL i
1480 VDU 12: FOR i=0 TO 24:
        VDU 31,0,i,col,157: NEXT
1490 ENDPROC
1497 REM
1498 REM Four procedures to draw trees
1499 REM
1500 DEF PROCtree1(x,y)
1510 VDU 31,x-3,y-1,147,154,238,255,164,31,x-2,y,147,153,181
1520 ENDPROC
1530 DEF PROCtree2(x,y)
1540 VDU 31,x-4,y-2,147,154,224,248,244,176,31,x-4,y-1,147,154,175,
     255,255,175,31,x-3,y,147,153,234,181,31,x-3,y+1,147,153,162,
     161
1550 ENDPROC
1560 DEF PROCtree3(x,y)
1570 VDU 31,x-4,y-4,147,154,248,254,255,252,176,31,x-4,y-3,147,154,
     171,255,255,191,161,31,x-2,y-2,147,234,255,31,x-2,y-1,147,234,
     255,31,x-2,y,147,163,163,161
1580 ENDPROC
1590 DEF PROCtree4(x,y)
1600 VDU 31,x-1,y-7,147,154,240,248,244,240,31,x-3,y-6,147,154,232,
     255,255,255,255,255,255,180,31,x-3,y-5,147,154,239,255,255,255,
     255,255,255,191,31,x-3,y-4,147,154,162,175,255,255,255,255,175,
     161
1610 VDU 31,x+1,y-3,147,255,255,31,x+1,y-2,147,255,255,31,x+1,y-1,
     147,255,255,31,x,y,147,174,175,175,173
1620 ENDPROC
1627 REM
1628 REM Five procedures to draw castles
1629 REM
1630 DEF PROCcastle1(x,y)
1640 VDU 31,x+1,y-3,145,153,244,244,180,31,x-2,y-2,145,153,244,244,
     244,255,255,181,31,x-2,y-1,145,153,255,255,255,255,255,181,31,
     x-1,y,145,157,148,160,255,146,234,255
1650 ENDPROC
1660 DEF PROCcastle2(x,y)
1670 VDU 31,x+4,y-7,145,153,240,160,240,160,240,31,x+4,y-6,145,153,
     255,252,255,252,255,31,x-2,y-5,145,153,240,160,240,160,240,160,
     255,157,151,165,150,255
1680 VDU 31,x-2,y-4,145,153,255,252,255,252,255,252,255,255,255,255,
     255,31,x-2,y-3,145,153,255,157,31,x+10,y-3,146,255
1690 VDU 31,x-2,y-2,145,153,255,157,31,x+10,y-2,146,255,31,x-1,y-1,
     145,255,157,31,x+6,y-1,148,248,253,176,146,255
1700 VDU 31,x-1,y,145,255,157,31,x+6,y,148,255,255,181,146,255
1710 ENDPROC
1720 DEF PROCcastle3(x,y)
```

```
1730 VDU 31,x+7,y-10,145,153,234,255,160,234,255,160,234,255,31,x+7,
     y-9,145,153,234,255,255,157,151,240,160,150,255
1740 VDU 31,x+7,y-8,145,153,234,255,255,157,151,175,160,150,255,31,
     x-2,y-7,145,153,234,255,160,234,255,160,234,255,160,234,255,
     255,157,31,x+16,y-7,150,255
1750 VDU 31,x-2,y-6,145,153,234,255,157,31,x+16,y-6,150,255,31,x-2,
     y-5,145,153,234,255,157,31,x+16,y-5,146,255
1760 VDU 31,x-2,y-4,145,153,234,255,157,31,x+16,y-4,146,255,31,x-2,
     y-3,145,153,234,255,157,31,x+16,y-3,146,255
1770 VDU 31,x-2,y-2,145,153,234,255,157,31,x+10,y-2,148,224,254,244,
     160,160,146,255,31,x-2,y-1,145,153,234,255,157,31,x+10,y-1,148,
     255,255,255,181,160,146,255,31,x-2,y,145,153,234,255,157,31,
     x+10,y,148,255,255,255,181,160,146,255
1780 ENDPROC
1790 DEF PROCcastle4(x,y)
1800 VDU 31,x+11,y-14,145,252,252,160,160,252,252,160,160,252,252,
     31,x+11,y-13,145,255,255,240,240,255,255,240,240,255,255
1810 VDU 31,x+11,y-12,145,255,157,31,x+17,y-12,151,224,160,160,150,
     255,31,x+11,y-11,145,255,157,31,x+17,y-11,151,255,181,160,150,
     255
1820 VDU 31,x-1,y-10,145,252,252,160,160,252,252,160,160,252,252,
     160,160,255,157,31,x+17,y-10,151,175,165,160,150,255,31,x-1,
     y-9,145,255,255,240,240,255,255,240,240,255,255,240,240,255,
     157,31,x+21,y-9,150,255
1830 VDU 31,x-1,y-8,145,255,157,31,x+21,y-8,150,255,31,x-1,y-7,145,
     255,157,31,x+21,y-7,146,255,31,x-1,y-6,145,255,157,31,x+21,y-6,
     146,255,31,x-1,y-5,145,255,157,31,x+21,y-5,146,255,31,x-1,y-4,
     145,255,157,31,x+21,y-4,146,255
1840 VDU 31,x-1,y-3,145,255,157,31,x+14,y-3,148,248,253,176,160,160,
     160,146,255,31,x-1,y-2,145,255,157,31,x+13,y-2,148,250,255,255,
     255,176,160,160,146,255,31,x-1,y-1,145,255,157,31,x+13,y-1,148,
     255,255,255,255,181,160,160,146,255
1850 VDU 31,x-1,y,145,255,157,31,x+13,y,148,255,255,255,255,181,160,
     160,146,255
1860 ENDPROC
1870 DEF PROCcastle5(x,y)
1880 VDU 31,x+14,y-18,145,224,240,240,160,160,224,240,240,160,160,
     224,240,240,31,x+14,y-17,145,234,255,255,160,160,234,255,255,
     160,160,234,255,255
1890 VDU 31,x+14,y-16,145,234,255,255,252,252,254,255,255,252,252,
     254,255,255,31,x+14,y-15,145,234,157,31,x+22,y-15,151,224,176,
     31,x+14,y-14,145,234,157,31,x+22,y-14,151,255,255
1900 VDU 31,x-1,y-13,145,224,240,240,160,160,224,240,240,160,160,
     224,240,240,160,160,234,157,31,x+22,y-13,151,175,175,31,x-1,
     y-12,145,234,255,255,160,160,234,255,255,160,160,234,255,255,
     160,160,234,157
1910 VDU 31,x-1,y-11,145,234,255,255,252,252,254,255,255,252,252,
     254,255,255,252,252,254,157,31,x-1,y-10,145,234,157,31,x-1,y-9,
     145,234,157,31,x-1,y-8,145,234,157,31,x-1,y-7,145,234,157
1920 VDU 31,x-1,y-6,145,234,157,31,x-1,y-5,145,234,157,31,x+19,y-5,
     148,224,31,x-1,y-4,145,234,157,31,x+18,y-4,148,248,255,253,176,
     31,x-1,y-3,145,234,157,31,x+17,y-3,148,232,255,255,255,253
1930 VDU 31,x-1,y-2,145,234,157,31,x+17,y-2,148,255,255,255,255,255,
     181,31,x-1,y-1,145,234,157,31,x+17,y-1,148,255,255,255,255,255,
     181,31,x-1,y,145,234,157,31,x+17,y,148,255,255,255,255,255,181
```

```
1940 ENDPROC
1947 REM
1948 REM Three procedures to draw men
1949 REM
1950 DEF PROCman1(x,y)
1960 SOUND 0,-5,4,2
1970 VDU 31,x-3,y-4,151,232,244,31,x-4,y-3,151,240,242,245,240,240,
     176,31,x-4,y-2,151,181,255,255,181,31,x-3,y-1,151,235,239,161,
     31,x-4,y,151,232,174,162,245
1980 PROCcheep(1): Birds=FALSE
1990 ENDPROC
2000 DEF PROCman2(x,y)
2010 SOUND 0,-5,4,2
2020 VDU 31,x-3,y-4,151,232,244,31,x-4,y-3,151,240,242,245,240,250,
     31,x-4,y-2,151,173,255,255,181,31,x-3,y-1,151,235,239,241,31,
     x-3,y,151,234,176,170,164
2030 ENDPROC
2040 DEF PROCman3(x,y)
2050 SOUND 0,-5,4,2: Birds=TRUE
2060 VDU 31,x-3,y-4,151,232,244,31,x-4,y-3,151,240,242,245,240,240,
     176,31,x-4,y-2,151,181,255,255,181,31,x-3,y-1,151,235,239,161,
     31,x-4,y,151,170,163,234,176
2070 ENDPROC
2077 REM
2078 REM Procedure to erase last man
2079 REM
2080 DEF PROCclearman(x,y)
2090 LOCAL y1
2100 FOR y1=y-5 TO y:
         PRINT TAB(x-4,y1);SPC(6);: NEXT
2110 ENDPROC
2116 REM
2117 REM Procedure to praise player for his courage,
2118 REM store his name, and CHAIN next program
2119 REM
2120 DEF PROCbrave
2130 PROCclear(134)
2140 PROCtell: PRINT Name$: PROCtell
2150 A%=LEN(Name$): $&408=Name$
2160 VDU 31,3,21,132,10,8,132,10,8,132,10,8,132,28,9,24,30,21
2170 CHAIN "CASTLE"
2180 ENDPROC
2187 REM
2188 REM Procedure to banish a cowardly knight
2189 REM
2190 DEF PROCcoward
2200 PROCclear(129)
2210 RESTORE 2930: PROCtell: PRINT Name$: PROCtell
2220 FOR I%=0 TO 24:
         VDU 31,3,I%,129: NEXT
2230 ENDPROC
2237 REM
2238 REM Procedure to tell a foolish knight to try again
2239 REM
2240 DEF PROCfool
```

```
2250 PROCclear(131)
2260 RESTORE 2970: PROCtell: PRINT Name$: PROCtell
2270 FOR I%=0 TO 24:
       VDU 31,3,I%,131: NEXT
2280 ENDPROC
2287 REM
2288 REM Error exit
2289 REM
2290 MODE 7: REPORT: IF ERR<>17 THEN
       PRINT " at ";ERL
2300 PRINT: END
2307 REM
2308 REM Data for Greensleeves music
2309 REM
2310 DATA 116,4,128,8,136,4,144,6,152,2,144,4,136,8,124,4,108,6,116,
     2,124,4,128,8,116,4,116,0,116,6,112,2,116,4,124,8,108,4,96,8
2320 DATA 116,4,128,8,136,4,144,6,152,2,144,4,136,8,124,4,108,6,116,
     2,124,4,128,6,124,2,116,4,112,6,104,2,112,4,116,8,116,0,116,4,
     116,0,116,12,-1
2330 DATA 156,12,156,0,156,6,152,2,144,4,136,8,124,4,108,6,116,2,
     124,4,128,8,116,4,116,0,116,6,112,2,116,4,124,8,108,4,96,12
2340 DATA 156,12,156,0,156,6,152,2,144,4,136,8,124,4,108,6,116,2,
     124,4,128,4,124,4,116,4,112,6,104,2,112,4,116,12,116,0,116,12,
     -1
2347 REM
2348 REM Data for text, its colour and position
2349 REM
2350 DATA    1,135,"Many years ago, in the days of myth"
2360 DATA    2,135,"and magic, young men would travel"
2370 DATA    3,135,"from far and wide to the court of"
2380 DATA    4,135,"King Arthur at the fabled city of",99
2390 DATA    9,135,"Some of these young men desired to"
2400 DATA   10,135,"join King Arthur and to become one"
2410 DATA   11,135,"of the Knights of the Round Table",-4
2420 DATA   13,135,"Many were the tests that were set"
2430 DATA   14,135,"for those who wished to become"
2440 DATA   15,135,"members of that select band of men,"
2450 DATA   16,135,"but of them all it was the final"
2460 DATA   17,135,"test which was the greatest test",-6
2470 DATA   19,135,"Close to Camelot was a forest where"
2480 DATA   20,135,"lived the sorceress Morgan le Fey",-3
2490 DATA   21,135,"and the final test was that the"
2500 DATA   22,135,"prospective knight should spend a"
2510 DATA   23,135,"day and a night alone in the forest",-6,99
2520 DATA    2,131,"You are such a person",-3
2530 DATA    4,131,"Before you enter the forest please"
2540 DATA    5,131,"give your name so that your deeds"
2550 DATA    6,131,"may be recorded for posterity"
2560 DATA    7,131,"and your valour may be remembered"
2570 DATA    8,131,"for as long as men talk of Camelot",-6
2580 DATA   10,131,"or, mayhap, that they may learn"
2590 DATA   11,131,"from your failure!",-3
2600 DATA   14,131,"Record your name below, and follow"
2610 DATA   15,131,"it by pressing the 'RETURN' key",99
2620 DATA    1,132,"It is spring and the peace and"
```

```
2630 DATA  2,132,"tranquillity of the forest is"
2640 DATA  3,132,"broken only by the sound of birds.",-3,99
2650 DATA  5,132,"As you walk amongst the trees",-1.5,99
2660 DATA  6,132,"you spy what looks like a castle"
2670 DATA  7,132,"in the distance.": -3,99
2680 DATA  1,132,"As you approach the castle",-0.5,99
2690 DATA  2,132,"you hear what sounds like a faint"
2700 DATA  3,132,"cry coming from the only window"
2710 DATA  4,132,"high up in the castle's tower",-4,99
2720 DATA  6,132,"You decide to investigate",-5,99
2730 DATA  1,132,"At the door of the castle you pause"
2740 DATA  2,132,"but at that very moment from above"
2750 DATA  3,132,"comes another cry of terror",-2,99
2760 DATA  5,132,"Will you enter the castle?"
2770 DATA  6,132,"(Type YES or NO)",99
2780 DATA  1,132,"Thou art truly brave ",99
2790 DATA  3,132,"This is the castle of Morgan le Fey"
2800 DATA  4,132,"which is bewitched and guarded"
2810 DATA  5,132,"within by dragons and evil spirits",-3
2820 DATA  7,132,"I shall be your guide, and you must"
2830 DATA  8,132,"use your skill to reach the"
2840 DATA  9,132,"uppermost room and then rescue the"
2850 DATA  10,132,"beautiful princess imprisoned there",-3
2860 DATA  12,132,"I shall draw a plan and you must"
2870 DATA  13,132,"use the four cursor control keys"
2880 DATA  14,132,"to tell me where you wish to go",-2
2890 DATA  16,132,"I also understand simple commands"
2900 DATA  17,132,"such as GET SWORD or OPEN DOOR"
2910 DATA  18,132,"but you will have to work these"
2920 DATA  19,132,"out for yourself!",99
2930 DATA  8,135,"Thou art a coward ",99
2940 DATA  10,135,"Never again shall thy face be seen"
2950 DATA  11,135,"by brave men and women in Camelot"
2960 DATA  13,135,"Begone, and never return!",-10,99
2970 DATA  8,132,"Thou art a fool ",99
2980 DATA  10,132,"If thou cannot say YES or NO to"
2990 DATA  11,132,"such a simple question, then what"
3000 DATA  12,132,"hope is there for thee in the"
3010 DATA  13,132,"castle of Morgan le Fey?"
3020 DATA  15,132,"Get thee back to Camelot and do not"
3030 DATA  16,132,"return here until thou hast gained"
3040 DATA  17,132,"some wisdom as well as courage!",-10,99
```

248

A.3 CASTLE

```
1 REM IMPORTANT!
2 REM Only those lines whose line numbers end in 0
3 REM (10, 20, 30, etc.) should be typed.
4 REM All other lines (1, 2, 3, etc.) are for
5 REM information only, and will make the program
6 REM too big if they are typed.
7 REM You can therefore use AUTO and ignore lines
8 REM which are not multiples of 10.
9 REM
10 *KEY10OLD|MGOTO1240|M
20 ON ERROR GOTO 1230
27 REM
28 REM Author:  Miles Ellis, 1983
29 REM
30 REM Copyright 1984, John Wiley & Sons, Limited
37 REM
38 REM Store name or initiate mode 2 title sequence
39 REM
40 IF A%>0 AND LEN($&408)=A% THEN
     Name$=$&408
   ELSE
     MODE 2: PROCtitle: A%=0
47 REM
48 REM Set colours and special cursor
49 REM
50 MODE 4:
   VDU 15,19,0,6;0;12,19,1,4;0;23;10,98,0;0;0;23;11,5,0;0;0;
57 REM
58 REM Get name if not passed from FINALTEST
59 REM
60 IF A%=0 THEN
     INPUT TAB(1,2)"What is your name? "Name$:
     IF LEN(Name$)>15 THEN
       PRINT TAB(1,2)
       "Please limit your name to 15 characters"TAB(0,2);:
       PROCwait(3): PRINT TAB(1,2);SPC(39): GOTO 60
     ELSE
       Name$=FNconvert(Name$): A%=LEN(Name$): $&408=Name$
67 REM
68 REM Get player's skill
69 REM
70 RESTORE 1410: PROCtell: PRINT
80 P$=GET$: PRINT TAB(1,10)P$;: P%=VAL(P$): IF P%<1 OR P%>8 THEN
     PRINT TAB(5,10)"From 1 to 8 I said!"TAB(0,10);: PROCwait(3):
     PRINT TAB(1,10)SPC(23): VDU 13: GOTO 80
87 REM
88 REM Set game level, dependent upon player's skill
89 REM
90 IF P%<3 THEN
     G%=1
   ELSE
     IF P%<7 THEN
       G%=2
     ELSE
       G%=3
```

```
100 VDU 23;8202;0;0;0;: PROCwait(.5): CLS: IF P%<4 THEN
      PROCtell: PROCcontinue
107 REM
108 REM Alter rate of flashing
109 REM
110 *FX9,3
116 REM
117 REM Set number of floors, maximum wait time before
118 REM spirits appear, and number of items in the castle
119 REM
120 *FX10,3
130 F%=2*G%+1: W%=900-100*P%: N%=4*(F%+1)-G%
137 REM
138 REM Clear screen and describe opening scenario
139 REM
140 VDU 12,19,0,1;0;19,1,3;0;
150 RESTORE 1470: PROCtell: PRINT Name$: PROCtell: PROCcontinue
157 REM
158 REM Clear screen and produce flashes and noises
159 REM
160 MODE 2: VDU 23;8202;0;0;0;: RESTORE 1530: PROCtell
170 ENVELOPE 1,1,-5,0,0,50,1,1,126,0,0,-126,0,0
180 TIME=0: REPEAT
      VDU 19,0,7;0;: SOUND &101,1,255,7: SOUND &100,-15,7,7:
      PROCwait(.1): VDU 19,0,1;0;: PROCwait(.1): UNTIL TIME>200
190 VDU 20: SOUND &10,0,0,0: SOUND &11,0,0,0: PROCtell
197 REM
198 REM Draw dragons, spirits, and skeletons
199 REM
200 PROCdragon(400,850,1): PROCdragon(150,300,2):
    PROCdragon(900,500,2): PROCwait(2): PROCtell
210 PROCspirit(706,358): PROCspirit(378,582): PROCspirit(850,562):
    PROCspirit(232,270): PROCspirit(1096,450): PROCwait(2)
220 PROCskeleton(150,470): PROCskeleton(590,318):
    PROCdragon(376,500,1): PROCskeleton(966,350): PROCtell
227 REM
228 REM Define restart key (f0) and CHAIN next program
229 REM
230 *KEY0MODE2: VDU15,23;8202;0;0;0;: RUN|M
240 VDU 28,2,31,19,27: ON ERROR OFF: CHAIN "CASTLE2"
247 REM
248 REM Procedure to wait t seconds
249 REM
250 DEF PROCwait(t)
260 t=TIME+100*t
270 REPEAT
      UNTIL TIME>t
280 ENDPROC
287 REM
288 REM Four functions to convert strings (as in FINALTEST)
289 REM
290 DEF FNconvert(n$)
300 LOCAL i,n,c$
310 n=LEN(n$): n$=FNupcase(n$,1,1)+FNlocase(n$,2,n)
320 FOR i=2 TO n
```

```
330   c$=MID$(n$,i,1): IF c$=" " OR c$="-" OR c$="'" THEN
          n$=MID$(n$,1,i)+FNupcase(n$,i+1,1)+MID$(n$,i+2)
340   NEXT
350 =n$
360 DEF FNupcase(n$,n1,n2)=FNcase(n$,n1,n2,-32)
370 DEF FNlocase(n$,n1,n2)=FNcase(n$,n1,n2,32)
380 DEF FNcase(n$,n1,n2,d)
390 LOCAL min,max,i,c,c$,a$
400 a$=STRING$(16," "): a$="": IF d<0 THEN
      min=97: max=122
    ELSE
      min=65: max=90
410 FOR i=n1 TO n2:
      c$=MID$(n$,i,1): c=ASC(c$)
420   IF c>=min AND c<=max THEN
        a$=a$+CHR$(c+d)
      ELSE
        a$=a$+c$
430   NEXT
440 =a$
447 REM
448 REM Procedure to control listing continuation
449 REM
450 DEF PROCcontinue
460 LOCAL x
470 *FX15,1
480 PRINT TAB(7,31);"Press any key to continue";: x=GET
490 ENDPROC
497 REM
498 REM Procedure to print text from DATA
499 REM
500 DEF PROCtell
510 LOCAL lin,line$
520 line$=STRING$(40," "): READ lin: REPEAT
      READ line$: PRINT TAB(1,lin);line$;: READ lin: IF lin<0 THEN
        PROCwait(-lin): READ lin
530   UNTIL lin>31
540 ENDPROC
547 REM
548 REM Procedure to produce Mode 2 title sequence
549 REM
550 DEF PROCtitle
560 LOCAL x,y,u,v
566 REM
567 REM Define half-width (mode 2) character sequence
568 REM for copyright message
569 REM
570 VDU 23,224,65,136,148,144,148,136,65,0
580 VDU 23,225,8,153,137,136,136,136,28,0
590 VDU 23,226,195,36,36,227,36,100,195,0
600 VDU 23,227,2,132,132,8,138,146,31,2
610 VDU 23,228,1,0,0,0,0,34,35,64
620 VDU 23,229,193,129,137,149,149,149,137,0
630 VDU 23,230,0,0,216,84,84,84,84,0
640 VDU 23,231,69,68,69,85,85,85,109,0
```

```
650 VDU 23,232,64,64,73,85,93,80,76,1
660 VDU 23,233,4,10,74,68,202,74,69,192
670 VDU 23,234,56,40,33,58,10,42,57,0
680 VDU 23,235,0,0,51,170,171,168,43,0
690 VDU 23,236,1,1,129,1,129,145,145,32
700 VDU 23,237,16,16,56,17,18,18,217,0
710 VDU 23,238,128,128,128,128,128,160,160,0
717 REM
718 REM Ensure normal flashing rate
719 REM
720 *FX9,25
730 *FX10,25
737 REM
738 REM Clear background to magenta
739 REM
740 VDU 23;8202;0;0;0;:: GCOL 0,133: CLG
746 REM
747 REM Change colour 0 to magenta and clear background
748 REM again; then play 1st part of Greensleeves
749 REM
750 VDU 19,0,5;0;: GCOL 0,128: CLG: RESTORE 1260: PROCtune
757 REM
758 REM Reset colour values for later colour "wipes"
759 REM
760 VDU 19,5,4;0;19,6,4;0;19,7,11;0;19,8,7;0;19,9,6;0;19,12,7;0;19,
    13,4;0;19,14,7;0;19,15,7;0;
767 REM
768 REM Draw title using coordinates held in DATA
769 REM
770 GCOL 0,15: RESTORE 1300: FOR I%=1 TO 17:
        READ x,y,u,v: PROCline(x,y,u,0,0,v): NEXT
780 PROCline(528,652,40,0,112,-212): PROCline(768,440,56,212,32,0):
    PROCline(832,652,72,-212,32,0)
790 FOR I%=1 TO 9:
        READ x,y,u,v: PROCline(x,y,u,0,0,v): NEXT
800 MOVE 852,320: MOVE 828,320: FOR I%=1 TO 26:
        READ x,y: PLOT 81,x,y: NEXT
810 PROCline(928,372,152,0,0,-28): PROCline(992,372,24,0,0,-212):
    PROCwait(1): RESTORE 1280: PROCtune
817 REM
818 REM Cycle through background colour wipes
819 REM
820 GCOL 1,129: CLG: PROCwait(.1): GCOL 1,130: CLG: PROCwait(.1)
830 GCOL 2,142: CLG: PROCwait(.1): GCOL 3,134: CLG: PROCwait(.1)
837 REM
838 REM After last background wipe, wipe title to blue
839 REM
840 GCOL 3,132: CLG: PROCwait(.1): GCOL 2,132: CLG: PROCwait(1)
847 REM
848 REM Produce three bands for background
849 REM
850 VDU 26,24,0;680;1279;1023;: GCOL 1,129: CLG: PROCwait(.5)
860 VDU 24,0;400;1279;679;: GCOL 1,137: CLG: PROCwait(.5)
870 VDU 24,0;0;1279;399;: GCOL 1,130: CLG: PROCwait(1.5)
877 REM
```

```
878 REM Produce yellow band at bottom
879 REM
880 VDU 24,0;0;1279;119;: GCOL 1,129: CLG: PROCwait(.5)
886 REM
887 REM Use characters 224-238 to display flashing
888 REM copyright notice on yellow background
889 REM
890 COLOUR 131: COLOUR 7: PRINT TAB(3,30);: FOR I%=224 TO 238:
    VDU I%: NEXT
897 REM
898 REM Play Greensleeves and stop flashing
899 REM
900 RESTORE 1260: PROCtune: VDU 19,7,4;0;: PROCtune
907 REM
908 REM Wipe out titles and reset normal colours
909 REM
910 VDU 26: GCOL 1,132: CLG: GCOL 2,132: CLG: VDU 20: GCOL 0,134:
    CLG
920 ENDPROC
927 REM
928 REM Procedure to play a tune stored in DATA
929 REM
930 DEF PROCtune
940 LOCAL a,p,d
950 ENVELOPE 1,1,0,0,0,0,0,0,15,5,0,-2,100,126
960 READ p: REPEAT
      READ d: IF d=0 THEN
        a=0
      ELSE
        a=1
970   SOUND 1,a,p,d: READ p: UNTIL p<0:
    PROCwait(2)
980 ENDPROC
987 REM
988 REM Procedure to fill a parallelogram
989 REM
990 DEF PROCline(x,y,u1,v1,u2,v2)
1000 VDU 29,x;y;: MOVE 0,0: MOVE u1,v1: PLOT 85,u2,v2:
     PLOT 85,u1+u2,v1+v2: VDU 29,0;0;
1010 ENDPROC
1017 REM
1018 REM Procedure to draw a dragon
1019 REM
1020 DEF PROCdragon(x,y,c)
1030 GCOL 1,c: VDU 29,x;y;
1040 MOVE 0,60: MOVE 50,60: PLOT 85,50,70: MOVE 75,85:
     PLOT 85,100,70: MOVE 70,70: PLOT 85,70,60: MOVE 50,60:
     PLOT 85,50,50
1050 MOVE 0,50: MOVE 50,50: PLOT 85,75,30: PLOT 85,70,60:
     PLOT 85,100,40: PLOT 85,100,70: PLOT 85,250,70: MOVE 250,85:
     PLOT 85,175,70: MOVE 175,85: PLOT 85,100,70
1060 MOVE 100,40: MOVE 250,70: PLOT 85,210,15: PLOT 85,285,60:
     PLOT 85,350,45: PLOT 85,330,60: PLOT 85,365,85
1070 MOVE 125,10: MOVE 100,10: PLOT 85,100,0: MOVE 140,0:
     PLOT 85,125,10: PLOT 85,140,40: PLOT 85,125,40
```

```
1080 MOVE 290,10: MOVE 265,10: PLOT 85,265,0: MOVE 305,0:
     PLOT 85,290,10: PLOT 85,305,40: PLOT 85,290,40: VDU 29,0;0;
1090 ENDPROC
1097 REM
1098 REM Procedure to draw a spirit
1099 REM
1100 DEF PROCspirit(x,y)
1110 GCOL 1,14: VDU 29,x;y;
1120 MOVE 30,90: MOVE 0,80: PLOT 85,60,80: PLOT 85,0,30:
     PLOT 85,60,30: MOVE 60,20: PLOT 85,48,30: PLOT 85,48,20:
     MOVE 36,30: MOVE 36,20: PLOT 85,24,30: PLOT 85,24,20
1130 MOVE 12,30: MOVE 12,20: PLOT 85,0,30: PLOT 85,0,20:
     PLOT 71,15,74: PLOT 71,36,74: PLOT 71,26,66: MOVE 15,56:
     PLOT 7,36,56: VDU 29,0;0;
1140 ENDPROC
1147 REM
1148 REM Procedure to draw a skeleton
1149 REM
1150 DEF PROCskeleton(x,y)
1160 GCOL 0,7: VDU 29,x;y;
1170 MOVE 30,90: MOVE 0,80: PLOT 85,60,80: PLOT 85,0,64:
     PLOT 85,12,60: MOVE 60,80: PLOT 85,48,60: PLOT 85,60,64
1180 MOVE 36,60: MOVE 48,60: PLOT 85,36,4: PLOT 85,48,10:
     PLOT 85,60,4: PLOT 85,60,10: MOVE 24,60: MOVE 12,60:
     PLOT 85,24,4: PLOT 85,12,10: PLOT 85,0,4: PLOT 85,0,10
1190 MOVE -15,30: MOVE -3,30: PLOT 85,-15,54: PLOT 85,-3,48:
     PLOT 85,12,60: PLOT 85,12,52: PLOT 85,48,60: PLOT 85,48,52:
     PLOT 85,75,54: PLOT 85,63,48: PLOT 85,75,30: PLOT 85,63,30
1200 MOVE 12,36: MOVE 48,36: PLOT 85,12,30: PLOT 85,48,30:
     PLOT 71,15,74: PLOT 71,36,74: PLOT 71,26,66: MOVE 15,56:
     PLOT 7,36,60: VDU 29,0;0;
1210 VDU 29,0;0;
1220 ENDPROC
1227 REM
1228 REM Error exit
1229 REM
1230 MODE 7: REPORT: IF ERR<>17 THEN
        PRINT " at line ";ERL
1240 A%=0: PRINT '"Type RUN to restart"
1250 END
1257 REM
1258 REM Data for Greensleeves music
1259 REM
1260 DATA 116,4,128,8,136,4,144,6,152,2,144,4,136,8,124,4,108,6,116,
     2,124,4,128,8,116,4,116,0,116,6,112,2,116,4,124,8,108,4,96,8
1270 DATA 116,4,128,8,136,4,144,6,152,2,144,4,136,8,124,4,108,6,116,
     2,124,4,128,6,124,2,116,4,112,6,104,2,112,4,116,8,116,0,116,4,
     116,0,116,12,-1
1280 DATA 156,12,156,0,156,6,152,2,144,4,136,8,124,4,108,6,116,2,
     124,4,128,8,116,4,116,0,116,6,112,2,116,4,124,8,108,4,96,12
1290 DATA 156,12,156,0,156,6,152,2,144,4,136,8,124,4,108,6,116,2,
     124,4,128,4,124,4,116,4,112,6,104,2,112,4,116,12,116,0,116,12,
     -1
1297 REM
1298 REM Data for coordinates of letters in title
```

```
1299 REM
1300 DATA   288,932,152,-28,352,932,24,-212
1310 DATA   528,932,24,-212,528,848,152,-44,656,932,24,-212
1320 DATA   768,932,24,-212,768,932,152,-28,768,848,112,-44,768,748,
     152,-28
1330 DATA   112,652,24,-212,112,652,152,-28,112,568,112,-44
1340 DATA   352,652,88,-28,384,652,24,-212,352,468,88,-28
1350 DATA   528,652,24,-212,656,652,24,-212
1360 DATA   800,536,88,-28
1370 DATA   1008,652,24,-212,1008,468,152,-28
1380 DATA   192,372,152,-28,256,372,24,-212
1390 DATA   432,372,24,-212,432,372,152,-28,432,288,112,-44,432,188,
     152,-28
1400 DATA   24,24,-24,-16,0,44,-16,-28,-116,28,16,-28,-40,0,24,-16,
     -24,-42,24,16,0,-44,16,28,100,-28,16,28,0,-44,24,16,-24,-52,24,
     -16,-40,0,16,-28,-116,28,-16,-28,0,44,-24,-16,24,28,-24,0
1407 REM
1408 REM Data for text to be displayed, etc.
1409 REM
1410 DATA   4,Before you start your difficult task,5,
     I must know how experienced you are,6,and what skills you have
1420 DATA   8,Please grade yourself on a scale,9,
     from 1 (beginner) to 8 (expert),99
1430 DATA   3,As you are not very experienced,4,
     perhaps I may be permitted to offer,5,
     you some advice before you begin your,6,
     adventures in the castle.,-4
1440 DATA   8,"First, you should know that every time",9,
     that anyone enters the castle the,10,
     corridors and stairways that lead from,11,
     the various doors are magically
1450 DATA   12,re-arranged.  You should not despair,13,
     "though, as there is always at least",14,
     one way to the tower room where the,15,princess is imprisoned.,
     -9
1460 DATA   17,"Secondly, you should remember that the",18,
     evil spirits will be searching for you,19,
     and that they cannot be defeated by,20,mere weapons.,99
1470 DATA   2,"When you open the door, ",99,3,
     "you can see nothing inside, but as",4,
     your eyes get used to the darkness.⌐,
     you can just see that you are in a,6,
     large and featureless hall.,-6
1480 DATA   8,The floor seems to have several,9,
     "objects lying upon it, but in the",10,
     gloom you cannot immediately see what,11,
     "they are; you can, however, see that"
1490 DATA   12,the hall has a great many doors,13,
     "leading from it, and clearly one of",14,
     these must lead you to the upper,15,
     floor from where the cry came.,-9
1500 DATA   17,As you move into the hall you brush,18,
     "against something, and with horror",19,
     "you realise that it is a skeleton,",20,clad in rusty armour!,
     -5
```

```
1510 DATA  22,You are about to turn away when you,23,
     notice some faint scratches on the,24,
     "wall beside the skeleton which, on"
1520 DATA  25,"closer examination, seem to be some",26,
     faded words.  You can just make out,27,
     "'magic', 'ring', and also what looks",28,
     like 'leather'.,-5,99
1530 DATA  1,Suddenly there is,2,a blinding flash,-0.5,99
1540 DATA  4,As your eyes begin,5,to recover their,6,
     sight you seem to,7,to see dragons,99
1550 DATA  7,to see dragons and,8,other strange and,9,
     terrifying shapes,10,which fill your,11,heart with dread.,99
1560 DATA  23,You decide to wait,24,until your courage,25,
     has returned.,99
```

A.4 CASTLE2

```
 1 REM IMPORTANT!
 2 REM Only those lines whose line numbers end in 0
 3 REM (10, 20, 30, etc.) should be typed.
 4 REM All other lines (1, 2, 3, etc.) are for
 5 REM information only, and will make the program
 6 REM too big if they are typed.
 7 REM You can therefore use AUTO and ignore lines
 8 REM which are not multiples of 10.
 9 REM
10 *KEY10OLD|MGOTO1360|M
20 ON ERROR GOTO 1350
27 REM
28 REM Author:  Miles Ellis, 1983
29 REM
30 REM Copyright 1984, John Wiley & Sons, Limited
40 DIM Door%(7,9),Item%(29),Item$(15)
50 DIM XX 3
57 REM
58 REM Read names of items found in the castle from DATA
59 REM
60 RESTORE 1900: FOR I=0 TO 15:
   READ Item$(I): NEXT:
   *FX15,1
66 REM
67 REM Define characters for items, spirits, dragons,
68 REM skeletons, player and Morgan le Fey
69 REM
70 VDU 23,224,0,0,0,126,6,6,6,0
80 VDU 23,225,0,0,0,16,56,16,0,0
90 VDU 23,226,16,40,68,130,132,88,32,24
100 VDU 23,227,0,0,64,64,254,64,64,0
110 VDU 23,228,16,16,56,56,16,16,16,16
120 VDU 23,229,56,124,84,108,124,68,56,56
130 VDU 23,230,0,0,0,0,24,60,189,126
140 VDU 23,231,0,16,16,56,56,124,124,254
150 VDU 23,232,0,16,40,0,40,0,40,16
160 VDU 23,233,56,40,56,56,40,56,16,0
170 VDU 23,234,16,56,56,0,56,56,0,56
180 VDU 23,235,0,0,0,2,255,2,0,0
190 VDU 23,236,0,8,66,16,132,41,128,82
200 VDU 23,237,0,0,16,40,40,16,0,0
210 VDU 23,238,56,124,84,108,124,68,124,124
220 VDU 23,239,124,124,124,84,84,0,0,0
230 VDU 23,240,56,124,84,108,68,56,254,254
240 VDU 23,241,186,186,186,56,56,56,56,108
250 VDU 23,242,56,124,84,108,68,56,124,238
260 VDU 23,243,170,170,186,40,40,40,40,108
270 VDU 23,244,16,56,221,63,255,55,2,6
280 VDU 23,245,144,241,249,255,254,252,228,12
290 VDU 23,246,9,143,159,255,127,63,39,48
300 VDU 23,247,8,28,187,252,255,236,64,96
310 VDU 23,248,56,52,60,60,56,24,255,255
320 VDU 23,249,188,188,60,36,228,228,134,134
330 VDU 23,250,28,44,60,60,28,24,255,255
340 VDU 23,251,61,61,60,36,39,39,97,97
```

```
350 VDU 23,252,28,44,60,60,156,152,255,255
360 VDU 23,253,60,60,60,100,100,196,204,12
370 VDU 23,254,56,52,60,60,57,25,255,255
380 VDU 23,255,60,60,60,38,38,35,51,48
387 REM
388 REM Ask if instructions needed and randomise RND
389 REM
390 CLS: PRINT TAB(0,2)"Do you require any"'"instructions? ";:
    A$=GET$: X%=RND(-TIME)
397 REM
398 REM Provide information if required
399 REM
400 IF A$="Y" THEN
      PRINT "Yes": PROCwait(0.5): MODE 1: VDU 23;8202;0;0;0;:
      PROCinfo: MODE 2: VDU 23;8202;0;0;0;: PROCdemo
    ELSE
      PRINT "No"
406 REM
407 REM Set up distribution of items and layout of castle,
408 REM and then draw ground floor plan
409 REM
410 PROCitems: PROCdoors: PROCsetup
417 REM
418 REM Store Item% and Door% in memory from &900
419 REM
420 K=&900: FOR I=0 TO N%:
      !K=Item%(I): K=K+4: NEXT
430 FOR I=0 TO F%:
      FOR J=0 TO 9:
        !K=Door%(I,J): K=K+4: NEXT:
      NEXT
437 REM
438 REM Store names of items and player in memory from &D00
439 REM
440 K=&D00: FOR I=0 TO 15:
      $K=Item$(I): K=K+LEN(Item$(I))+1: NEXT:
    $K=$&408
447 REM
448 REM Chain next (and last!) program
449 REM
450 ON ERROR OFF: CHAIN "Castle"
457 REM
458 REM Procedure to create layout of castle passages
459 REM
460 DEF PROCdoors
470 LOCAL d%,d1%,foe%,f%,t%
477 REM
478 REM Clear Door% array
479 REM
480 FOR I%=0 TO F%:
      FOR J%=0 TO 9:
        Door%(I%,J%)=0: NEXT:
      NEXT
486 REM
487 REM Set up the main entrance (0,5) and the door to
```

```
488 REM the tower (a random door on the top floor)
489 REM
490 Door%(0,5)=&7000080: Door%(F%,RND(10)-1)=&5AA00FF
497 REM
498 REM Create a (random) chain from ground floor to top
499 REM
500 FOR I%=0 TO F%-1
510   REPEAT
        d%=RND(10)-1: UNTIL Door%(I%,d%)=0
520   REPEAT
        d1%=RND(10)-1: UNTIL Door%(I%+1,d1%)=0
527   REM
528   REM Define guardian and store relevant details
529   REM
530   foe%=FNfoe(I%,d%,0): Door%(I%,d%)=foe% OR (256*(I%+1)+d1%)
540   foe%=FNfoe(I%+1,d1%,foe%):
      Door%(I%+1,d1%)=foe% OR (256*I%+d%)
550   NEXT
557 REM
558 REM Create (random) links between all remaining doors
559 REM
560 FOR I%=0 TO F%:
      FOR J%=0 TO 9
570     IF Door%(I%,J%)<>0 THEN
          GOTO 620
580     REPEAT
          d%=RND(10)-1: IF I%<F% THEN
            f%=I%+RND(F%+1-I%)-1
          ELSE
            f%=I%
590       UNTIL Door%(f%,d%)=0 AND 10*f%+d%<>10*I%+J%
597     REM
598     REM Define guardian and store relevant details
599     REM
600     foe%=FNfoe(I%,J%,0): Door%(I%,J%)=foe% OR (256*f%+d%)
610     foe%=FNfoe(f%,d%,foe%): Door%(f%,d%)=foe% OR (256*I%+J%)
620     NEXT:
      NEXT
630 ENDPROC
637 REM
638 REM Procedure to define guardian for a passage
639 REM
640 DEF FNfoe(f%,d%,foe%)
650 LOCAL c%,s%,m%,fo%
656 REM
657 REM foe% is zero on first entry for a passage, but
658 REM contains the details for the other end otherwise
659 REM
660 fo%=foe%
667 REM
668 REM If skeleton already assigned then return same
669 REM
670 IF (fo% AND &7000000)=&7000000 THEN
      =fo%
677 REM
```

```
678 REM If dragon already assigned then check direction
679 REM
680 IF fo%<>0 THEN
      GOTO 720
686 REM
687 REM No guardian yet - 1 in 4 is a skeleton, and
688 REM some of these are magic
689 REM
690 IF RND(4)=1 THEN
      fo%=&7000000 OR RND(F%) DIV 3*&40000: GOTO 730
697 REM
698 REM Determine strength, colour, magic, etc. of dragon
699 REM
700 s%=f%+RND(G%+5): IF RND(f%+2)>2 THEN
      c%=2: m%=RND(P%+f%)
    ELSE
      c%=1: m%=0
710 fo%=c%*&1000000 OR s%*&100000 OR m%*&10000
717 REM
718 REM Ensure that dragon faces in the correct direction
719 REM
720 IF d%<5 THEN
      fo%=fo% OR &10000000
    ELSE
      fo%=fo% AND &FFFFFFF
727 REM
728 REM Establish whether passage has a trapdoor
729 REM
730 IF foe%=0 AND G%>=RND(5*F%) THEN
      fo%=fo% OR &800
740 =fo%
747 REM
748 REM Procedure to define position of items in the castle
749 REM
750 DEF PROCitems
760 LOCAL c,s,m,full
767 REM
768 REM Read item qualities from DATA
769 REM
770 FOR I%=0 TO N%
776    REM
777    REM There are only 16 discrete items, so if there are
778    REM more than 16 items the DATA must be read again
779    REM
780    IF I% MOD 16=0 THEN
         RESTORE 1910
787    REM
788    REM Store magic and strength in packed form in XX
789    REM
790    !XX=0: READ c,s,m: ?XX=c+16*(RND(F%+1)-1): XX?1=m+16*s
797    REM
798    REM Store (random) position in packed form in XX
799    REM
800    XX?2=RND(14)+2: XX?3=RND(16)+11
807    REM
```

```
808    REM Check if this position is free
809    REM
810    full=FALSE: FOR J%=0 TO I%-1
820      IF (Item%(J%) AND &FFFF00F0)=(!XX AND &FFFF00F0) THEN
           full=TRUE
830      NEXT
837    REM
838    REM If position is occupied then try again
839    REM
840    IF full THEN
           GOTO 800
850    Item%(I%)=!XX: NEXT
857 REM
858 REM Set item 5 (sword) as being already held by player
859 REM
860 Item%(5)=Item%(5) OR &80
870 ENDPROC
877 REM
878 REM Procedure to explain about the game and its commands
879 REM
880 DEF PROCinfo
890 LOCAL c
900 VDU 19,0,6;0;19,3,4;0;: CLS: COLOUR 3: Ttell=1: Twait=10:
    RESTORE 1370: PROCtell: PROCcontinue
910 COLOUR 130: CLS: c=3: FOR I=1 TO 5:
        COLOUR c: PROCtell: c=4-c: NEXT:
    PROCcontinue
920 ENDPROC
927 REM
928 REM Procedure to demonstrate items, creatures, etc.
929 REM
930 DEF PROCdemo
940 LOCAL c,s,m,ch
950 Ttell=0: Twait=0: COLOUR 3: PROCtell: PRINT: PRINT
957 REM
958 REM Draw items using information read from DATA
959 REM
960 RESTORE 1910: FOR I=0 TO 15:
        READ c,s,m: ch=FNchar(I)
970    PROCwait(0.5): COLOUR c: PRINT TAB(5)CHR$ch;: COLOUR 6:
       PRINT " "Item$(I): NEXT:
    PROCcontinue
977 REM
978 REM Draw dragons, spirits and skeletons
979 REM
980 CLS: COLOUR 7: RESTORE 1830: PROCtell: FOR I=1 TO 2:
        VDU 17,I,32,244,245: NEXT:
    PROCwait(1)
990 COLOUR 7: PROCtell: FOR I=14 TO 12 STEP -1:
        VDU 17,I,32,11,238,8,10,239: NEXT:
    PROCwait(1)
1000 COLOUR 7: PROCtell: FOR I=1 TO 2:
        VDU 32,11,242,8,10,243: NEXT
1007 REM
1008 REM Draw Morgan le Fey
```

```
1009 REM
1010 PROCwait(1): PROCtell: PROCcontinue: VDU 28,0,31,19,30,12,26
1017 REM
1018 REM Draw demonstration wall, and then add a door
1019 REM
1020 COLOUR 7: PROCtell: MOVE 120,172: GCOL 0,1: DRAW 1152,172:
     PROCwait(2)
1030 PROCtell: MOVE 600,172: GCOL 0,4: DRAW 679,172
1040 ENDPROC
1047 REM
1048 REM Procedure to draw a plan of the ground floor
1049 REM
1050 DEF PROCsetup
1060 LOCAL x,y,dx,dy
1067 REM
1068 REM Draw walls
1069 REM
1070 VDU 18,0,128,18,0,1,26,16,5,25,4,120;932;25,1,1032;0;25,1,0;
     -644;25,1,-1032;0;25,1,0;644;18,0,4
1077 REM
1078 REM Draw doors using coordinates read from DATA
1079 REM
1080 RESTORE 1920: FOR I%=0 TO 9:
         READ x,y,dx,dy: VDU 25,4,x;y;25,1,dx;dy;: NEXT
1087 REM
1088 REM Draw all items positioned on the ground floor
1089 REM
1090 FOR I=1 TO N%:
         IF (Item%(I) AND &F0)=0 THEN
         PROCdrawitem(I)
1100     NEXT:
     T%=0: Q%=1: VDU 4,17,2,28,0,31,19,26
1110 Ttell=0: Twait=0: RESTORE 1890: PROCtell: PRINT: PRINT: A%=0
1120 ENDPROC
1127 REM
1128 REM Procedure to draw an item in its correct place
1129 REM
1130 DEF PROCdrawitem(n)
1140 LOCAL x,y,c,ch
1147 REM
1148 REM Unpack colour and coordinates
1149 REM
1150 !XX=Item%(n): c=(?XX) AND &0F: x=(XX?2)*64: y=(XX?3)*32:
     n=n MOD 16
1157 REM
1158 REM Obtain character used for plotting this item
1159 REM
1160 ch=FNchar(n)
1167 REM
1168 REM Plot item in correct position and colour
1169 REM
1170 GCOL 3,c: MOVE x,y: PRINT CHR$ch;
1180 ENDPROC
1186 REM
1187 REM Function to obtain character used to plot an item
```

```
1188 REM as rubies, emeralds and diamonds differ only in colour
1189 REM
1190 DEF FNchar(n)
1200 IF n>3 THEN
        =222+n
     ELSE
       IF n=0 THEN
          =224
       ELSE
          =225
1207 REM
1208 REM Procedure to control listing continuation
1209 REM
1210 DEF PROCcontinue
1220 LOCAL x
1230 *FX15,1
1240 COLOUR 1: PRINT TAB(Twait,31);"Any key to continue";: x=GET
1250 ENDPROC
1257 REM
1258 REM Procedure to display text read from DATA
1259 REM
1260 DEF PROCtell
1270 LOCAL lin,line$
1280 line$=STRING$(20," "): READ lin: REPEAT
        READ line$: PRINT TAB(Ttell,lin);line$;: READ lin:
        IF lin<0 THEN
           PROCwait(-lin): READ lin
1290    UNTIL lin>31
1300 ENDPROC
1307 REM
1308 REM Procedure to wait t seconds
1309 REM
1310 DEF PROCwait(t)
1320 t=TIME+100*t
1330 REPEAT
        UNTIL TIME>t
1340 ENDPROC
1347 REM
1348 REM Error exit
1349 REM
1350 MODE 7: REPORT: IF ERR<>17 THEN
        PRINT " at line ";ERL
1360 PRINT '"Press f0 key to restart": END
1367 REM
1368 REM Data for text listing, etc.
1369 REM
1370 DATA   1,"As you move around the castle you will"
1380 DATA   2,"find various items lying on the floor.",-3
1390 DATA   4,"Most of these will be of some use in"
1400 DATA   5,"fighting with dragons or warding off"
1410 DATA   6,"any evil spirits that may find you but"
1420 DATA   7,"some of them are totally useless!",-6
1430 DATA   9,"You will have to find out for yourself"
1440 DATA   10,"what is valuable and what is not.",-3
1450 DATA   12,"For your Final Test in the forest you"
```

```
1460 DATA  13,"were (naturally) carrying a sword with"
1470 DATA  14,"which to defend yourself and you still"
1480 DATA  15,"have it with you.  You may also"
1490 DATA  16,"collect anything that you find which"
1500 DATA  17,"you think may be useful.",-9
1510 DATA  19,"Some of the objects in the castle have"
1520 DATA  20,"magic powers which they will endow you"
1530 DATA  21,"with for as long as you are holding"
1540 DATA  22,"them.  It is impossible to get through"
1550 DATA  23,"some of the doors in the castle unless"
1560 DATA  24,"you have sufficient magic power and,"
1570 DATA  25,"of course, an evil spirit cannot be"
1580 DATA  26,"harmed by any ordinary weapon.",-12
1590 DATA  28,"You should also beware of any green"
1600 DATA  29,"dragons as they too have magic powers!",-2,99
1610 DATA  1,"I shall draw a plan of each room of"
1620 DATA  2,"the castle that you enter.",-3
1630 DATA  4,"You can instruct me to move around the"
1640 DATA  5,"room by use of the four cursor control"
1650 DATA  6,"keys, or to carry out various other"
1660 DATA  7,"actions by typing one of the following"
1670 DATA  8,"commands:",-6,99
1680 DATA  10,"GET something from the floor",-1
1690 DATA  11,"DROP something that you are carrying",-1
1700 DATA  12,"OPEN a door",-2,99
1710 DATA  14,"I only need the first letter of the"
1720 DATA  15,"command and enough letters of any"
1730 DATA  16,"other words for me to identify them,"
1740 DATA  17,"but they must be in capitals.",-6
1750 DATA  19,"Finally, I will give you a list of"
1760 DATA  20,"what you are carrying (if you have"
1770 DATA  21,"forgotten) if you type",99
1780 DATA  23,"INVENTORY",-5,99
1790 DATA  25,"(or just I).  This extra work will"
1800 DATA  26,"use up some of our joint energy"
1810 DATA  27,"though, so don't ask too often!",-4,99
1820 DATA  3,"These are the items",4,"that you may find",5,
     "in the castle:",-2,99
1830 DATA  3,"You may also meet",5,"Dragons",99,8,"Spirits",99
1840 DATA  11,"Skeletons",99,13,"or even Morgan le",14,
     "Fey herself!",99
1850 DATA  17,"I shall now draw you",18,"a plan of the ground",19,
     "floor of the castle"
1860 DATA  20,"showing the objects",21,"to be found there",-3
1870 DATA  23,"I shall draw the",24,"walls in red",-1,99
1880 DATA  28,"while the doors will",29,"be in blue.",-1,99
1890 DATA  0,"Please wait while",1,"I prepare myself",99
1897 REM
1898 REM Data for names of items to be found in the castle
1899 REM
1900 DATA  Axe,Ruby,Emerald,Diamond,Belt,Sword,Cross,Skull,Hat,Salt,
     Necklace,Shield,Lamp,Spear,Feathers,Ring
1907 REM
1908 REM Data for colour, strength and magic of items
1909 REM
```

```
1910 DATA   3,14,0,1,0,9,2,0,4,7,0,0,5,1,0,3,11,0,6,3,7,7,1,2,4,0,3,
     7,0,0,1,0,3,6,8,0,3,2,0,6,10,0,7,0,0,3,0,15
1917 REM
1918 REM Data for coordinates of doors
1919 REM
1920 DATA   312,932,79,0,600,932,79,0,888,932,79,0,1152,743,0,-79,
     1152,551,0,-79,967,288,-79,0,679,288,-79,0,391,288,-79,0,120,
     472,0,79,120,664,0,79
```

A.5   Castle

```
  1 REM IMPORTANT!
  2 REM Only those lines whose line numbers end in 0
  3 REM (10, 20, 30, etc.) should be typed.
  4 REM You can therefore use AUTO and ignore lines
  5 REM which are not multiples of 10.
  6 REM
  7 REM This program MUST then be compacted to remove
  8 REM non-essential spaces or it will be too big
  9 REM
 10 *KEY10OLD|MGOTO1570|M
 20 ON ERROR GOTO 1560
 27 REM
 28 REM Author:  Miles Ellis, 1983
 29 REM
 30 REM Copyright 1984, John Wiley & Sons, Limited
 40 ENVELOPE 1,1,2,-2,2,10,20,10,1,0,0,0,50,50
 50 DIM Door%(7,9),Item%(29),Item$(15),Sx%(3),Sy%(3),XX 3
 56 REM
 57 REM Set up Item%, Door%, Item$ and Name$ from information
 58 REM stored in areas from &900 and &D00 by CASTLE2
 59 REM
 60 CLS: K%=&900: FOR I%=0 TO N%:
       Item%(I%)=!K%: K%=K%+4: NEXT
 70 FOR I%=0 TO F%:
       FOR J%=0 TO 9:
         Door%(I%,J%)=!K%: K%=K%+4: NEXT:
       NEXT
 80 K%=&D00: FOR I%=0 TO 15:
       Item$(I%)=$K%: K%=K%+LEN($K%)+1: NEXT:
     Name$=$K%
 87 REM
 88 REM Set up initial conditions
 89 REM
 90 S%=0: Z%=0: M%=1: O%=1: E%=7: S$=STRING$(20," "): *FX11,0
100 C=5: S=5+G%: M=0: W=11: *FX4,1
106 REM
107 REM Draw ground floor plan (if necessary) and plot
108 REM player at open main entrance (with skeleton)
109 REM
110 PROCplan: PROCexit(5)
117 REM
118 REM Main program loop
119 REM
120 TIME=0: REPEAT
127     REM
128     REM Take action if a key has been pressed
129     REM
130     C%=INKEY(0): IF C%>135 AND C%<140 THEN
           PROCmove
         ELSE
           IF C%<>-1 THEN
             PROCgetcom
137     REM
138     REM Move spirits (if any present)
139     REM
```

```
140    IF T%>0 THEN
          PROCmovespirit
147    REM
148    REM Create a new spirit if maximum wait time exceeded
149    REM
150    IF C%<>-1 THEN
          TIME=0
       ELSE
         IF TIME>W% THEN
            PROCgetspirit: TIME=0
157    REM
158    REM If strength is exhausted then player must die!
159    REM
160    IF S<.1 THEN
          RESTORE 1720: PROCtune: GOTO 1550
167    REM
168    REM Calculate and print score
169    REM
170    H%=(C+S)*(M+W+M%): VDU 4: PRINT TAB(4,31)"Score: ";H%;" ";:
       VDU 5
177    REM
178    REM Repeat unless tower floor has been reached
179    REM
180    UNTIL Z%>F%
187 REM
188 REM Success! Print congratulations and play jolly tune
189 REM
190 MODE 1: COLOUR 129: CLS: RESTORE 1750: PROCtune:
    PRINT TAB(2,4)"Arise Sir ";Name$;"!": PROCwt(3):
    PRINT TAB(2,7)"You scored ";H%,TAB(2,30);: GOTO 1570
197 REM
198 REM Procedure to draw floor plan including any items
199 REM
200 DEF PROCplan: LOCAL x,y,dx,dy,c
210 T%=0: Q%=1: VDU 20,26,5: IF A%=0 THEN
       ENDPROC
217 REM
218 REM Draw walls
219 REM
220 GCOL 0,128: GCOL 0,1: CLG: MOVE 120,932: PLOT 1,1032,0:
    PLOT 1,0,-644: PLOT 1,-1032,0: PLOT 1,0,644
227 REM
228 REM Choose door for dungeon and set door colour
229 REM
230 K%=RND(10): IF Z%<0 THEN
      c=1
    ELSE
      c=4
237 REM
238 REM Draw doors using coordinates read from DATA
239 REM
240 RESTORE 1600: FOR I%=1 TO 10:
       READ x,y,dx,dy: IF I%=K% THEN
         GCOL 0,4
       ELSE
```

```
          GCOL 0,c
250    MOVE x,y: PLOT 1,dx,dy: NEXT
257 REM
258 REM Draw all items on this floor
259 REM
260 FOR I%=0 TO N%:
       IF (Item%(I%) AND &F0)=Z%*16 THEN
         PROCdrawitem(I%)
270    NEXT:
    ENDPROC
277 REM
278 REM Procedure to draw an item in its correct place
279 REM
280 DEF PROCdrawitem(n): LOCAL x,y,c,ch
287 REM
288 REM Unpack colour and coordinates
289 REM
290 !XX=Item%(n): c=?XX AND &0F: x=XX?2*64: y=XX?3*32: n=n MOD 16
297 REM
298 REM Establish correct character for this item
299 REM
300 IF n>3 THEN
      ch=222+n
    ELSE
      IF n=0 THEN
        ch=224
      ELSE
        ch=225
307 REM
308 REM Plot item
309 REM
310 GCOL 3,c: MOVE x,y: PRINT CHR$ch;: ENDPROC
317 REM
318 REM Procedure to open a door and draw player beside it
319 REM
320 DEF PROCexit(d): LOCAL x,y,dx,dy
330 PROCopen(d): B%=SGN(X%-650): A%=249+B%: PROCman: PROCmtq:
    ENDPROC
337 REM
338 REM Procedure to draw a door opening, and its guardian
339 REM
340 DEF PROCopen(d): LOCAL x,y,a,inc,dx,dy,du,dv,c
347 REM
348 REM Determine position of door and direction of opening
349 REM
350 IF d<3 THEN
      x=312+288*d: y=932: a=0: X%=x+8: Y%=y-4
    ELSE
      IF d<5 THEN
        x=1152: y=743-192*(d-3): a=-PI/2: X%=x-64: Y%=y-7
      ELSE
        IF d<8 THEN
          x=967-288*(d-5): y=288: a=PI: X%=x-71: Y%=y+64
        ELSE
          x=120: y=472+192*(d-8): a=PI/2: X%=x+8: Y%=y+72
```

```
360 inc=PI/16: GCOL 0,4: dx=79*COS(a): dy=79*SIN(a)
367 REM
368 REM Draw door opening
369 REM
370 FOR I%=1 TO 8:
      a=a+inc: du=79*COS(a): dv=79*SIN(a): MOVE x,y: PLOT 3,dx,dy:
      dx=du: dy=dv: MOVE x,y: PLOT 1,dx,dy: NEXT
377 REM
378 REM No guardian on dungeon door
379 REM
380 IF Z%<0 THEN
      ENDPROC
387 REM
388 REM Calculate position of guardian (if any)
389 REM
390 IF d<5 THEN
     x=x+8
    ELSE
     x=x-64
400 IF d<3 OR d>7 THEN
     y=y+40
    ELSE
      IF d<5 THEN
        y=y-40
      ELSE
        y=y-8
407 REM
408 REM Extract colour of guardian
409 REM
410 !XX=Door%(Z%,d): c=XX?3: IF c=0 THEN
      ENDPROC
417 REM
418 REM Red or green dragon (left facing)
419 REM
420 IF c>15 THEN
      VDU 18,3,c-16,25,4,x;y;244,245: ENDPROC
427 REM
428 REM Red or green dragon (right facing)
429 REM
430 IF c<5 THEN
      VDU 18,3,c,25,4,x-64;y;246,247: ENDPROC
440 IF d<5 OR d>7 THEN
      y=y+32
447 REM
448 REM Skeleton (or Morgan le Fey)
449 REM
450 VDU 18,3,c,25,4,x;y;235+c,10,8,236+c: ENDPROC
457 REM
458 REM Procedure to draw a man
459 REM
460 DEF PROCman: VDU 18,3,E%,25,4,X%;Y%;A%,8,10,A%+1: ENDPROC
467 REM
468 REM Procedure to move the player (man)
469 REM
470 DEF PROCmove: LOCAL c1,c2,w
```

```
480 S%=G%: D%=B%: U%=X%: V%=Y%
487 REM
488 REM Calculate next position
489 REM
490 w=277-2*C%: IF C%<138 THEN
      w=w-1: D%=w-3: U%=X%-32*D%
    ELSE
      V%=Y%-32*w: w=w+2
497 REM
498 REM Check if move will be into a wall or a door
499 REM
500 IF FNwall(w)=w THEN
      GOTO 530
507 REM
508 REM Move man
509 REM
510 PROCman: A%=502-A%: X%=U%: Y%=V%: IF B%<>D% THEN
      B%=D%: A%=249+B%
520 PROCman: SOUND 0,-4,5,2: ENDPROC
527 REM
528 REM Check if move is through an open door
529 REM
530 c1=POINT(X1,Y1): c2=POINT(X2,Y2)
540 IF c1=0 AND c2=0 THEN
      PROCenter(X1,Y1,X2,Y2): ENDPROC
547 REM
548 REM Print error message
549 REM
550 S=.95*S: RESTORE 1610: PROCsay(1): IF c1=4 AND c2=4 THEN
      PRINT "door!"
    ELSE
      PRINT "wall!"
560 PROCcont: ENDPROC
567 REM
568 REM Function to determine player's relationship with walls
569 REM
570 DEF FNwall(d)
576 REM
577 REM Calculate number of any wall within one step
578 REM in the current direction
579 REM
580 X1=X%: X2=X%+56: Y1=Y%-60: Y2=Y%:
    ON d+1GOTO 590,620,600,610,590
590 IF X%=128 THEN
      X1=120: X2=120: =4
600 IF X%=1088 THEN
      X1=1152: X2=1152: =2
610 IF Y%=352 THEN
      Y1=288: Y2=288: =3
620 IF Y%=928 THEN
      Y1=932: Y2=932: =1
630 =0
637 REM
638 REM Procedure to create a new spirit
639 REM
```

```
640 DEF PROCgetspirit
647 REM
648 REM Are maximum number already active?
649 REM
650 IF T%=S% THEN
      ENDPROC
657 REM
658 REM Find one which is not active
659 REM
660 T%=T%+1: R%=0: REPEAT
      R%=R%+1: UNTIL Q% MOD (R%+2)>0:
    Q%=Q%*(R%+2)
667 REM
668 REM Calculate a suitable point of appearance
669 REM
670 K%=320+8*RND(20): L%=SGN(610-X%): Sx%(R%)=X%+L%*K%:
    K%=160+4*RND(30): L%=SGN(650-Y%): Sy%(R%)=Y%+L%*K%: PROCspirit:
    SOUND R%,1,245-10*R%,255: ENDPROC
677 REM
678 REM Procedure to draw a spirit
679 REM
680 DEF PROCspirit:
    VDU 18,3,15-R%,25,4,Sx%(R%);Sy%(R%);238,8,10,239: ENDPROC
687 REM
688 REM Procedure to move all spirits currently present
689 REM
690 DEF PROCmovespirit: LOCAL x,y,dx,dy
700 FOR R%=1 TO S%:
      IF Q% MOD (R%+2)>0 THEN
        NEXT:
      ENDPROC
710   x=Sx%(R%): dx=X%-x: y=Sy%(R%): dy=Y%-y
717   REM
718   REM Move spirit towards player
719   REM
720   IF ABS(dx)>ABS(dy) THEN
        x=x+8*R%*SGN(dx)
      ELSE
        y=y+8*R%*SGN(dy)
730   IF ABS(X%-x)>60 OR ABS(Y%-y)>60 THEN
        PROCspirit: Sx%(R%)=x: Sy%(R%)=y: PROCspirit: NEXT:
      ENDPROC
736   REM
737   REM Spirit is close to player - if player is strong
738   REM enough then repel spirit, otherwise weaken player
739   REM
740   C=.97*C: IF M>3*R% THEN
        S=.9*S: SOUND 16+R%,0,0,1: PROCspirit: T%=T%-1:
        Q%=Q% DIV (R%+2): PROCgetspirit
      ELSE
        IF M>0 THEN
          S=.99*S
        ELSE
          S=.95*S
747   REM
```

```
748    REM If player is very weak then set him flashing
749    REM
750    IF S<1 THEN
          PROCman: E%=15: PROCman
760    NEXT:
    ENDPROC
767 REM
768 REM Procedure to silence all spirit wailing
769 REM
770 DEF PROCquiet: FOR I%=1 TO T%:
       SOUND 16+I%,0,0,1: NEXT:
    ENDPROC
777 REM
778 REM Procedure to obtain and act on a command
779 REM
780 DEF PROCgetcom
790 VDU 4,28,0,31,19,26,31,3,0,17,3: C$=CHR$(C%):
    ON INSTR("OGDI",C$)+1GOTO 860,800,810,820,830
800 PROCopn: ENDPROC
810 PROCget: ENDPROC
820 PROCdrop: ENDPROC
827 REM
828 REM Print list of items held
829 REM
830 PRINT "Inventory": PRINT
840 FOR I%=0 TO N%:
       IF (Item%(I%) AND &80)<>0 THEN
          PRINT Item$(I% MOD 16);: PROCwt(1)
850    NEXT:
    PRINT: PROCcont: C=.9*C: ENDPROC
860 PRINT C$;: INPUT ""S$: RESTORE 1650: PROCsay(1): ENDPROC
867 REM
868 REM Function to obtain the name of an item
869 REM
870 DEF FNitem: LOCAL n
880 PROCmtq: C$=GET$: n=INSTR("AREDBSCSHSNSLSFR",C$)-1: PRINT C$;
890 IF n=5 THEN
       S$=GET$: n=2*INSTR("WKAHP",S$)+3: IF n=3 THEN
          n=-3
900 IF n=1 THEN
       S$=GET$: n=14*INSTR("UI",S$)-13
910 IF n<-1 THEN
       PRINT S$;
920 IF n<0 THEN
       RESTORE 1650: PROCsay(1): =-1
930 PRINT CHR$(8);Item$(n): PROCmtq: =n
936 REM
937 REM Procedure to enter a doorway and fight its guardian
938 REM (if necessary) before entering the passage
939 REM
940 DEF PROCenter(x1,y1,x2,y2): LOCAL c,d,p,m,s,f,t
950 IF Z%<0 THEN
       PROCquiet: Z%=0: PROCplan: PROCman: ENDPROC
957 REM
958 REM Unpack details of guardian
```

```
 959 REM
 960 d=FNdoor(x1,y1,x2,y2): !XX=Door%(Z%,d): c=XX?3 MOD 16: p=XX?2:
     IF c=5 THEN
        M=M*O%
 967 REM
 968 REM If nothing there, or zero strength, enter passage
 969 REM
 970 IF c=0 OR p=0 THEN
        f=XX?1: d=?XX: PROCtunnel(f,d): ENDPROC
 977 REM
 978 REM Noise and flashing for battle
 979 REM
 980 t=TIME+c MOD 7*50: REPEAT
        VDU 19,0,c MOD 4;0;: SOUND 0,-15,4,3: PROCwt(.1):
        VDU 19,0,7;0;: SOUND 0,-15,5,2: PROCwt(.1): UNTIL TIME>t:
     VDU 20
 986 REM
 987 REM Calculate effect of any magical clash,
 988 REM and then of any physical battle
 989 REM
 990 C=C+.01*c*C: s=(p DIV 16)*(3+RND(1)): m=(p MOD 16)*(c MOD 6):
     IF m>M THEN
        GOTO 1030
     ELSE
        IF s>(C+S+W) THEN
          GOTO 1040
 997 REM
 998 REM Victory! Morgan le Fey is defeated!
 999 REM
1000 IF c=5 THEN
        PROCquiet: S=S+s+m: Z%=F%+1: T%=0: ENDPROC
1007 REM
1008 REM Unpack details of passage
1009 REM
1010 c=c DIV 7*7: XX?2=0: XX?3=c: Door%(Z%,d)=!XX: f=(XX?1 AND 7):
     d=?XX: !XX=Door%(f,d): XX?2=0: XX?3=c: Door%(f,d)=!XX:
     S=S+.1*s: IF S>1 THEN
        E%=7
1017 REM
1018 REM Enter passage
1019 REM
1020 PROCtunnel(f,d): ENDPROC
1027 REM
1028 REM Player is defeated by magical powers
1029 REM
1030 IF c=7 THEN
        RESTORE 1710: PROCsay(5): ENDPROC
1037 REM
1038 REM Player is defeated by dragon or Morgan le Fey
1039 REM
1040 IF c=5 THEN
        C=.5*C: S=.5*S: M=M DIV O%: RESTORE 1700: GOTO 1060
1050 RESTORE 1690: PROCsay(1): IF s>5*S THEN
        S=.75*S: PRINT "badly";
     ELSE
```

```
          S=.9*S: PRINT "slightly";
1060 PROCsay(1): IF S<1 THEN
          PROCman: E%=15: PROCman
1070 ENDPROC
1077 REM
1078 REM Function to determine the number of a door
1079 REM
1080 DEF FNdoor(x1,y1,x2,y2)
1090 IF x1=120 THEN
          =8+(y2 DIV 600)
1100 IF x1=1152 THEN
          =4-(y2 DIV 600)
1110 IF y1=288 THEN
          =7-(x2 DIV 400)
1120 =x2 DIV 400
1127 REM
1128 REM Procedure to move along a tunnel to another doorway
1129 REM
1130 DEF PROCtunnel(f,d): LOCAL n,dx,dy
1137 REM
1138 REM Deal with any possible trapdoor
1139 REM
1140 PROCquiet: n=38: IF f>7 THEN
          f=f-7: n=RND(80-P%*G%): IF n>38 THEN
          n=38
1146 REM
1147 REM Establish direction of travel (left/right,
1148 REM and up/down/level)
1149 REM
1150 IF B%<0 THEN
          X%=0: dx=32
     ELSE
          X%=1216: dx=-32
1160 IF f>Z% THEN
          Y%=160: dy=20
     ELSE
          IF f<Z% THEN
            Y%=920: dy=-20
          ELSE
            Y%=540: dy=0
1167 REM
1168 REM Move man across screen
1169 REM
1170 CLG: FOR I%=1 TO n:
          PROCman: SOUND 0,-4,5,2: PROCwt(.1): PROCman: A%=502-A%:
          X%=X%+dx: Y%=Y%+dy: NEXT:
     IF n<38 THEN
          PROCdungeon: ENDPROC
1180 IF d<>128 THEN
          GOTO 1200
     ELSE
          RESTORE 1620: PROCsay(1): C$=GET$
1187 REM
1188 REM Player has left castle - does he wish to return?
1189 REM
```

```
1190 IF C$="Y" THEN
        PRINT "Yes": d=5
     ELSE
        PRINT "No": PROCwt(2): CLS: RESTORE 1740: GOTO 1550
1197 REM
1198 REM Draw new floor plan and continue game
1199 REM
1200 Z%=f: PROCplan: PROCexit(d): TIME=0: ENDPROC
1207 REM
1208 REM Procedure to process an OPEN command
1209 REM
1210 DEF PROCopn
1220 PRINT "Open door": PROCwt(1): VDU 12,26,5: PROCmtq
1230 IF FNwall(0) AND POINT(X1,Y1)=4 AND POINT(X2,Y2)=4 THEN
        GOTO 1240
     ELSE
        C=.95*C: RESTORE 1640: PROCsay(1): ENDPROC
1240 d=FNdoor(X1,Y1,X2,Y2): PROCopen(d)
1250 ENDPROC
1257 REM
1258 REM Procedure to drop man through trapdoor into the dungeon
1259 REM
1260 DEF PROCdungeon
1270 REPEAT
        PROCman: PROCwt(.05): PROCman: Y%=Y%-20: UNTIL Y%<63:
     RESTORE 1630: PROCsay(1)
1280 FOR I%=0 TO N%:
        Item%(I%)=Item%(I%) AND &FFFFFF7F: NEXT
1290 X%=128+64*RND(14): Y%=352+32*RND(9): Z%=-1: M%=0: O%=1: W=0:
     M=0: PROCplan: PROCwt(4-G%): PROCman: VDU 19,4,1;0;: ENDPROC
1297 REM
1298 REM Procedure to process a GET command
1299 REM
1300 DEF PROCget
1310 PRINT "Get ";: I%=FNitem: IF I%<0 THEN
        ENDPROC
1320 IF M%=6 THEN
        RESTORE 1670: GOTO 1360
1330 !XX=0: XX?3=Y% DIV 32-1: XX?2=X% DIV 64: ?XX=16*Z%
1340 IF (Item%(I%) AND &FFFF00F0)=!XX THEN
        !XX=Item%(I%): Item%(I%)=!XX OR &80: K%=XX?1: GOSUB 1410:
        M%=M%+1: ENDPROC
1350 I%=I%+16: IF I%<=N% THEN
        GOTO 1340
     ELSE
        RESTORE 1660
1360 PROCsay(1): ENDPROC
1367 REM
1368 REM Procedure to process a DROP command
1369 REM
1370 DEF PROCdrop
1380 PRINT "Drop ";: I%=FNitem: IF I%<0 THEN
        ENDPROC
1390 IF (Item%(I%) AND &80)<>0 THEN
        !XX=Item%(I%): XX?3=Y% DIV 32-1: XX?2=X% DIV 64:
```

```
          ?XX=16*Z%+?XX MOD 16: Item%(I%)=!XX: K%=-XX?1: GOSUB 1410:
          M%=M%-1: ENDPROC
1400 I%=I%+16: IF I%<=N% THEN
          GOTO 1390
     ELSE
          RESTORE 1680: PROCsay(1): ENDPROC
1406 REM
1407 REM Lines 1410 and 1420 are used by GOSUB statements
1408 REM at lines 1340 and 1390 in order to save space
1409 REM
1410 W=W+K% DIV 16: M=M+K% MOD 16: PROCwt(1): VDU 12,26,5:
     PROCdrawitem(I%): IF I%=14 THEN
          O%=3-O%
1420 RETURN
1427 REM
1428 REM Procedure to wait for t seconds
1429 REM
1430 DEF PROCwt(t): t=TIME+100*t: REPEAT
          UNTIL TIME>t:
     ENDPROC
1437 REM
1438 REM Procedure to control listing continuation
1439 REM
1440 DEF PROCcont: LOCAL x
1450 PROCmtq: COLOUR 6: PRINT TAB(0,5);"Any key to continue";:
     x=GET: VDU 12,26,5: ENDPROC
1457 REM
1458 REM Procedure to display text read from DATA
1459 REM
1460 DEF PROCsay(c): LOCAL n
1470 VDU 4,28,0,31,19,26,17,c: READ n: REPEAT
          READ S$: PRINT TAB(0,n);S$;: READ n: IF n<0 THEN
          PROCwt(-n): READ n
1480     UNTIL n>31:
     IF n<100 THEN
          PROCcont
1490 ENDPROC
1497 REM
1498 REM Procedure to clear keyboard buffer
1499 REM
1500 DEF PROCmtq: *FX15,1
1510 ENDPROC
1517 REM
1518 REM Procedure to play a tune from notes read from DATA
1519 REM
1520 DEF PROCtune: LOCAL a,p,d
1530 PROCquiet: READ p: REPEAT
          READ d: IF d=0 THEN
          a=0
     ELSE
          a=-15
1540     SOUND 1,a,p,d: READ p: UNTIL p<0:
     ENDPROC
1547 REM
1548 REM Common exit for death or cowardice
```

```
1549 REM
1550 PROCsay(1): PRINT ;H%: PROCcont
1557 REM
1558 REM Error exit
1559 REM
1560 MODE 7: REPORT: IF ERR<>17 THEN
        PRINT " at line ";ERL
1567 REM
1568 REM Entrypoint after a BREAK
1569 REM
1570 PRINT '"Press f0 key to rerun": *FX4,0
1580 *FX12,0
1590 END
1597 REM
1598 REM Data for coordinates of doors
1599 REM
1600 DATA 312,932,79,0,600,932,79,0,888,932,79,0,1152,743,0,-79,
        1152,551,0,-79,967,288,-79,0,679,288,-79,0,391,288,-79,0,120,
        472,0,79,120,664,0,79
1607 REM
1608 REM Data for text, etc. to be displayed
1609 REM
1610 DATA 1,You can't just walk,2,through the ,100
1620 DATA 0,That was the front,1,door of the castle!,3,
        Do you wish to go,4,back inside?,100
1630 DATA 0,You have fallen,1,through a concealed,2,
        trapdoor into the,3,dungeon!,-5,100
1640 DATA 2,You can't reach,3,any doors!,99
1650 DATA 2,I don't understand!,99
1660 DATA 2,None within reach!,99
1670 DATA 2,You can't carry,3,any more!,99
1680 DATA 2,You haven't any!,99
1690 DATA 1,The dragon ,100,2,wounds you and you,3,
        can't get past him!,99
1700 DATA 1,Morgan le Fey is far,2,too powerful for you,99
1710 DATA 2,Some unseen force,3,drives you back!,99
1717 REM
1718 REM Data for "Gypsy Lament" to be played when the player
        dies
1719 REM
1720 DATA 32,12,32,0,32,12,52,18,32,6,24,6,16,6,12,6,4,6,12,24,32,
        12,64,12,60,18,52,6,44,6,24,6,32,3,44,3,36,6,32,24,32,0,32,12,
        48,12,52,18,36,6,32,6,12,6,16,3,32,3,24,3,16,3,4,24,-1
1727 REM
1728 REM Data for text, etc. to be displayed at player's death
1729 REM
1730 DATA 0,It is all over.,1,You are dead!,-2
1740 DATA 3,You scored ,100
1746 REM
1747 REM Data for "Hail! Hail! The Gang's all here!" to be played
1748 REM when the player reaches the tower
1749 REM
1750 DATA 108,8,108,0,108,6,100,2,100,0,100,4,92,4,72,8,72,0,72,2,
        80,2,88,2,72,2,80,4,72,4,72,0,72,2,80,2,88,2,72,2,80,4,72,4,
        108,8,108,0,108,6,100,2,100,0,100,4,92,4,72,8,72,0,72,2,80,2,
        88,2,92,2,100,4,120,4,92,16,-1
```

Appendix B

How The Final Test works

B.1 THE OVERALL STRUCTURE

The Final Test consists of four programs, of which only the last (Castle) needs any detailed explanation.

FINALTEST serves no purpose other than to provide a wide range of mode 7 graphics displays, to provide a (historical!) background to the game, and to request the player's name. It then loads and runs CASTLE (i.e. it "chains" CASTLE).

CASTLE reproduces the mode 7 opening title sequence using mode 2 (unless it has been chained from FINALTEST), asks for the player's name (unless already provided) and his skill level. It uses his skill level to determine certain overall game parameters (P%, G%, F%, N% and W%, see figure 15.1), provides a further demonstration of mode 2 graphics, and then chains CASTLE2.

CASTLE2 sets up the user-defined characters, creates the tunnel "maze" that links the floors of the castle, determines what type of creature shall guard each door and where the various items shall be placed. It also provides some guidance on how to play the game, if requested. It then chains Castle.

Castle is the program that actually plays the game.

B.2 THE DATA BASE

The game is controlled by a number of variables and arrays. Foremost amongst these are the 26 resident integer variables (see figure 15.1) and three arrays which are set up by CASTLE2.

The array Door% determines the form of the castle. The first subscript defines the floor in the range 0 to F%, where F% is either 3, 5 or 7 depending upon the game level. The second subscript defines the door in the range 0 to 9. The array is set up by CASTLE2, which first sets up a (random) set of passages from floor 0 up to floor F%, in steps of one floor; there is, therefore, certain to be at least one route to the top. One door on the top floor is selected as the "winning" door to the tower; this is guarded by Morgan le Fey herself. Door 5 on the ground floor is the main entrance. The remaining doors are connected at random, by connecting each unconnected ground floor door to a random door (and vice-versa), then repeating the process for floor 1, etc.

Every element of Door% is set up as follows:

```
&xcsmffdd
```

where   dd is the door number (0–9) at the other end of the tunnel
          ff is the floor (0–7) at the other end of the tunnel
          m is the magic power of the tunnel's guardian (0–15)
          s is the strength of the tunnel's guardian (0–15)
          c is the colour of the tunnel's guardian
          x is used to determine which way a dragon is facing

There are two special doors – 128 indicates that this is the main entrance on the ground floor, while 255 indicates that this is the entrance to the tower.

Some of the tunnels have 8 added to the floor number; this indicates the presence of a trapdoor to the dungeon! The number of such trapdoors depends upon the player's skill. At the lowest level (1) there is a 1 in 15 chance that a tunnel will contain a trapdoor; since there are only four floors, and hence 19 tunnels, there will probably be one such trapdoor. At the highest level (8) the chance of a tunnel having a trapdoor has risen to 3 in 35; as there are now eight floors and 39 tunnels there is a strong likelihood of several trapdoors existing!

The type and strength of the tunnel guardians is set up at random according to certain rules which affect the probability of particular actions.

Thus 1 in 4 (approximately) are skeletons, whose colour is white. These have no strength, but their magic power is either 0, 4 or 8. For a level 1 game (player levels 1 and 2) about half have no magic and the rest have 4; there are no class 8 skeletons for beginners! For level 2 (player levels 3–6) the proportions are around 2:3:1, while at level 3 only one-quarter have no magic, with the others equally divided.

On the ground floor all dragons are red and have no magic; on higher floors the proportion of green dragons gradually increases, until floor 7 (used only at game level 3) has, on average, three green dragons to every red one.

The algorithms for determining both strength and magic depend upon the player's skill level and the floor on which the dragon was first set up. The values can range from 1 to 15. Morgan le Fey has both magical and physical strengths of ten.

In a similar way, the array Item% contains details of the various items to be found in the castle. The subscript ranges from 0 to N%, where N% is 15 for a (four-floor) level 1 game, 22 for a (six-floor) level 2 game and 29 for a (eight-floor) level 3 game. There are only 16 different types of item to be found, so levels 2 and 3 allow more than one copy of some items. Each element of Item% is set up as follows:

```
&fcsmxxyy
```

where   f is the floor on which the item is to be found (or where it used to be)
          c is its colour
          s is its strength factor (0–14)
          m is its magic factor (0–15)
          xx is the x co-ordinate on the floor (3–16)
          yy is the y co-ordinate on the floor (12–27)

The colour, strength and magic power of each type of item are stored in DATA statements in CASTLE2 (as are their names), and are READ from there and inserted into the appropriate parts of each array element.

The floor is set to a random value in the range 0–N%, thus distributing the items around the castle.

The position on the floor is also set up on a random basis, but in order to allow each co-ordinate to be stored in a single byte (i.e. in the range 0–255) the value stored cannot be the graphical co-ordinate but is a representation of the character position. A refinement is that items are not, initially, placed next to walls as this could lead to their being "hidden" by the player as he comes out of a door.

The various parts of Door% and Item% are extracted and inserted by direct byte addressing, using the special four-byte area whose address is stored in XX. This technique is described in detail in section 17.4

The final array is Item$, which simply contains the names of all the items to be found in the castle.

B.3   THE GAME

The game itself contains four main elements – moving around the castle, fighting off various creatures, collecting weapons and/or magical items, and processing requests.

The player figure is moved in the way described in chapter 12 using the four character pairs (248,249), (250,251), (252,253), (254,255). Before each move a check is made to see if it will result in collision with a wall (coloured red) or a door (coloured blue), and if so an error message is printed.

When a player passes through a door the relevant element of Door% is used to determine where he is to come out. This determines whether he is to go up, down or straight across the screen, and also enables the correct floor plan to be produced.

If the tunnel contains a trapdoor then the number of steps the player must take before he reaches it is calculated. This is a random number in the range 1–79 for a player with a skill level of 1, and a random number in the range 1–56 for one with a skill level of 8. There are 38 steps taken to cross the screen, and, therefore, the higher the player's skill the greater the likelihood of his falling through the trapdoor.

If he falls into the dungeon then he loses all his possessions and the door is only visible for a brief period; the higher the skill, the shorter the time the player has to spot the door. The door is made invisible by means of a VDU 19 statement (see line 1290), and therefore the *logical* colour remains unaltered; the program can thus see it, but you can't.

The method used to process requests to open a door, collect or drop an item, or to get an inventory listing, was described in section 10.4.

If a door is to be opened then the relevant element of Door% gives the *colour* of its guardian, and this directly indicates which character is to be drawn there. When a dragon is defeated it dies and the colour part of Door% is set to 0 (as is the corresponding door at the other end of the tunnel); the tunnel is then unguarded. A skeleton has no physical strength, but some have magical powers. When defeated they lose their magic but still remain at their post (they are after all already dead!). If you defeat Morgan le Fey you have finished the game and will receive suitable rewards.

Items to be collected have their floor increased by eight and are removed from the screen in the usual way by being plotted again using GCOL 3,c (where c is their colour). Items to be dropped have the current player co-ordinates (suitably scaled) inserted in their position fields, and the floor reset to the actual floor. They are plotted in the usual way.

The player has four variables which define his power. These are C (his courage), S (his strength), W (his weapon strength) and M (his magical strength).

Initially his courage is set to 5, his strength to 6, 7 or 8, depending on the game level, and his weapon strength to 11 because he starts with a sword; he has no magical items to begin with. Whenever he collects an item its strength and magic factors are added to W and M, respectively; when he drops an item then he loses the corresponding values.

The player's own courage and strength are altered as a result of his fights. If he attempts to enter a guarded tunnel then his courage will be increased slightly – by how much depends upon the type of his adversary.

The guardian's magic is then multiplied by two (if a green dragon) or five (if Morgan le Fey) and compared with the player's magic (M). If he is facing Morgan le Fey then feathers will double his magic power; otherwise they have no effect on anything! If he wins this magical battle then the sum of C, S and W is compared with the guardian's strength, multiplied by a random number in the range 3 to 3.999999999. If he wins this battle then he enters the tunnel.

If the player defeats Morgan le Fey then he adds her physical *and* magical powers to his strength. If he defeats anyone (anything?) else then he adds 10% of their physical strength to his strength.

If he is defeated by Morgan le Fey he loses 50% of both his courage and his strength. If he is defeated by a dragon then there are two possibilities. If its strength is more than five times the player's strength (S) then he is "badly wounded" and loses 25% of his strength, otherwise he is only "slightly wounded" and loses 10% of his strength.

Finally we come to the spirits. If a player does nothing for a period of time (8 seconds for a beginner, but only 1 second for a player with level 8 skill) then a spirit will appear. Either one, two or three spirits may appear in total – each more vicious than the last; the number depends upon the game level. No spirits can appear until the player has made his *first* move.

The spirits move more or less directly towards the player until they get close enough to attack him. Their co-ordinates are kept in the arrays Sx% and Sy%, and either the x or y co-ordinate is altered by 8, 16 or 24 units in the appropriate direction, depending on the spirit; the spirit is then moved in the usual way, thus making the three spirits move at different speeds.

When the spirit is within 60 units of the player (in both directions) it stops moving and attacks the player. Every time that the main loop is executed the player's courage is reduced by 3% before his magic is compared with that of the spirit (which is 3, 6 or 9). If his magic is greater than the spirit's then the spirit is "thrown" to some distance away, but it comes straight back! If the spirit's magic is greater, then the player loses 1% of his strength unless he has no magic powers at all; in that case he loses 5% of his strength every time.

Spirits can very rapidly reduce a powerful player to a pitiful wreck – especially if he has no magic!

Finally, we should mention that if, as a result of spirit attacks or fights with other creatures, the player's strength (S) falls below 1 then he starts to get very weak and "flickers" on the screen. When his strength falls below 0.1 he dies.

There are a number of aspects of the game that are not detailed above, but all the major features are described – you should be able to work out the rest by yourself!

Appendix C

Four utility programs

The four programs listed in this appendix are available in cassette tape form from your local bookshop, computer store or the publisher.

C.1 SLIST

The following program has been used to produce all the well-laid-out program listings in this book. To use it, the program to be listed should first be loaded as usual. You should then type

```
PRINT ~TOP
```

to find out the highest address used by the program code in *hexadecimal*. If this is less than 6700 (which it almost certainly is) then type

```
PAGE =&6700
```

to alter PAGE to &6700 (see section 17.3). If you now load (or chain) SLIST then it will be loaded starting at this address and can be run without destroying the program which is to be listed.

   Note that if you have typed SLIST yourself and have not compacted it (see Appendix C.2) then the relevant address should be &6300.

   The SLIST program will first ask how many characters (maximum) are to be listed on each line. It will then ask if the program to be listed starts at &E00 (the cassette-based system default); if it does not then it will ask for the start address, which you may give in either decimal or hexadecimal (preceded by &, as usual). It will then ask if the listing is to be sent to a printer as well as to the screen, and if so will ask how many lines are to be printed per page.

   The program will then be listed in the structured form used throughout this book.

   If the printer is not in use then the listing will be in page mode and will pause after approximately every 20 lines. If the printer is in use then a form feed character will be sent to the printer before the start of printing and after every nth line, where n is the number of lines per page specified (unless this was zero, in which case printing is continuous).

If the TOP of the program to be listed is more than &6700 then it will be necessary to list the program in two parts.

First you should make sure that you have a SAVEd copy of the program.

Now delete parts of the program, starting at the end. A well-written program will have DATA statements and/or PROCedures at the end and these should be deleted in appropriate groups of lines (i.e. all consecutive DATA statements, or a complete procedure). Keep checking the value of TOP until it is below &6700 (or whatever address SLIST will be loaded at).

You can now list this first part of the program using SLIST.

Once this has been done you should reset PAGE to its normal value and load the complete program again. Now delete all those lines that were listed before. Finally, run SLIST to list the last part of the program.

```
 10 DIM Token% 125
 17 REM
 18 REM Author:  Miles Ellis, 1983
 19 REM
 20 REM Copyright 1984, John Wiley & Sons, Limited
 30 MODE 7: PROCinit
 40 REPEAT
      PROCline: UNTIL NoMore
 50 IF Printing THEN
      VDU 3
    ELSE
      VDU 15
 60 END
 70 DEF PROCinit
 80 VDU 12: FOR I%=7 TO 8:
      PRINT TAB(12,I%)CHR$141;CHR$130;"SUPER LISTER": NEXT
 90 PRINT TAB(1,11)CHR$129;"(c) 1984, John Wiley & Sons, Limited"
100 Table=&80: Size=&83: Start=&87: End=&89
110 ?(Start+1)=&80: ?(End+1)=&83: IF ?&8071=0 THEN
      ?Start=&6D: ?End=&58
    ELSE
      ?Start=&71: ?End=&6B
120 FOR Pass=0 TO 2 STEP 2
130    P%=Token%
140    [OPT Pass
150    LDA &601: STA &70: LDA &602: STA &71 \Address of Byte%
160    LDY #0: LDA (&70),Y: STA &82 \Value of Byte%
170    LDA &604: STA &72: LDA &605:
       STA &73 \Address of tkn$ information block
180    LDA #&3F: STA &84: STA &85: STA &86 \Store ??? in &84-&86
190    LDA Start: STA &80: LDA Start+1:
       STA &81 \Store start of table
200    .Loop INY: LDA (Table),Y \Get next byte
210    AND #&80: BEQ Loop \Check if token
220    LDA (Table),Y: EOR &82: BEQ Save \Check if correct token
230    INY: INY: STY Size:
       LDY #0 \Skip over token and action pointer
240    LDA Table: CLC: ADC Size: STA Table: LDA Table+1: ADC #0:
       STA Table+1 \Update start of table
250    LDA Table: SEC: SBC End: LDA Table+1: SBC End+1:
       BCC Loop \Check for end of table
260    LDA #&84: STA Table: LDA #0: STA Table+1:
       LDY #3 \Invalid token - return ???
270    .Save TYA: TAX: LDY #3:
       STA (&72),Y \Move string length to X and store
280    LDY #0: LDA (&72),Y: STA &74: INY: LDA (&72),Y: STA &75:
       LDY #0 \Store address of tkn$ in &74,&75
290    .Copy LDA (Table),Y: STA (&74),Y: INY: DEX:
       BNE Copy \Copy string to tkn$
300    RTS: ]NEXT
310 PRINT TAB(3,15)CHR$130;"What line width do you want?";CHR$131;
320 INPUT ""Width%
330 IF Width%<20 OR Width%>120 THEN
      PRINT TAB(3,14)CHR$129;"Line width must be >=20 and <=120";
      TAB(33,15)SPC(7);TAB(33,15);: GOTO 320
```

```
340 PRINT TAB(3,18)CHR$130;"Does program start at &E00 (Y/N)?";
    CHR$131;
350 A$=GET$: PRINT A$
360 IF A$="Y" OR A$="y" THEN
      Next%=&E00
    ELSE
      PRINT TAB(3,19)CHR$130;"Where does it start?";CHR$131;:
      INPUT ""A$: Next%=EVAL(A$)
370 PRINT TAB(3,21)CHR$130;"Is printer output required (Y/N)?";
    CHR$131;
380 A$=GET$: PRINT A$
390 Printing=A$="Y" OR A$="y"
400 PageLen%=&7FFFFFFF: IF Printing THEN
      PRINT TAB(3,22)CHR$130;"How many lines per page (or 0)?";
      CHR$131;: INPUT ""PageLen%: IF PageLen%<=0 THEN
        PageLen%=&7FFFFFFF
410 Last%=Width%-6: Tab%=6
420 NoMore=FALSE: Forst=FALSE: Loopnd=FALSE: Ifst=FALSE:
    AssCode=FALSE
430 Line$=STRING$(Last%+8," "): LineNum%=1
440 IF Printing THEN
      VDU 2,15
    ELSE
      VDU 14
450 CLS
460 ENDPROC
470 DEF PROCline
480 Colon%=0: Brkpt%=0: Char%=1: Line$="": Paren%=0: Text=FALSE:
    Data=FALSE: Rem=FALSE: Dim=FALSE: Continued=FALSE
490 IF Next%?1=&FF THEN
      NoMore=TRUE: ENDPROC
500 a%=5: PRINT 256*Next%?1+Next%?2;
510 Next%=Next%+4: Byte%=?Next%
520 REPEAT
530   IF Byte%<&80 OR Text OR Data THEN
        PROCchar
      ELSE
        PROCtoken
540   IF Char%<=Last% THEN
        GOTO 560
550   IF Colon%>0 THEN
        PROCbreak(Colon%)
      ELSE
        IF Brkpt%>0 THEN
          PROCbreak(Brkpt%)
        ELSE
          PROCbreak(-Last%)
560   Next%=Next%+1: Byte%=?Next%: UNTIL Byte%=&D
570 IF Forst THEN
      PROClist(2): Forst=FALSE
    ELSE
      IF Ifst THEN
        PROClist(IfTab%-Tab%): Ifst=FALSE
      ELSE
        IF Loopnd THEN
```

```
            PROClist(-2): Loopnd=FALSE
         ELSE
            IF Char%>1 THEN
                PROClist(0)
580 ENDPROC
590 DEF PROCbreak(n%)
600 LOCAL num%,n1%
610 n1%=ABS(n%)
620 IF NOT Continued THEN
        PRINT TAB(Tab%);
630 PRINT LEFT$(Line$,n1%);FNendline
640 num%=LEN(Line$)-n1%: IF MID$(Line$,n1%+1,1)=" " THEN
        num%=num%-1
650 Line$=RIGHT$(Line$,num%)
660 Colon%=0: Brkpt%=0: Char%=num%+1
670 IF n%<0 THEN
        Continued=TRUE: Last%=Width%
    ELSE
        Continued=FALSE: Last%=Width%-Tab%
680 ENDPROC
690 DEF PROClist(n%)
700 IF Char%-1<=Last% THEN
        GOTO 720
710 IF Colon%>0 THEN
        PROCbreak(Colon%)
    ELSE
      IF Brkpt%>0 THEN
         PROCbreak(Brkpt%)
      ELSE
         PROCbreak(-Last%)
720 IF Continued THEN
        Continued=FALSE: Last%=Width%-Tab%
    ELSE
        PRINT TAB(Tab%);
730 PRINT Line$;FNendline
740 Tab%=Tab%+n%: Last%=Last%-n%
750 Line$="": Colon%=0: Brkpt%=0: Char%=1
760 ENDPROC
770 DEF FNendline
780 LineNum%=LineNum%+1
790 IF Printing AND LineNum%>PageLen% THEN
        LineNum%=1: =CHR$1+CHR$12
800 =""
810 DEF PROCchar
820 IF Byte%<>32 OR Text OR Data OR Rem OR Dim OR AssCode THEN
        Line$=Line$+CHR$(Byte%): Char%=Char%+1
830 IF Byte%=32 AND (Rem OR AssCode) THEN
        Brkpt%=Char%-1: ENDPROC
840 IF (((Byte%=44) AND NOT (Text OR Paren%)) OR ((Byte%=59 OR
    Byte%=39 OR Byte%=41) AND NOT (Text OR Data))) AND
    (Next%?1<>58 AND Next%?1<>41) THEN
        Brkpt%=Char%-1: ENDPROC
850 IF Byte%=40 THEN
        Paren%=Paren%+1: ENDPROC
860 IF Byte%=41 THEN
```

```
          Paren%=Paren%-1: ENDPROC
 870 IF Byte%=34 THEN
          Text=NOT Text: ENDPROC
 880 IF Byte%=91 THEN
          AssCode=TRUE: ENDPROC
 890 IF Byte%=93 THEN
          AssCode=FALSE: ENDPROC
 900 IF Byte%<>58 OR Text THEN
          ENDPROC
 910 Colon%=Char%-1: Data=FALSE: Dim=FALSE
 920 IF Forst THEN
          PROClist(2): Forst=FALSE
      ELSE
        IF Loopnd THEN
          PROClist(-2): Loopnd=FALSE
        ELSE
          Line$=Line$+" ": Char%=Char%+1
 930 ENDPROC
 940 DEF PROCtoken
 950 LOCAL lnum%,p%,p1%,tkn$,op
 960 tkn$=STRING$(8," "): op=FALSE
 970 IF Byte%=&8D THEN
          lnum%=(Next%?2 AND &3F)+(Next%?1 AND &30 EOR &10)*4+(Next%?3
          AND &3F)*256+(Next%?1 AND &40 EOR &40)*4096:
          Char%=Char%+LEN(STR$(lnum%)): Line$=Line$+STR$(lnum%):
          Next%=Next%+3: ENDPROC
 980 IF Byte%=&8B THEN
          PRINT TAB(Tab%);Line$;FNendline'TAB(ElseTab%);"ELSE";
          FNendline: Line$="": Colon%=0: Brkpt%=0: Char%=1:
          IF Loopnd THEN
            Loopnd=FALSE: Tab%=Tab%-2: Last%=Last%+2
 990 IF Byte%=&8B THEN
          ENDPROC
1000 IF Byte%<&85 OR Byte%=&88 OR Byte%=&8C OR (Byte%=&B8 AND
     Next%?1<>80) THEN
          op=TRUE: IF NOT AssCode THEN
            Line$=Line$+" ": Brkpt%=Char%: Char%=Char%+1
1010 CALL Token%,Byte%,tkn$:
     REM M/c code routine to put character form of token (in Byte%)
     into tkn$
1020 Line$=Line$+tkn$: Char%=Char%+LEN(tkn$)
1030 IF RIGHT$(tkn$,1)="(" THEN
          Paren%=Paren%+1: ENDPROC
1040 IF Byte%=&8C AND Ifst THEN
          ElseTab%=Tab%: PROClist(2): ENDPROC
1050 IF Byte%=&8C THEN
          Ifst=TRUE: IfTab%=Tab%: ElseTab%=Tab%: PROClist(2): ENDPROC
1060 IF Byte%=&F5 THEN
          PROClist(2): ENDPROC
1070 IF NOT AssCode AND (op OR Byte%<&88 OR (Byte%>&D3 AND
     Byte%<>&F2) OR Byte%=&AC) AND (Next%?1<>58) THEN
          Line$=Line$+" ": IF Char%<Last% THEN
            Brkpt%=Char%: Char%=Char%+1
1080 IF Byte%=&E3 THEN
          Forst=TRUE: ENDPROC
```

```
1090 IF Byte%=&ED OR Byte%=&FD THEN
        Loopnd=TRUE: ENDPROC
1100 IF Byte%=&DC THEN
        Data=TRUE: ENDPROC
1110 IF Byte%=&F4 THEN
        Rem=TRUE: IF Next%?1=32 THEN
        Next%=Next%+1
1120 IF Byte%=&DE THEN
        Dim=TRUE: IF Next%?1=32 THEN
        Next%=Next%+1
1130 ENDPROC
```

C.2 COMPACTER

This program produces the minimum sized Basic or Assembly language program, compatible with its being re-edited or otherwise altered. The COMPACTER program should be loaded above the program to be compacted at &7100 by typing

```
PAGE =&7100
```

and then loading the program. Before doing this, if you have a large program you should check that it does not go beyond &7100 by typing

```
PRINT ~TOP
```

to obtain the TOP address in hexadecimal. If this is greater than &7100 then the COMPACTER cannot be used, except, possibly, in two stages, as described below.

The COMPACTER will ask for the start address of the program (if it is not &E00) in the same way as with SLIST (see C.1), and also asks whether comments are to be removed. It will then work through the program removing all non-essential spaces. Essential spaces are those in character strings, DATA statements or REMarks (or assembly language comments), and those whose context makes them essential. Thus the statement

```
IF Flag(N) AND X=17 THEN PRINT "Get lost!"
```

will be compacted to

```
IFFlag(N)ANDX=17THENPRINT"Get lost!"
```

whereas the statement

```
IF Flag AND X=A THEN PRINT "Get lost!"
```

will become

```
IFFlag ANDX=A THENPRINT"Get lost!"
```

During its execution the COMPACTER will display the line number currently being compacted (so that you know it's doing something!), and at the end will display details of the old and new program sizes and the consequent size reduction.

The compacted program can then be saved, after first resetting the value of PAGE.

A very large program whose TOP is more than &7100 may, possibly, be compacted by first deleting sufficient lines to reduce the TOP to less than &7100 and then compacting it. The missing lines can then be retyped and the complete program compacted again.

Note that the above description assumes that a compacted COMPACTER is being used. If you have typed the program yourself then experiment 17.3 explains how to use it to compact itself, or you could simply load the COMPACTER at &6F00 instead of &7100.

```
   7 REM
   8 REM Author:  Miles Ellis, 1983
   9 REM
  10 REM Copyright 1984, John Wiley & Sons, Limited
  20 MODE 7: PROCinit
  30 PROCcompress
  40 END
  50 DEF PROCinit
  60 VDU 12: FOR I%=7 TO 8:
        PRINT TAB(10,I%)CHR$141;CHR$130;"BASIC COMPACTER": NEXT
  70 PRINT TAB(1,11)CHR$129;"(c) 1984, John Wiley & Sons, Limited"
  80 TIME=0: REPEAT
        UNTIL TIME>150
  90 PRINT TAB(3,15)CHR$130;"Do you want to remove comments?";
     CHR$131;
 100 A$=GET$: PRINT A$
 110 NoComments=A$="Y" OR A$="y"
 120 PRINT TAB(3,18)CHR$130;"Does program start at &E00?";CHR$131;
 130 A$=GET$: PRINT A$
 140 IF A$="Y" OR A$="y" THEN
        Start%=&E00
     ELSE
        PRINT TAB(3,19)CHR$130;"Where does it start?";CHR$131;:
        INPUT """A$: Start%=EVAL(A$)
 150 ENDPROC
 160 DEF PROCcompress
 170 LOCAL top%,size%,line%
 180 Next%=Start%: Shift%=0: AssCode=FALSE
 190 PRINT TAB(9,22)CHR$131;"Compacting line";CHR$129
 200 REPEAT
 210    Text=FALSE: Data=FALSE: Rem=FALSE: Dim=FALSE: Name=FALSE:
        AssLabel=FALSE: AssRem=FALSE
 220    PRINT TAB(26,22)SPC(6);TAB(26,22)256*Next%?1+Next%?2;
 230    !(Next%-Shift%)=!Next%: line%=Next%-Shift%: Len%=line%?3:
        Next%=Next%+4: Byte%=?Next%
 240    REPEAT
 250      IF Byte%=32 THEN
             PROCspace: GOTO 380
 260      IF (Byte%>=65 AND Byte%<=90) OR (Byte%>=97 AND Byte%<=122)
          OR (Name AND (Byte%>=48 AND Byte%<=57)) THEN
             Name=TRUE: GOTO 370
          ELSE
             Name=FALSE
 270      IF Byte%=58 THEN
             Data=FALSE: Dim=FALSE: AssRem=FALSE: GOTO 370
 280      IF Byte%=34 THEN
             Text=NOT Text: GOTO 370
 290      IF Byte%=&DC THEN
             Data=TRUE: GOTO 370
 300      IF Byte%=&F4 THEN
             Rem=TRUE: IF NoComments THEN
                PROCremove: GOTO 390
 310      IF Byte%=&DE THEN
             Dim=TRUE: GOTO 370
 320      IF Byte%=&8D THEN
```

```
          !(Next%-Shift%)=!Next%: Next%=Next%+3: GOTO 380
330     IF Byte%=91 THEN
          AssCode=TRUE: GOTO 370
340     IF Byte%=93 THEN
          AssCode=FALSE: GOTO 370
350     IF Byte%=92 AND AssCode THEN
          AssRem=TRUE: IF NoComments THEN
            PROCremove: GOTO 390
360     IF Byte%=46 AND AssCode AND NOT AssRem THEN
          AssLabel=TRUE
370     ?(Next%-Shift%)=Byte%
380     Next%=Next%+1: Byte%=?Next%
390     UNTIL Byte%=&D
400    line%?3=Len%: IF Len%=4 THEN
         Shift%=Shift%+4
410   UNTIL Next%?1=&FF
420 top%=Next%+1: ?(top%-Shift%-1)=&D: ?(top%-Shift%)=&FF:
    size%=top%-Start%+1
430 VDU 28,0,24,39,15,12,26
440 PRINT TAB(1,15)CHR$131;"Original program starts at";CHR$129;
    "&";~Start%
450 PRINT TAB(18,16)CHR$131;"ends    at";CHR$129;"&";~top%
460 PRINT TAB(18,17)CHR$131;"occupies";CHR$129;size%;CHR$131;
    "bytes"
470 PRINT TAB(0,19)CHR$131;"Compacted program starts at";CHR$129;
    "&";~Start%
480 PRINT TAB(18,20)CHR$131;"ends    at";CHR$129;"&";~top%-Shift%
490 PRINT TAB(18,21)CHR$131;"occupies";CHR$129;size%-Shift%;
    CHR$131;"bytes"
500 PRINT TAB(0,23)CHR$130;"Program has been reduced by";CHR$129;
    Shift%;CHR$130;"bytes"
510 ENDPROC
520 DEF PROCremove
530 IF ?(Next%-Shift%-1)=58 THEN
      PROCshift
540 REPEAT
550   PROCshift: Next%=Next%+1: Byte%=?Next%
560   UNTIL Byte%=&D OR (AssCode AND (Byte%=58 OR Byte%=93))
570 IF Byte%=93 THEN
      AssCode=FALSE
580 ENDPROC
590 DEF PROCspace
600 IF Text OR Data OR Rem OR Dim OR AssLabel OR AssRem OR (Name
    AND Next%?1>&7F) THEN
      Name=FALSE: AssLabel=FALSE: ?(Next%-Shift%)=Byte%: ENDPROC
610 Name=FALSE: PROCshift
620 ENDPROC
630 DEF PROCshift
640 Shift%=Shift%+1: Len%=Len%-1
650 ENDPROC
```

C.3 ENVELOPE

This program is intended to greatly simplify the use of the SOUND and ENVELOPE statements. A full description of its use is given in the last section (16.4) of chapter 16.

```
10 *KEY10OLD|MRUN|M
20 DIM Env(12),Snd(1,2),Emin(12),Emax(12),Smin(2),Smax(2)
30 ON ERROR GOTO 2200
37 REM
38 REM Author:  Miles Ellis, 1983
39 REM
40 REM Copyright 1984, John Wiley & Sons, Limited
50 MODE 7: PROCinit: MODE 1: PROCsetup
60 REPEAT
     Key%=GET
70   IF Key%=32 THEN
        PROCplay
80   IF Key%=81 THEN
        PROCquiet
90   IF Key%=69 THEN
        PROCenv(TRUE)
100  IF Key%=83 THEN
        PROCsound(TRUE)
110  IF Key%=78 THEN
        PROCnoise(TRUE)
120  IF Key%=68 THEN
        PROCdraw
130  IF Key%=136 OR Key%=137 OR Key%=13 THEN
        PROCnext
140  IF (Key%>=48 AND Key%<=57) OR Key%=45 THEN
        PROCvalue
150  UNTIL Key%=88
160 MODE 7
170 *FX4,0
180 END
190 DEF PROCinit
200 VDU 12: FOR I%=6 TO 7:
     PRINT TAB(10,I%)CHR$141;CHR$130;"ENVELOPE SHAPER": NEXT
210 PRINT TAB(1,10)CHR$129;"(c) 1984, John Wiley & Sons, Limited"
220 TIME=0: REPEAT
     UNTIL TIME>150
230 PRINT TAB(0,14)CHR$130;"This program will display both pitch"
240 PRINT CHR$130;"and amplitude envelopes for the first"
250 PRINT CHR$130;"two seconds of the sound created."
260 PRINT 'CHR$130;"You may alter this period if you wish"
270 PRINT CHR$130;"to between 1 and 20 seconds."
280 PRINT 'CHR$130;"Do you wish to change the period?";CHR$131;
290 A$=GET$: PRINT A$
300 IF A$="Y" OR A$="y" THEN
     PRINT CHR$130;"To what (in seconds)?";CHR$131;: INPUT ""Tmax
   ELSE
     Tmax=2
310 IF Tmax<1 OR Tmax>20 THEN
     PRINT TAB(0,22)CHR$129;"Between 1 and 20 seconds please";
     SPC(8);TAB(0,22);: TIME=0: REPEAT
        UNTIL TIME>150:
     PRINT SPC(32);TAB(0,22);: GOTO 300
   ELSE
     Tmax=100*Tmax
320 FOR I%=1 TO 9:
```

```
        Env(I%)=0: NEXT
330 Env(0)=1: Env(7)=126: Env(8)=-10: Env(10)=-4: Env(11)=126:
    Env(12)=100
340 FOR I%=0 TO 2:
        Snd(0,I%)=0: NEXT
350 Snd(1,0)=1: Snd(1,1)=89: Snd(1,2)=5
360 CLS
370 PRINT TAB(9,3)CHR$134;"Use keys as follows:"
380 PRINT ''CHR$129;"     E";CHR$131;
    "to modify envelope parameters"
390 PRINT 'CHR$129;"     S";CHR$131;
    "to modify sound (1) parameters"
400 PRINT 'CHR$129;"     N";CHR$131;
    "to modify sound (0) parameters"
410 PRINT 'CHR$129;"     D";CHR$131;"to draw updated graphs"
420 PRINT 'CHR$129;"space";CHR$131;"to sound";CHR$136;"both";
    CHR$137;"channels"
430 PRINT 'CHR$129;"     Q";CHR$131;
    "for quiet - i.e. to stop sound"
440 PRINT 'CHR$129;"   ESC";CHR$131;"to restart program"
450 PRINT 'CHR$129;"     X";CHR$131;
    "to exit - i.e. to end program"
460 FOR I%=0 TO 12:
        READ Emin(I%),Emax(I%): NEXT
470 FOR I%=0 TO 2:
        READ Smin(I%),Smax(I%): NEXT
480 Opsys=FNos
490 *FX15,1
500 PRINT TAB(6,24)CHR$133;"Press any key to continue": X%=GET
510 ENDPROC
520 DEF FNos
530 IF !&E8B3=&30312E30 THEN
        =0.1
    ELSE
        =1
540 DEF PROCsetup
550 LOCAL tmax
560 VDU 19,1,6;0;19,2,4;0;19,3,1;0;5
570 COLOUR 1: GCOL 0,1
580 MOVE 112,259: DRAW 112,1023: MOVE 0,1023: PRINT "255":
    MOVE 0,643: PRINT "128"
590 tmax=0.01*Tmax: @%=&20104: MOVE 112,259: DRAW 1200,259:
    MOVE 532,247: PRINT 0.5*tmax: MOVE 1032,247: PRINT tmax:
    MOVE 748,247: PRINT "(secs)": @%=4
600 VDU 24,116;260;1116;1023;29,112;256;
610 PROCcursor(FALSE): VDU 4
620 PRINT TAB(0,26)"ENVELOPE    1,    1,"
630 FOR I%=1 TO 6:
        PRINT Env(I%);",";: NEXT:
    PRINT "   (pitch)"
640 FOR I%=7 TO 11:
        PRINT Env(I%);",";: NEXT:
    PRINT Env(12);"   (ampl.)"
650 PRINT TAB(0,30)"SOUND    1,    1,   89,    5";TAB(32,30);"(music)"
660 PRINT TAB(0,31)"SOUND    0,    0,    0,    0";TAB(32,31);"(noise)";
```

```
670 EnvUpd=FALSE: SndUpd=FALSE: NseUpd=FALSE
680 PROCdraw: *FX4,1
690 ENDPROC
700 DEF PROCcursor(on)
710 IF on THEN
      VDU 23;10,0,0;0;0;23;11,7,0;0;0;
    ELSE
      VDU 23;8202;0;0;0;
720 ENDPROC
730 DEF PROCplay
740 PROCquiet: PROCclear
750 ENVELOPE 1,Env(0),Env(1),Env(2),Env(3),Env(4),Env(5),Env(6),
    Env(7),Env(8),Env(9),Env(10),Env(11),Env(12)
760 SOUND &100,Snd(0,0),Snd(0,1),Snd(0,2)
770 SOUND &101,Snd(1,0),Snd(1,1),Snd(1,2)
780 ENDPROC
790 DEF PROCquiet
800 SOUND &10,0,0,1: SOUND &11,0,0,1
810 ENDPROC
820 DEF PROCclear
830 IF EnvUpd THEN
      PROCenv(FALSE)
    ELSE
      IF SndUpd THEN
        PROCsound(FALSE)
      ELSE
        IF NseUpd THEN
          PROCnoise(FALSE)
840 ENDPROC
850 DEF PROCenv(on)
860 IF SndUpd OR NseUpd THEN
      PROCclear
870 IF on THEN
      COLOUR 3
    ELSE
      COLOUR 1
880 PRINT TAB(0,26)"ENVELOPE    1,";: PROCcursor(on)
890 EnvUpd=on: Cpos=0: Cx=15: Cy=26: COLOUR 1
900 ENDPROC
910 DEF PROCsound(on)
920 IF EnvUpd OR NseUpd THEN
      PROCclear
930 IF on THEN
      COLOUR 3
    ELSE
      COLOUR 1
940 PRINT TAB(0,30)"SOUND    1,";: PROCcursor(on)
950 SndUpd=on: Cpos=0: Cx=10: Cy=30: COLOUR 1
960 ENDPROC
970 DEF PROCnoise(on)
980 IF EnvUpd OR SndUpd THEN
      PROCclear
990 IF on THEN
      COLOUR 3
    ELSE
```

```
        COLOUR 1
1000 PRINT TAB(0,31)"SOUND   0,";: PROCcursor(on)
1010 NseUpd=on: Cpos=0: Cx=10: Cy=31: COLOUR 1
1020 ENDPROC
1030 DEF PROCnext
1040 IF Key%=136 THEN
        Cpos=Cpos-1
     ELSE
        Cpos=Cpos+1
1050 IF Cpos<0 THEN
        PROCerror: Cpos=0: ENDPROC
1060 IF SndUpd THEN
        Cy=30: GOTO 1100
     ELSE
        IF NseUpd THEN
          Cy=31: GOTO 1100
1070 IF Cpos>12 THEN
        PROCerror: Cpos=12: ENDPROC
1080 IF Cpos=0 THEN
        Cx=15: Cy=26
     ELSE
        IF Cpos<7 THEN
          Cx=5*(Cpos-1): Cy=27
        ELSE
          Cx=5*(Cpos-7): Cy=28
1090 PRINT TAB(Cx,Cy);: ENDPROC
1100 IF Cpos>2 THEN
        PROCerror: Cpos=2: ENDPROC
1110 Cx=5*(Cpos+2): PRINT TAB(Cx,Cy);
1120 ENDPROC
1130 DEF PROCvalue
1140 LOCAL n,neg,val,max
1150 PRINT CHR$(Key%);SPC(3);TAB(Cx+1,Cy);
1160 IF Key%=45 THEN
        neg=TRUE: val=0: n=0
     ELSE
        neg=FALSE: val=Key%-48: n=1
1170 REPEAT
1180    Key%=GET: IF (Key%<48 AND Key%<>13) OR Key%>57 THEN
          PROCerror: GOTO 1180
1190    IF Key%=13 THEN
          n=3
        ELSE
          PRINT CHR$(Key%);: n=n+1: val=10*val+Key%-48
1200    UNTIL n=3
1210 IF neg THEN
        val=-val
1220 IF NOT FNvalid(val) THEN
        PROCerror: PRINT TAB(Cx,Cy);"   0";TAB(Cx,Cy);: ENDPROC
1230 IF EnvUpd THEN
        Env(Cpos)=val: max=12
     ELSE
        IF SndUpd THEN
          Snd(1,Cpos)=val: max=2
        ELSE
```

```
           Snd(0,Cpos)=val: max=2
1240 IF Cpos=0 AND NOT EnvUpd THEN
         PROCselect
1250 IF Cpos<max THEN
         PROCnext
     ELSE
         PRINT TAB(Cx,Cy);
1260 ENDPROC
1270 DEF FNvalid(n)
1280 LOCAL min,max
1290 IF EnvUpd THEN
         min=Emin(Cpos): max=Emax(Cpos)
     ELSE
         min=Smin(Cpos): max=Smax(Cpos)
1300 IF SndUpd AND Cpos=0 THEN
         min=0
     ELSE
       IF NseUpd AND Cpos=1 THEN
         max=7
1310 =n>=min AND n<=max
1320 DEF PROCselect
1330 LOCAL y
1340 IF Snd(0,0)<1 OR Snd(1,0)<1 THEN
         ENDPROC
1350 PROCerror: IF SndUpd THEN
         y=31
     ELSE
         y=30
1360 COLOUR 3: PRINT TAB(10,y)"   0";: TIME=0: REPEAT
         UNTIL TIME>100
1370 COLOUR 1: PRINT TAB(10,y)"    0";: Snd(31-y,0)=0
1380 ENDPROC
1390 DEF PROCerror
1400 ENVELOPE 2,1,5,-1,5,1,2,1,127,0,0,-127,126,126
1410 SOUND 2,2,255,5
1420 ENDPROC
1430 DEF PROCdraw
1440 PROCclear
1450 Tstep=Env(0) MOD 128
1460 CLG: PROCamp: PROCpitch
1470 ENDPROC
1480 DEF PROCamp
1490 IF Snd(1,0)=1 THEN
         Dur=Snd(1,2)
     ELSE
       IF Snd(0,0)=1 THEN
         Dur=Snd(0,2)
       ELSE
         Dur=0
1500 IF Dur<0 OR Dur=255 OR 5*Dur>Tmax THEN
         Dur=Tmax
     ELSE
         Dur=5*Dur
1510 GCOL 0,2: MOVE 0,0
1520 PROCattack: PROCdecay: PROCsustain: PROCrelease
```

```
1530 ENDPROC
1540 DEF PROCattack
1550 LOCAL aa,ala,at
1560 aa=Env(7): ala=Env(11)
1570 IF aa<=0 THEN
       at=0
     ELSE
       at=Tstep*ala/aa: IF at<0 THEN
         at=0
1580 IF at>Dur THEN
       ala=Dur*ala/at: at=Dur
1590 Xenv=1000*at/Tmax: Yenv=3*ala
1600 MOVE Xenv,Yenv: PLOT 85,Xenv,0
1610 Time=at: Level=ala
1620 ENDPROC
1630 DEF PROCdecay
1640 LOCAL ad,ald,dt
1650 IF Time>=Dur THEN
       ENDPROC
1660 ad=Env(8)
1670 IF ad=0 THEN
       ald=Env(11): dt=Dur-Time
     ELSE
       ald=Env(12): dt=Tstep*(ald-Level)/ad: IF dt<0 THEN
         dt=0
1680 Xenv=Xenv+1000*dt/Tmax: Yenv=3*ald
1690 PLOT 85,Xenv,Yenv: PLOT 85,Xenv,0
1700 Tie>=Dur OR Level=0 THEN
       ENDPROC
1750 as=Env(9): st=Dur-Time: als=Level+st*as/Tstep
1760 IF als<0 THEN
       als=0: st=-Tstep*Level/as
1770 Xenv=Xenv+1000*st/Tmax: Yenv=3*als
1780 PLOT 85,Xenv,Yenv: PLOT 85,Xenv,0
1790 Time=Time+st: Level=als
1800 ENDPROC
1810 DEF PROCrelease
1820 LOCAL ar,rt
1830 IF Level=0 OR Time>=Tmax THEN
       ENDPROC
1840 ar=Env(10)
1850 IF ar=0 THEN
       rt=Tmax-Time: Xenv=1000
     ELSE
       rt=-Tstep*Level/ar: Xenv=Xenv+1000*rt/Tmax: Yenv=0
1860 PLOT 85,Xenv,Yenv: IF Yenv>0 THEN
       PLOT 85,Xenv,0
1870 Time=Time+rt: IF Time>Tmax THEN
       Time=Tmax
1880 ENDPROC
1890 DEF PROCpitch
1900 LOCAL repeat,phase,pi,pn,ndur
1910 IF Snd(1,0)=0 THEN
       ENDPROC
1920 ndur=Snd(0,2): IF ndur<0 OR ndur=255 OR 5*ndur>Tmax THEN
```

```
          ndur=1000
       ELSE
          ndur=5000*ndur/Tmax
1930 Ynorm=3*Snd(1,1): IF Time>Dur THEN
       Xmax=Xenv
       ELSE
       Xmax=1000*Dur/Tmax
1940 IF Env(10)=0 THEN
       Xmax=1000
1950 GCOL 0,3: MOVE 0,Ynorm
1960 repeat=Env(0)<128
1970 Xenv=0
1980 REPEAT
1990    Yenv=Ynorm: DRAW Xenv,Yenv: phase=1
2000    REPEAT
2010      pi=Env(phase): pn=Env(phase+3): IF pn=0 AND Opsys<1 THEN
             pn=256
2020      PROCpdraw(pi,pn)
2030      phase=phase+1: UNTIL phase>3 OR Xenv>=Xmax
2040    UNTIL Xenv>=Xmax OR (Xenv=0 AND phase>3)
2050 IF Xenv<Xmax THEN
       DRAW Xmax,Yenv
2060 IF Xmax<ndur AND Snd(0,0)<0 THEN
       DRAW ndur,Yenv
2070 ENDPROC
2080 DEF PROCpdraw(pi,pn)
2090 LOCAL xinc,yinc,xnext,ynext,xstep,ystep
2100 xinc=1000*pn*Tstep/Tmax: yinc=3*pn*pi: IF Xenv+xinc>Xmax THEN
       yinc=yinc*(Xmax-Xenv)/xinc: xinc=Xmax-Xenv
2110 REPEAT
2120    xnext=Xenv+xinc: ynext=Yenv+yinc
2130    IF ynext>=0 AND ynext<766 THEN
          Xenv=xnext: Yenv=ynext: DRAW Xenv,Yenv: xinc=0: GOTO 2180
2140    IF ynext<0 THEN
          ystep=-Yenv
       ELSE
          ystep=765-Yenv
2150    xstep=xinc*ystep/yinc
2160    Xenv=Xenv+xstep: Yenv=Yenv+ystep: DRAW Xenv,Yenv:
       Yenv=765-Yenv: DRAW Xenv,Yenv
2170    xinc=xinc-xstep: yinc=yinc-ystep
2180    UNTIL xinc<=0
2190 ENDPROC
2200 IF ERR=17 THEN
       RUN
     ELSE
       MODE 7: REPORT: PRINT " at ";ERL: GOTO 170
2210 DATA  1,255,-128,127,-128,127,-128,127,0,255,0,255,0,255,-127,
     127,-127,127,-127,0,-127,0,0,126,0,126
2220 DATA  -15,1,0,255,-1,255
```

C.4 SHAPES

This program enables the user to easily define his own characters in either mode 1 (40 characters per line) or mode 2 (20 characters per line). Its use is described in some detail in chapter 12, section 12.2.

```
 10 DIM Def%(7,7)
 20 ON ERROR GOTO 1860
 27 REM
 28 REM Author:  Miles Ellis, 1983
 29 REM
 30 REM Copyright 1984, John Wiley & Sons, Limited
 40 MODE 7: PROCinit
 50 REPEAT
 60   MODE M%: PROCdefine
 70   UNTIL NoMore
 80 MODE 7: IF Save OR List THEN
    PROCsave
 90 *FX4,0
100 END
110 DEF PROCinit
120 VDU 12: FOR I%=6 TO 7:
    PRINT TAB(11,I%)CHR$141;CHR$130;"SHAPE DEFINER": NEXT
130 PRINT TAB(1,10)CHR$129;"(c) 1984, John Wiley & Sons, Limited"
140 TIME=0: REPEAT
    UNTIL TIME>150:
    Table%=TOP-1371
150 PRINT TAB(1,14)CHR$131;"You may start with:"
160 PRINT TAB(4,16)CHR$134;"a) Blank user-defined characters"
170 PRINT TAB(4,17)CHR$134;"b) Saved user-defined characters"
180 PRINT TAB(4,18)CHR$134;"c) Pre-set user-defined characters"
190 PRINT TAB(1,20)CHR$131;"Which do you require (a/b/c)?";CHR$134;
200 A$=GET$: PRINT A$
210 IF A$="A" OR A$="a" THEN
    PROCblank
    ELSE
      IF A$="B" OR A$="b" THEN
        PROCsaved
      ELSE
        IF A$<>"C" AND A$<>"c" THEN
          PROCerror: VDU 31,32,20,32,8: GOTO 200
220 PRINT TAB(1,23)CHR$131;"Which MODE do you want (1/2)?";CHR$129;
230 A$=GET$: PRINT A$: M%=VAL(A$)
240 IF M%<1 OR M%>2 THEN
    PROCerror: VDU 31,32,23,32,8: GOTO 230
250 NoMore=FALSE: Save=FALSE: List=FALSE: @%=3
260 PROCvdu: *FX4,1
270 ENDPROC
280 DEF PROCblank
290 FOR I%=Table% TO Table%+1333 STEP 43
300   FOR J%=I% TO I%+28 STEP 4
310     ?J%=32: J%?1=32: J%?2=48
320     NEXT:
    NEXT
330 ENDPROC
340 DEF PROCsaved
350 LOCAL file%,byte%,table%
360 PRINT TAB(1,21)CHR$133;"Please position tape and then RETURN":
    *MOTOR1
370 VDU 28,0,24,39,22
```

```
380 REPEAT
      UNTIL GET=&D:
    *MOTOR0
390 PRINT TAB(1,0)CHR$133;"PLAY then RETURN": REPEAT
      UNTIL GET=&D
400 file%=OPENIN("CharDefs"): table%=Table%
410 *OPT1,1
420 *OPT2,1
430 byte%=BGET#(file%): FOR I%=0 TO 31
440   FOR J%=1 TO 16:
        byte%=BGET#(file%): NEXT
450   FOR J%=1 TO 8:
        FOR K%=0 TO 2:
          byte%=BGET#(file%): table%?K%=byte%: NEXT
460     byte%=BGET#(file%): table%=table%+4: NEXT
470   table%=table%+11: NEXT:
    CLOSE #file%
480 VDU 12,26
490 ENDPROC
500 DEF PROCerror
510 ENVELOPE 1,1,5,-1,5,1,2,1,127,0,0,-127,126,126
520 SOUND 1,1,255,5
530 ENDPROC
540 DEF PROCdefine
550 IF M%=1 THEN
      PROCsetup1
    ELSE
      PROCsetup2
560 PROCchoose: Kept=FALSE
570 REPEAT
      Key%=GET
580   IF Key%=88 THEN
        PROCfill(TRUE): GOTO 660
590   IF Key%=32 THEN
        PROCfill(FALSE): GOTO 660
600   IF Key%=83 THEN
        PROCkeep: GOTO 660
610   IF Key%=136 AND U%>Xmin% THEN
        PROCcursor(FALSE): U%=U%-80: GOTO 650
620   IF Key%=137 AND U%<Xmax% THEN
        PROCcursor(FALSE): U%=U%+80: GOTO 650
630   IF Key%=138 AND V%>Ymin% THEN
        PROCcursor(FALSE): V%=V%-Ystep%: GOTO 650
640   IF Key%=139 AND V%<Ymax% THEN
        PROCcursor(FALSE): V%=V%+Ystep%
650   PROCcursor(TRUE)
660   UNTIL Key%=81 OR Kept
670 IF FNmore THEN
      GOTO 560
680 ENDPROC
690 DEF PROCsetup1
700 VDU 19,1,6;0;19,3,3;0;23;8202;0;0;0;
710 CLS: COLOUR 1: FOR I%=0 TO 15
720   PRINT TAB(28,I%+4)224+2*I%;SPC(4);225+2*I%: NEXT
730 COLOUR 3: FOR I%=0 TO 15
740   VDU 31,32,I%+4,224+2*I%,31,39,I%+4,225+2*I%: NEXT
```

```
 750 GCOL 0,1: MOVE 28,320: DRAW 28,960: DRAW 668,960: DRAW 668,320:
     DRAW 28,320
 760 FOR I%=400 TO 880 STEP 80
 770   MOVE 28,I%: DRAW 668,I%: NEXT
 780 FOR I%=108 TO 588 STEP 80
 790   MOVE I%,960: DRAW I%,320: NEXT
 800 X%=32: Y%=4: A%=32: B%=39: Cx%=480: Cy%=284
 810 Xmin%=32: Xmax%=592: Ymin%=396: Ymax%=956: Ystep%=80
 820 COLOUR 1:
     PRINT TAB(1,26)"Use cursor control keys to move cursor"
 830 ENDPROC
 840 DEF PROCsetup2
 850 VDU 19,1,6;0;19,2,3;0;23,8202;0;0;0;
 860 CLS: COLOUR 1: FOR I%=0 TO 15
 870   PRINT TAB(12,I%+4)224+2*I%: NEXT
 880 COLOUR 3: FOR I%=0 TO 15
 890   VDU 31,16,I%+4,224+2*I%,9,9,225+2*I%: NEXT
 900 GCOL 0,1: MOVE 28,480: DRAW 28,800: DRAW 668,800: DRAW 668,480:
     DRAW 28,480
 910 FOR I%=520 TO 760 STEP 40
 920   MOVE 28,I%: DRAW 668,I%: NEXT
 930 FOR I%=108 TO 588 STEP 80
 940   MOVE I%,800: DRAW I%,480: NEXT
 950 X%=16: Y%=4: A%=16: B%=19: Cx%=576: Cy%=444
 960 Xmin%=36: Xmax%=596: Ymin%=516: Ymax%=796: Ystep%=40
 970 COLOUR 1:
     PRINT TAB(0,22)"Use cursor control"'"keys to move cursor"
 980 ENDPROC
 990 DEF PROCchoose
1000 LOCAL table%,h%,t%,n%
1010 COLOUR 1: IF M%=1 THEN
     PRINT TAB(1,28)"Press RETURN to select character"
     ELSE
     PRINT TAB(0,25)"Press RETURN to"'"select character"
1020 VDU 31,X%,Y%,23;10,0,0;0;0;23,11,7,0;0;0;
1030 REPEAT
     Key%=GET
1040   IF Key%=136 AND X%=B% THEN
          X%=A%: GOTO 1080
1050   IF Key%=137 AND X%=A% THEN
          X%=B%: GOTO 1080
1060   IF Key%=138 AND Y%<19 THEN
          Y%=Y%+1: GOTO 1080
1070   IF Key%=139 AND Y%>4 THEN
          Y%=Y%-1
1080   PRINT TAB(X%,Y%);
1090   UNTIL Key%=&D:
     VDU 23;8202;0;0;0;
1100 Char%=216+2*Y%: IF X%=B% THEN
     Char%=Char%+1
1110 IF M%=1 THEN
     PRINT TAB(1,28)SPC(32);TAB(1,23)"Character ";
     ELSE
     PRINT TAB(0,25)SPC(15)'SPC(16);TAB(0,18)"Char ";
1120 PRINT Char%;: COLOUR 3: VDU 32,Char%,5
```

```
1130 table%=Table%+43*(Char%-224)
1140 FOR J%=0 TO 7:
        V%=Ymax%-J%*Ystep%
1150   h%=?table%-48: IF h%<0 THEN
          h%=0
1160   t%=table%?1-48: IF t%<0 THEN
          t%=0
1170   n%=100*h%+10*t%+table%?2-48
1180   FOR I%=7 TO 0 STEP -1
1190     U%=Xmin%+80*I%: Def%(I%,J%)=n% MOD 2: n%=n% DIV 2:
          PROCfill(Def%(I%,J%)): PROCcursor(FALSE): NEXT
1200   table%=table%+4: NEXT
1210 U%=Xmin%: V%=Ymax%: PROCcursor(TRUE): VDU 4
1220 IF M%=1 THEN
       PRINT TAB(1,28)"Press space to clear element, X to fill"'
       " Press S to save definition, Q to quit": VDU 5: ENDPROC
1230 PRINT TAB(0,25)"Space to clear"'"   X to fill"'
     "   S to save"'"   Q to quit": VDU 5
1240 ENDPROC
1250 DEF PROCfill(on)
1260 LOCAL u%,v%,x%,y%
1270 IF on THEN
       GCOL 1,2
     ELSE
       GCOL 2,1
1280 MOVE U%-4*M%,V%+4: PLOT 0,80,0: PLOT 81,-80,-Ystep%:
     PLOT 81,80,0
1290 MOVE U%,V%: PROCcursor(TRUE)
1300 u%=(U%-Xmin%) DIV 80: v%=(Ymax%-V%) DIV Ystep%
1310 x%=Cx%+4*M%*u%: y%=Cy%-4*v%
1320 GCOL 0,3: IF on THEN
       Def%(u%,v%)=1: PLOT 69,x%,y%
     ELSE
       Def%(u%,v%)=0: PLOT 71,x%,y%
1330 ENDPROC
1340 DEF PROCcursor(on)
1350 IF on THEN
       GCOL 0,1
     ELSE
       GCOL 0,POINT(U%,V%)
1360 IF M%=1 THEN
       MOVE U%+24,V%-24
     ELSE
       MOVE U%+8,V%-4
1370 PRINT "+": MOVE U%,V%
1380 ENDPROC
1390 DEF PROCkeep
1400 LOCAL table%,h%,t%,n%
1410 table%=Table%+43*(Char%-224)
1420 FOR J%=0 TO 7:
       n%=0
1430   FOR I%=0 TO 7:
         n%=2*n%+Def%(I%,J%): NEXT
1440   h%=n% DIV 100: IF h%=0 THEN
         h%=32
```

```
          ELSE
             h%=h%+48
1450    t%=(n% DIV 10) MOD 10: IF t%=0 AND h%=32 THEN
             t%=32
          ELSE
             t%=t%+48
1460    ?table%=h%: table%?1=t%: table%?2=n% MOD 10+48
1470    table%=table%+4: NEXT
1480 PROCvdu: Kept=TRUE
1490 VDU 4,31,X%,Y%,Char%
1500 ENDPROC
1510 DEF FNmore
1520 IF M%=1 THEN
          VDU 4,28,1,31,39,26
       ELSE
          VDU 4,28,0,31,19,22
1530 CLS: COLOUR 3: IF M%=1 THEN
          PRINT "Another character definition? ";
       ELSE
          PRINT "Another character? ";
1540 A$=GET$: COLOUR 1: PRINT A$;: IF A$="N" OR A$="n" THEN
          GOTO 1570
       ELSE
          IF A$<>"Y" AND A$<>"y" THEN
             GOTO 1530
1550 CLS: VDU 26: IF M%=1 THEN
          PRINT TAB(1,26)"Use cursor control keys to move cursor"
       ELSE
          PRINT TAB(0,22)"Use cursor control"'"keys to move cursor"
1560 =TRUE
1570 COLOUR 3: IF M%=1 THEN
          PRINT '"Do you want to change modes? ";
       ELSE
          PRINT "Change modes? ";
1580 A$=GET$: COLOUR 1: PRINT A$;: IF A$="Y" OR A$="y" THEN
          M%=3-M%: =FALSE
1590 NoMore=TRUE: COLOUR 3: IF M%=1 THEN
          PRINT '"Do you want to save the definitions? ";
       ELSE
          PRINT '"Save definitions? ";
1600 A$=GET$: COLOUR 1: PRINT A$;: Save=A$="Y" OR A$="y":
       IF Save THEN
          =FALSE
1610 COLOUR 3: IF M%=1 THEN
          PRINT '"Do you want to list them? ";
       ELSE
          PRINT '"List definitions? ";
1620 A$=GET$: COLOUR 1: PRINT A$;: List=A$="Y" OR A$="y"
1630 =FALSE
1640 DEF PROCsave
1650 LOCAL file%,byte%,table%,vdu%,line$
1660 FOR I%=6 TO 7:
          PRINT TAB(11,I%)CHR$141;CHR$130;"SHAPE DEFINER": NEXT
1670 PRINT TAB(1,10)CHR$129;"(c) 1984, John Wiley & Sons, Limited"
1680 table%=Table%-12: IF Save THEN
```

```
          vdu%=21
       ELSE
          vdu%=17: GOTO 1740
 1690 PRINT TAB(1,14)CHR$133;"Please position tape and then RETURN":
      *MOTOR1
 1700 REPEAT
         UNTIL GET=&D:
      *MOTOR0
 1710 *OPT1,1
 1720 PRINT TAB(1,16)CHR$133;: file%=OPENOUT("CharDefs"):
      BPUT #file%,&A: BPUT #file%,&D
 1730 PRINT TAB(1,18)CHR$131;"File will be called";CHR$134;
      "CharDefs": VDU 28,2,24,39,20
 1740 FOR I%=0 TO 31
 1750    IF List THEN
            PRINT TAB(1,vdu%)CHR$130;"VDU 23,";224+I%;",";TAB(3,vdu%+1)
            CHR$134;: GOTO 1790
 1760    line$=STR$(32735+I%)+"VDU"
 1770    FOR J%=1 TO 8:
            byte%=ASC(MID$(line$,J%,1)): BPUT #file%,byte%: NEXT
 1780    FOR J%=5 TO 11:
            byte%=table%?J%: BPUT #file%,byte%: NEXT
 1790    FOR J%=12 TO 42:
            byte%=table%?J%: IF List THEN
               VDU byte%
            ELSE
               BPUT #file%,byte%
 1800    NEXT
 1810    IF Save THEN
            BPUT #file%,&A: BPUT #file%,&D
         ELSE
            PRINT TAB(1,24)CHR$129;"Press any key for next character";:
            X%=GET: PRINT TAB(1,24)SPC(33);
 1820    table%=table%+43: NEXT:
      IF Save THEN
         CLOSE #file%
 1830 VDU 28,0,24,39,13,12,26
 1840 IF Save THEN
         PRINT TAB(4,15)CHR$131;"Definitions saved in";CHR$134;
         "CharDefs"''''
      ELSE
         PRINT TAB(0,20);
 1850 ENDPROC
 1860 *FX4,0
 1870 MODE 7: REPORT: PRINT " at line ";ERL: END
32734 DEF PROCvdu
32735 VDU 23,224,064,160,174,226,174,170,174,000
32736 VDU 23,225,232,168,168,204,170,170,236,000
32737 VDU 23,226,064,160,128,132,138,136,170,068
32738 VDU 23,227,194,162,162,166,170,170,198,000
32739 VDU 23,228,224,128,142,234,142,136,238,000
32740 VDU 23,229,230,132,132,238,132,132,132,000
32741 VDU 23,230,064,160,134,138,170,166,098,014
32742 VDU 23,231,168,168,168,238,170,170,170,000
32743 VDU 23,232,228,064,068,068,068,068,228,000
```

```
32744 VDU 23,233,036,032,036,036,164,164,068,012
32745 VDU 23,234,168,168,234,202,236,170,170,000
32746 VDU 23,235,132,132,132,132,132,132,228,000
32747 VDU 23,236,160,224,234,238,174,170,170,000
32748 VDU 23,237,160,160,238,234,234,170,170,000
32749 VDU 23,238,064,160,164,170,170,170,068,000
32750 VDU 23,239,224,160,174,234,138,142,136,008
32751 VDU 23,240,064,160,174,170,170,238,098,034
32752 VDU 23,241,224,160,174,234,200,168,168,000
32753 VDU 23,242,224,160,142,232,046,162,238,000
32754 VDU 23,243,228,068,078,068,068,068,070,000
32755 VDU 23,244,160,160,170,170,170,170,238,000
32756 VDU 23,245,160,160,170,170,170,234,068,000
32757 VDU 23,246,160,160,170,170,234,238,170,000
32758 VDU 23,247,160,160,234,078,228,174,170,000
32759 VDU 23,248,160,160,170,074,074,070,066,014
32760 VDU 23,249,224,032,046,066,132,136,238,000
32761 VDU 23,250,228,172,164,164,164,164,238,000
32762 VDU 23,251,238,170,034,102,194,138,238,000
32763 VDU 23,252,046,104,104,172,162,226,044,000
32764 VDU 23,253,110,130,134,196,172,168,072,000
32765 VDU 23,254,068,170,170,070,162,170,068,000
32766 VDU 23,255,000,000,000,000,000,066,066,004
32767 ENDPROC
```

Appendix D

A quick summary of BBC Basic

This appendix lists all the Basic keywords and functions that appear in BBC Basic with a *very* brief description of their purpose, their syntax, and where they are described in this book. Only the main reference is given here – the Index gives a more complete set of references. Items which are unique to BBC Basic, or whose use is significantly different from other Basic dialects, are preceded by an asterisk.

Keyword	Type	Purpose	Syntax	Main Ref.
ABS	function	absolute value	ABS(x)	8.2
ACS	function	arc-cosine	ACS(x)	8.2
*ADVAL	function	analogue-to-digital	ADVAL(n)	10.1
AND	operator	logical/bitwise	l1 AND l2	
ASC	function	numeric (ASCII) code	ASC(s$)	9.3
ASN	function	arc-sine	ASN(x)	8.2
ATN	function	arc-tangent	ATN(x)	8.2
*AUTO	command	automatic line numbering	AUTO m,n	2.1
*BGET#	function	read byte	BGET #ch	15.5
*BPUT#	command	write byte	BPUT #ch,n	15.5
CALL	command	m/c code subroutine call	CALL n,....	
*CHAIN	command	load and run Basic program	CHAIN "name"	1.4
CHR$	function	character code	CHR$(n)	9.3
CLEAR	command	clear memory	CLEAR	Ch.14 hints
*CLG	command	clear graphics screen	CLG	5.2

Keyword	Type	Purpose	Syntax	Main Ref.
*CLOSE#	command	close file	CLOSE #ch	15.3
*CLS	command	clear text screen	CLS	5.1
*COLOUR	command	select text colour	COLOUR c	5.1
COS	function	cosine	COS(x)	8.2
*COUNT	function	count of characters output	COUNT	7.6
DATA	command	define data for READ	DATA....	4.2
*DEF	command	define a PROC or FN	DEF ...	8.2
*DEG	function	radians to degrees	DEG(x)	2.1
DELETE	command	delete program lines	DELETE n1,n2	14.1
DIM	command	dimension an array	DIM a(n)	8.5
DIV	operator	integer divide	n DIV m	5.2
*DRAW	command	draw a line	DRAW x,y	10.1
*ELSE	keyword	used in an IF statement	IF...THEN...ELSE	4.2
END	command	end of program	END	4.2
*ENDPROC	command	end of procedure	ENDPROC	16.2
*ENVELOPE	command	sound envelope definition	ENVELOPE...	15.3
*EOF#	function	test for end of file	EOF #ch	17.2
*EOR	operator	bitwise Exclusive OR	n EOR m	
*ERL	function	line number of last error	ERL	9.3
*ERR	function	error number of last error	ERR	8.2
*EVAL	function	evaluate an expression	EVAL(s$)	
EXP	function	exponential	EXP(x)	
*EXT#	function	length of file	EXT#(ch)	17.2
FALSE	function	logical value FALSE	FALSE	8.4
*FN	keyword	part of a function name	FNname	6.1
FOR	command	initiate a FOR loop	FOR n=a TO b STEP c	11.4
*GCOL	command	select graphics colour	GCOL n,c	7.7
GET	function	input an ASCII code	GET	7.7
*GET$	function	input a character	GET$	
GOSUB	command	go to a subroutine	GOSUB n	10.2
GOTO	command	unconditional jump	GOTO n	17.3
*HIMEM	pseudo-var.	top of available memory	HIMEM	10.1
*IF	command	decision making	IF ... THEN ...	7.7
*INKEY	function	input an ASCII code	INKEY(n)	7.7
*INKEY$	function	input a character	INKEY$(n)	

Keyword	Type	Purpose	Syntax	Main Ref.
INPUT	command	input an item	INPUT . . .	7.2
INPUT#	command	read from a file	INPUT #ch,. . .	15.3
*INSTR	function	match strings	INSTR(a$,b$)	10.4
INT	function	whole number part	INT(x)	8.2
LEFT$	function	left-hand part of string	LEFT$(s$,n)	9.2
LEN	function	length of string	LEN(s$)	9.2
LET	command	assignment	LET x= . . .	6.2
LIST	command	list a program	LIST n,m	2.1
*LISTO	command	select listing style	LISTO n	
LN	function	natural logarithm	LN(x)	8.2
LOAD	command	load a Basic program	LOAD "name"	1.4
*LOCAL	command	define local variables	LOCAL v1,v2,. . .	6.4
LOG	function	common logarithm	LOG(x)	8.2
*LOMEM	pseudo-var.	bottom of available memory	LOMEM	17.3
MID$	function	extract sub-string	MID$(s$,n,m)	9.2
MOD	operator	modulus (remainder)	n MOD m	8.5
*MODE	command	select graphics mode	MODE n	2.2
*MOVE	command	position graphics cursor	MOVE x,y	5.2
NEW	command	clear memory for new program	NEW	2.1
NEXT	command	ends a FOR loop	NEXT	6.1
NOT	operator	bitwise inversion operator	NOT n	17.2
*OLD	command	recover program after BREAK	OLD	4.4
ON	command	multiple choice	ON x GOTO n1,n2,. . .	10.4
*OPENIN	function	open input file	OPENIN("name")	15.3
*OPENOUT	function	open output file	OPENOUT("name")	15.3
*OPT	command	used with assembly code	OPT n	
OR	operator	logical/bitwise OR	l1 OR l2	10.1
*PAGE	pseudo-var.	start address of program	PAGE	17.3
PI	constant	3.14159265 (π)	PI	8.2
*PLOT	command	general plotting command	PLOT k,x,y	11.1
*POINT	function	screen colour	POINT(x,y)	12.2
POS	function	horizontal cursor position	POS	
PRINT	command	output items	PRINT . . .	7.1
PRINT#	command	write a file	PRINT #ch,. . .	15.3
*PROC	keyword	part of a procedure name	PROCname	4.2

Keyword	Type	Purpose	Syntax	Main Ref.
*PTR#	command	select disc file	PTR #ch	8.2
*RAD	function	degrees to radians	RAD(x)	7.6
READ	command	read items from DATA	READ...	4.5
REM	command	comment	REM...	2.1
RENUMBER	command	renumber program lines	RENUMBER n,m	10.3
*REPEAT	command	initiate a REPEAT loop	REPEAT	
*REPORT	command	print last error message	REPORT	
RESTORE	command	reset pointer to DATA items	RESTORE n	7.6
RETURN	command	return from subroutine	RETURN	
RIGHT$	function	right-hand part of string	RIGHT$(s$,n)	9.2
RND	function	random number generator	RND(n)	8.3
RUN	command	start program execution	RUN	2.1
SAVE	command	save a program in a file	SAVE "name"	1.5
SGN	function	sign of a number	SGN(x)	8.2
SIN	function	sine	SIN(x)	8.2
*SOUND	command	sound generator	SOUND c,a,p,d	3.1
SPC	keyword	spaces with PRINT/INPUT	SPC(n)	7.5
SQR	function	square root	SQR(x)	8.2
STEP	keyword	part of a FOR statement	FOR...TO...STEP...	10.3
STOP	command	stop program execution	STOP	
STR$	function	number to characters	STR$(x)	9.3
*STRING$	function	multiple strings	STRING$(s$,n)	9.1
TAB	keyword	tabulation in PRINT/INPUT	TAB(x,y)	7.5
TAN	function	tangent	TAN(x)	8.2
*THEN	keyword	used in an IF statement	IF...THEN...	10.1
*TIME	pseudo-var.	internal elapsed time	TIME	7.7
TO	keyword	part of a FOR statement	FOR...TO...	6.1
*TOP	function	top of program space	TOP	17.3
*TRACE	command	trace statement execution	TRACE n	17.2
TRUE	function	logical value TRUE	TRUE	10.3
*UNTIL	command	ends a REPEAT loop	UNTIL c	
*USR	function	obey m/c code routine	USR(n)	
VAL	function	character to number	VAL(s$)	9.3
*VDU	command	general screen output	VDU n,...	11.5
*VPOS	function	vertical cursor position	VPOS	
*WIDTH	command	set line width	WIDTH n	17.1

Index

309

310